CorelDRA... Sh...

KEY	USE
Alt+F7	Opens the Move dialog box
F8	Selects the Text tool
Ctrl+F8	Opens the PowerLine roll-up
Alt+F8	Opens the Rotate & Skew dialog box
F9	Toggles between the Normal and Preview display modes
Shift+F9	Toggles between editable preview and wireframe view
Ctrl+F9	Opens the Contour roll-up
Alt+F9	Opens the Stretch & Mirror dialog box
F10	Selects the Shape tool
Ctrl+F10	Opens the Node Edit roll-up
Alt+F10	Aligns selected text to baseline
F11	Opens the Fountain Fill dialog box
Shift+F11	Opens the Uniform Fill dialog box
F12	Opens the Outline Pen dialog box
Shift+F12	Opens the Outline Color dialog box
Ctrl+F12	Opens the Object Data roll-up

Computer users are not all alike.
Neither are SYBEX books.

We know our customers have a variety of needs. They've told us so. And because we've listened, we've developed several distinct types of books to meet the needs of each of our customers. What are you looking for in computer help?

If you're looking for the basics, try the **ABC's** series. For a more visual approach, select full-color **Quick & Easy** books.

Running Start books are two books in one: a fast-paced tutorial, followed by a command reference.

Mastering and **Understanding** titles offer you a step-by-step introduction, plus an in-depth examination of intermediate-level features, to use as you progress.

Our **Up & Running** series is designed for computer-literate consumers who want a no-nonsense overview of new programs. Just 20 basic lessons, and you're on your way.

SYBEX **Encyclopedias, Desktop References,** and **A to Z** books provide a *comprehensive reference* and explanation of all of the commands, features, and functions of the subject software.

Sometimes a subject requires a special treatment that our standard series don't provide. So you'll find we have titles like **Advanced Techniques, Handbooks, Tips & Tricks,** and others that are specifically tailored to satisfy a unique need.

You'll find SYBEX publishes a variety of books on every popular software package. Looking for computer help? Help Yourself to SYBEX.

For a complete catalog of our publications:

SYBEX Inc.
2021 Challenger Drive, Alameda, CA 94501
Tel: (510) 523-8233/(800) 227-2346 Telex: 336311
Fax: (510) 523-2373

SYBEX is committed to using natural resources wisely to preserve and improve our environment. This is why we have been printing the text of books like this one on recycled paper since 1982.

This year our use of recycled paper will result in the saving of more than 15,300 trees. We will lower air pollution effluents by 54,000 pounds, save 6,300,000 gallons of water, and reduce landfill by 2,700 cubic yards.

In choosing a SYBEX book you are not only making a choice for the best in skills and information, you are also choosing to enhance the quality of life for all of us.

The SYBEX Instant Reference Series

Instant References are available on these topics:

AutoCAD Release 12
for Windows

CorelDRAW 3

dBASE

dBASE IV 2.0 Programmer's

DOS 5

DOS 6

DR DOS 6

Excel 4 for Windows

Harvard Graphics 3

Harvard Graphics
for Windows

Lotus 1-2-3 Release 2.3 &
2.4 for DOS

Lotus 1-2-3 Release 4
for Windows

Lotus 1-2-3 for Windows

Microsoft Access

Norton Desktop for DOS

Norton Desktop for
Windows 2.0

Norton Utilities 7

OS/2 2.1

PageMaker 4.0
for the Macintosh

Paradox 4 Programmer's

Paradox 4 User's

PC Tools 8

Quattro Pro for Windows

SQL

Windows 3.1

Windows NT

Word for Windows,
Version 2.0

WordPerfect 5.1 for DOS

WordPerfect 5.1 for
Windows

WordPerfect 6 for DOS

CorelDRAW 4
Instant Reference

Gordon Padwick

SYBEX®

San Francisco • Paris • Düsseldorf • Soest

Acquisitions Editor: David J. Clark
Developmental Editor: Kenyon Brown
Editor: Brendan Fletcher
Project Editor: Kathleen Lattinville
Technical Editor: Erik Ingenito
Book Designer: Ingrid Owen
Production Artist: Lisa Jaffe
Screen Graphics: Cuong Le
Typesetter: Alissa Feinberg
Proofreader/Production Assistant: Janet MacEachern
Indexer: Nancy Guenther
Cover Designer: Archer Design
Cover Illustrator: David Brickley, Shooting Brick Productions
Screen reproductions produced with Collage Complete.
Collage Complete is a trademark of Inner Media Inc.
SYBEX is a registered trademark of SYBEX Inc.

Library of Congress Card Number: 93-85060
ISBN: 0-7821-1307-9

Manufactured in the United States of America
First Printing
10 9 8 7 6 5 4 3 2 1

To Melissa

Acknowledgments

Although there is only one name on the cover of this book, many people contributed to it. My thanks particularly go to Kenyon Brown, developmental editor, for his overall guidance; to Brendan Fletcher, editor, for many helpful suggestions and skillful editing; to Erik Ingenito, technical editor, for his meticulous review of all the procedures in this book; and to Kathleen Lattinville, project editor, for firmly but kindly keeping me on schedule and coordinating the efforts of all the people involved.

This book would not have been possible without the support of many people at Corel Corporation, particularly Janie Sullivan, for providing me pre-release copies of CorelDRAW 4.

While working with CorelDRAW 4, I used a Gateway 2000 4DX2-66V computer running MS-DOS 6.0 and Windows 3.1. I used a CD Porta-Drive from CD Technology to access CorelDRAW files on compact disk and the Corel Quick Tour, and a Soundblaster 16 ASP from Creative Technology to work with the sound capabilities in CorelSHOW and CorelMOVE. All the screen captures were made with the help of Collage Complete from Inner Media. I wrote the text in Microsoft Word 5.0 on a Zenith Model 241 computer.

My thanks, as always, go to my wife, Kathy, for her encouragement and patience during the long hours I spent in front of my computers while writing this book.

Table of Contents

Introduction

xxi

Part 1

CorelDRAW

Part 2

CorelCHART

Part 3
CorelPHOTO-PAINT

Part 4
CorelSHOW

Part 5

CorelTRACE

Part 6

CorelMOVE

Appendix

File Formats Supported by Corel Graphics

Index

Introduction

If you have used earlier versions of CorelDRAW, you will be delighted with version 4. With the introduction of version 3, CorelDRAW became a package of graphics applications. Version 4 greatly improves the integration between these applications, enhances them with additional capabilities, and adds the completely new CorelMOVE animation application. Some 750 typefaces and 18,000 clip art images are included.

Most graphics packages are quite a challenge to new users, not because they are particularly difficult to use, but because there is so much to learn. This certainly is the case with CorelDRAW. That is why you need this Instant Reference.

When you buy CorelDRAW, you get a complete package of eight applications:

- CorelDRAW, now expanded with many desktop publishing and technical illustration features, is covered in Part 1 of this book.

- CorelCHART, a program you can use to produce many types of two-dimensional and three-dimensional charts and graphs, now enhanced with many of the data manipulation capabilities found in leading spreadsheet programs, is covered in Part 2.

- CorelPHOTO-PAINT, a paint-type graphics program you can use to create as well as enhance bitmap graphics, including color and black-and-white scanned images, by using photography-like retouching techniques. The new version includes color separations and other prepress capabilities. CorelPHOTO-PAINT is covered in Part 3.

- CCAPTURE, a utility you can use to capture on-screen images, is covered in Part 3.

- CorelSHOW, a program that allows you to create slides and overhead transparencies and run a slide show on your computer monitor. The new version, which allows you to include sound in on-screen presentations and provides enhanced control of objects in a slide, is covered in Part 4.

- CorelTRACE, a utility that converts color and black-and-white bitmap images into vector images, is much easier to use than the previous version. CorelTRACE is covered in Part 5.

- CorelMOSAIC, a utility that simplifies selecting objects to import into CorelDRAW, is included in Part 1, the CorelDRAW section.

- CorelMOVE, a new application you can use to create animated presentations with sound, is covered in Part 6.

While there are still some rough edges, all the applications are much better integrated than before. If you take the time to become familiar with one, the others will be quite easy to learn.

What This Book Contains

Within each part, tasks and major features are listed in alphabetical order. Throughout the book, step-by-step procedures show you how to successfully complete a wide variety of tasks.

When you are working with one of the applications in the CorelDRAW package, you will usually find it easy to turn to the relevant section of the book and locate information relating to your current activity. If that fails, turn to the index at the back of the book to find the information you need.

If you are already familiar with CorelDRAW 3, most of CorelDRAW 4 will be familiar. Entries that refer to material that is new in CorelDRAW 4, or changed significantly, are marked with the symbol you see here.

As its title suggests, this book provides a fast way for you to gain clear and specific information about the major tasks you will encounter while working with the CorelDRAW package. It is not intended to be a comprehensive reference, so it does not deal with alternative methods of accomplishing an objective. Be prepared to explore beyond what is covered in this book and you will find many hidden treasures. You will find a lot more about CorelDRAW 4 in Rick Altman's *Mastering CorelDRAW 4*, also published by SYBEX.

Who Should Read This Book

Whether you use or plan to use CorelDRAW frequently or infrequently, this book is for you. It is the book to keep by the side of your computer for ready access. Its step-by-step procedures will save you a great deal of time.

The book makes certain assumptions. It assumes you have a job to do and a limited time in which to get it done; it assumes you know what you want to do, but are uncertain how to do it with CorelDRAW. The book assumes that you have some experience with computer graphics, perhaps with an earlier version of CorelDRAW or with another graphics package, and that you are comfortable working with Windows applications.

How to Use This Book

Use this book to help solve specific problems and also as a means of expanding your knowledge about CorelDRAW.

When you need to do something you are not sure about, look it up here. Generally, you will find a step-by-step procedure that tells you exactly what to do, or which you can easily modify to accomplish your specific task. Save yourself time in the future by marking the page where you found the information you used.

To expand your knowledge of CorelDRAW, open the book at random. Quite often you will come across something that is new to you. Look over the information so that you get a general idea of what is there. If you think it might be useful to you in the future, mark the page so that you can easily find it again.

CorelDRAW on CD-ROM

The CorelDRAW package contains a set of floppy disks that contain the eight separate applications, some typefaces, and some clip art. The package also contains two CD-ROMs that contain the eight separate applications, some 750 typefaces and 18,000 clip art images, and also the Corel Quick Tour.

If you do not already have a CD-ROM drive, now you can justify buying one. You need it to access most of the typefaces and clip art Corel supplies, and to see the animated Quick Tour of all eight applications. Installing CorelDRAW from CD-ROM is a snap! Instead of shuffling disk after disk, just slip in the CD-ROM drive, type **INSTALL**, and that's all. Most of the typefaces and clip art are not copied to your hard disk, so you avoid the problem of consuming disk space with data you use only rarely.

Notes and Cross-References

Notes follow many procedures in this book. Notes provide information that supplements that given before or within a procedure. Make a habit of reading any notes that follow a procedure you are using.

To avoid unnecessary repetition, the book makes frequent use of cross-references. Cross-references to alphabetical entries are set in italics for easy identification. When a cross-reference is to an entry in another part in the book, that part is identified; otherwise the cross-reference is to an entry in the same section.

In some cases, references are made to headings within an alphabetical entry. In these cases, the heading name referred to appears in quotation marks. Refer to the heading for further information.

Part 1

CorelDRAW

CorelDRAW is the principal component of the CorelDRAW PC Illustration Package. CorelDRAW itself is a versatile, yet easy-to-use, vector-based application you can use to create a wide range of illustrative material, ranging from simple, single-page diagrams to multipage documents that combine illustrations and text.

You can use CorelDRAW's tools to create straight lines, curves, rectangles, ellipses, and text. You can control the thickness, color, and style of lines, and you can fill closed shapes with color, fountain fills, patterns, and textures. Alternatively, you can use Corel-DRAW's tools to modify text and graphics imported in many formats to suit your needs.

CorelDRAW's capabilities extend beyond those of most graphics applications by offering pressure-sensitive drawing, object cloning, the ability to create graphics databases, prepress tools including color separations, and a host of other capabilities.

You can take advantage of the 750 fonts supplied on CD-ROM with CorelDRAW, and you have access to 18,000 clip art images and symbols you can use as they are or modify according to your needs.

2   CorelDRAW

ALIGNMENT AND PLACEMENT AIDS

CorelDRAW has several ways to help you align and place objects
exactly. The information here applies to graphic and text objects.
See *Formatting Text* for information about aligning text.

Finding the Cursor Position

The left end of the status line shows the coordinates of the cursor.
See *Screen* for information about how to display the status line.

Using the Crosshair Cursor

Use the non-printing crosshair cursor to visually align objects vertically and horizontally. You can place the crosshair cursor at any
point and see its coordinates in the status line. To display the
crosshair cursor:

1.   Choose **Special ➤ Preferences**.

2.   In the Preferences dialog box, click the **Cross Hair Cursor**
check box, then click **OK**.

3.   After using the crosshair cursor, repeat steps 1 and 2 to
return to the normal cursor.

Using the Grid

Use the grid to place objects exactly at grid points. See *Grid* for information about setting up the grid. To display the grid:

1.   Choose **Layout ➤ Grid Setup** to display the Grid Setup
dialog box.

2.   At the bottom of the dialog box, click the **Show Grid**
check box.

3.   Click the **Snap To Grid** check box, if appropriate.

4.   Click **OK** to accept the grid setup.

NOTES   To avoid clutter, not all grid points are shown on the screen. However, when snap-to-grid is enabled, objects snap to invisible grid points as well as to those that are visible.

You can turn the snap-to grid on or off from the Layout menu by clicking Snap To and then clicking Grid.

Creating Guidelines

Use guidelines to align objects. You can place horizontal and vertical guidelines on the screen by eye, or by typing exact coordinates. Guidelines will not appear when you print your drawing.

To place guidelines by eye:

1.   Make sure the rulers are displayed (see *Displaying Rulers* below).

2.   To place a horizontal guideline, point into the horizontal ruler; to place a vertical guideline, point into the vertical ruler.

3.   Press the mouse button and drag down from the horizontal ruler, or to the right from the vertical ruler, until the guideline is correctly placed. You can see the guideline coordinates in the status line.

4.   Repeat steps 2 and 3 to place additional guidelines.

To place guidelines with more precision:

1.   Choose **Layout ➤ Guidelines Setup** to display the Guidelines dialog box.

2.   In the **Guidelines** dialog box, click either the **Horizontal** or **Vertical** option button.

3.   To define the guideline position, choose or type the position in the **Ruler Position** text box, then click **Add**.

To move an existing guideline by eye:

1.   Point with the **Pick** tool onto the guideline you want to move.

2.   Drag the guideline to the new position.

To move an existing guideline with more precision:

1.   Double-click on the guideline to open the **Guidelines** dialog box with the guideline's position displayed.

2.   Select or type the new coordinate in the **Ruler Position** text box, then click **Move**.

To remove a guideline:

1.   Point with **Pick** tool onto the guideline you want to remove.

2.   Drag the guideline up, or to the left, into the ruler.

Nudging Objects into Position

You can nudge an object to move it vertically or horizontally by an incremental distance you can define.

1.   Set the nudge increment, as described in *Preferences*.

2.   Using the **Pick** tool, select the object you wish to nudge.

3.   Press ↑, ↓, →, or ← according to the direction you wish to move the object.

NOTES   You can nudge an object, even if it has been snapped.

Displaying Rulers

You can display a horizontal ruler at the top of the drawing area and a vertical ruler at the left of the drawing area. You can choose zero points for the rulers and the unit of measurement they display. To display or hide the rulers, choose **Display ➤ Show Rulers**.

NOTES   The ruler zero points and measurement units are the same as those for the grid (see *Grid*).

Dotted lines in the rulers show the position of the cursor.

Snapping Objects to the Grid and to Guidelines

When you are placing objects, moving them, or reshaping them, you can do so with precision by snapping them to the grid or to guidelines. To activate or deactivate snapping:

1.   Display the grid or guidelines as required (see "Using the Grid" and "Creating Guidelines" above).

2.   Choose **Layout ➤ Snap To** to display a secondary menu.

3.   In the secondary menu, click any combination of **Grid**, **Guidelines**, and **Objects** to activate or deactivate snapping.

NOTES   When an object is close to a grid point, it snaps to that point if snap-to-grid is active. When an object is close to a guideline, it snaps to that line if snap-to-guidelines is active. If snap-to-grid and snap-to-guidelines are both active, snap-to-guidelines has priority.

Snapping to Objects

Snapping an object to another object allows you to accurately position one object, the moving object, relative to another, the stationary object. To snap one object to another:

1.   Decide which node on the stationary object you want to snap the moving object to. See the notes below for information about selecting a node.

2.   Choose **Layout ➤ Snap To ➤ Objects**.

3. Use the **Pick** tool to point to the moving object at the exact point on it that you want to snap to a node on the stationary object. In editable preview, you can select a point anywhere on a filled object. In wireframe view and in editable preview for unfilled objects, you must select a point on the object's outline.

4. Drag the moving object until it is close to a node on the stationary object.

NOTES The stationary object has nodes to which you can snap the moving object. These nodes are visible when the object is selected. If necessary, you can add nodes to the stationary object (see *Shaping and Reshaping an Object*).

Aligning Objects to Each Other

1. Select two or more objects. The object you select last is the one the other objects will be aligned to.

2. Choose **Arrange ➤ Align** to display the **Align** dialog box.

3. Click one of the vertical alignment option buttons or one of the horizontal alignment option buttons, or one of each, then click **OK**. The objects move into alignment.

NOTES You can also use Arrange ➤ Align to align an object to the center of the page or to the nearest grid point.

Using Objects as Guides

You can create an object on the guides layer of a drawing, and use it as an alignment aid for precise positioning of objects on drawing layers. To create a guide object and move an existing object so that it snaps to the guide object:

1. Choose **Layout ➤ Layers Roll-Up** to display the Layers roll-up (see *Layering a Drawing*).

2. In the Layers roll-up, click **Guides** to access the guides layer.

3. On the guides layer, draw the objects you want to use as guides. These objects appear as dashed outlines. If necessary, add nodes at places on these objects to which you want to snap objects on drawing layers (see *Shaping and Reshaping an Object*).

4. In the Layers roll-up, select a drawing layer. You can still see the dashed outline of guide objects.

5. If necessary, turn on snap-to-objects by choosing **Layout ➤ Snap To ➤ Objects**.

6. Point onto the place on the existing object that you want to snap to a node on the guide object. Press the mouse button and drag until the cursor is close to a node on the guide object. The existing object snaps to the node on the guide object.

NOTES   You can also snap a new object to a guide object. After step 5, select the tool with which you will draw the new object, move the cursor close to a node on the guide object, and start drawing. The first node of the new object snaps to the node on the guide object.

AUTOJOIN

AutoJoin allows you to easily place a node on one object in exactly the same position as a node on another object, so that the two objects are joined. The default AutoJoin distance is five pixels.

Joining Lines or Curves

1. Use the **Pick** tool to select a line or curve.

2. Using the **Pencil** tool, point to within the AutoJoin distance of one of the nodes on the selected line or curve.

3. Draw a line or curve. The new line or curve is joined to the first.

NOTES   See *Drawing an Object* for information about drawing lines and curves. See *Preferences* for information about the AutoJoin distance.

BLENDING OBJECTS

You can blend one object into another through a series of intermediate objects that progressively change their shapes and attributes. The blend can follow a straight or curved path.

Figure 1.1 shows two objects: the two objects blended along a straight line, and the same objects blended along a curve.

Basic Blending

1. Using the **Pick** tool, select the two objects to be blended.

2. Choose **Effects ➤ Blend Roll-Up** to display the Blend roll-up shown in Figure 1.2.

3. In the Blend roll-up, specify the number of blend steps and the rotation of the blend, then click **Apply** to create the blend.

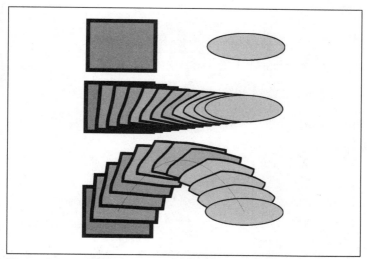

Figure 1.1: Two objects: a blend on a straight line, and a blend on a curved line

NOTES The number specified in the Blend roll-up's Steps text box determines how many intermediate objects are created between the two objects being blended. If you specify five steps, the entire blend consists of seven objects, the two objects being blended and five intermediate objects.

The angle specified in the Blend roll-up's Rotation text box determines the rotation of the blend as a whole. Suppose you specify three steps and a rotation of 180 degrees. With three intermediate objects, there are four steps in the progression from the first object to the last. Each intermediate object rotates 45 degrees (180 divided by 4).

When you click one of the intermediate objects, the entire blend is selected. At the same time, the two arrow buttons in the Blend roll-up change from white to black. Click the left black arrow button and then click Show Start to select the object at the start of the blend. Do the same with the right arrow to identify the end object.

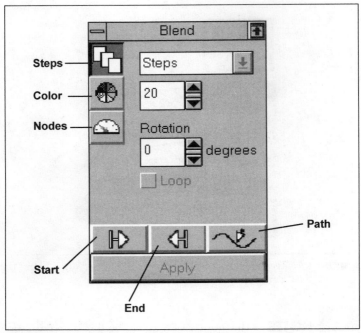

Figure 1.2: The Blend roll-up for choosing steps

Blending along a Path

You can create a blend along a path, specifying either the number of blend steps or the spacing between the steps.

1. Draw a path for the blend.

2. Use the **Pick** tool to select the two objects to be blended.

3. In the Blend roll-up, click the **Path** button and then click **New Path**.

4. Click the blend path with the arrow cursor.

5. Click the **Full Path** check box in the roll-up if you want the blend to extend along the full length of the path.

6. Click the **Rotate All** check box in the roll-up if you want the blended objects to rotate along the path.

7. If you want to specify the number of blend steps, choose or type the number in the text box. If you want to specify the space between blend steps, choose **Spacing** in the list box at the top of the roll-up then choose or type the spacing in the text box.

8. Click **Apply** to create the blend.

NOTES   After you have created a blend on a path, you can select the blend and the path by clicking one of the intermediate objects. To select the path alone, click the Path icon in the roll-up, and then click Show Path. To detach the path from the blend, click the Path icon and then click Detach From Path.

Blending Colored Objects

Two objects that have different color fills or outlines can be smoothly blended. You can preview the color blend.

1. With the **Pick** tool, select the two objects to be blended.

2. In the Blend roll-up, choose or type the number of blend steps.

3. In the Blend roll-up, click the **Colorwheel** icon to display color progression as in Figure 1.3. The straight line in the colorwheel indicates the progression of color changes that will occur.

4. To create a rainbow effect by having the colors progress around the outside of the colorwheel, click the **Rainbow** check box. Then click either color-direction button to choose between clockwise and counterclockwise progression around the colorwheel.

5. Click **Apply** to create the blend.

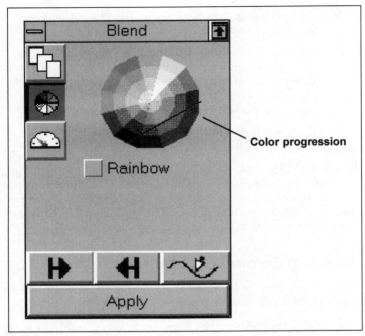

Figure 1.3: The Blend roll-up for colors

Reversing the Blend Order

You can change the appearance of blends between filled objects by interchanging the start and end objects.

1. Use the **Pick** tool to select the blended object by clicking on one of the intermediate blend objects.

2. Choose **Arrange ➤ Order ➤ Reverse Order**.

Selecting Nodes on Start and End Objects

CorelDRAW automatically selects the first node on the start and end objects as the basis of a blend. You can change the blend by selecting a different node on each object.

1. Use the **Pick** tool to select the blended object.

2. In the Blend roll-up, click the **Nodes** icon to display node information as shown in Figure 1.4, then click the **Map Nodes** button to show the nodes on one of the blended objects.

3. Click the node you want to use on the starting or ending object (whichever is selected).

4. Click on the node you want to use on the other object.

5. Click **Apply** to redraw the blend based on the new nodes.

6. Click a blank area of the screen to display the blend without the blend nodes showing.

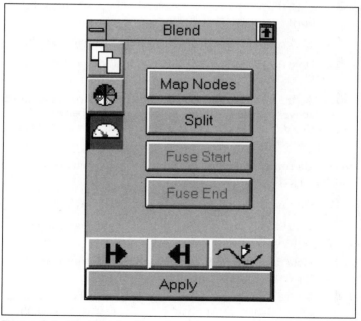

Figure 1.4: The Blend roll-up for choosing nodes

Clearing a Blend

1. Select the blend with the **Pick** tool.

2. Choose **Effects ➤ Clear Blend**.

Creating a Compound Blend

A compound blend is a blend between any object in a blend and another object. To create a compound blend between an intermediate object in an existing blend and another object:

1. Start with a blend and another separate object.

2. Using the **Pick** tool, click an intermediate object to select the entire blend.

3. Click the **Nodes** icon in the Blend roll-up, and then click **Split**.

4. Click on an intermediate object in the blend to select it.

5. Hold down the Shift key and use the **Pick** tool to select the separate object.

6. Set the blend parameters in the Blend roll-up, as explained above, then click **Apply**. A blend is created between the selected intermediate object in the first blend and the separate object.

To create a compound blend between the start or end object in an existing object and another object:

1. Start with a blend and another separate object.

2. Use the **Pick** tool to select the start or end node on the existing blend.

3. Hold down the Shift key and use the **Pick** tool to select the separate object.

4. Set the blend parameters in the Blend roll-up, as explained above, then click **Apply**. A blend is created between the selected intermediate object in the first blend and the separate object.

CHARACTER ATTRIBUTES

You can select conventional character attributes for any text you create in CorelDRAW: typeface (by name), size (0.7 to 2160 points), style (normal, bold, italic, or bold italic), and placement (normal, superscript, or subscript). In addition, you can control each character's outline (width, pen shape, and color), and choose a fill color, pattern, or texture.

You can also copy attributes from one character to another.

Setting Conventional Attributes

1. Use the **Text** tool to select artistic or paragraph text characters whose attributes you want to change.

2. Choose **Text ➤ Text Roll-Up** to display the Text roll-up shown in Figure 1.5, or choose **Text ➤ Character** to display the Character Attributes dialog box.

3. In either the roll-up or the dialog box, select the typeface, size, style, and placement.

4. Click **Apply** in the roll-up, or click **OK** in the dialog box, to apply the attributes to the selected text.

NOTES   In the Text roll-up, you can click Paragraph to display the Paragraph dialog box in which you can select alignment.

The Character Attributes dialog box shows examples of characters with the chosen attributes.

Setting Outline and Fill Attributes

To choose an outline width, pen shape, and fill:

1. Use the **Text** tool to select artistic or paragraph text characters.

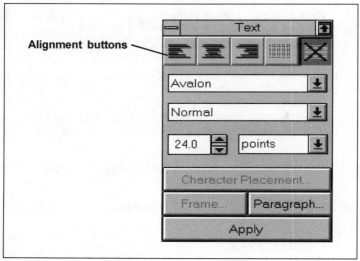

Alignment buttons

Figure 1.5: The Text roll-up

2. Use the procedures described in *Outlining an Object* to change the line width and color.

3. Use the procedures described in *Filling an Object* to change the fill.

Copying Attributes

You can copy any combination of conventional attributes, outline pen, outline color, and fill from selected characters or objects to other characters.

1. Use the **Pick** tool to select the characters you wish to change.

2. Choose **Edit ➤ Copy Attributes From**.

3. In the Copy Attributes dialog box, click one or more check boxes to select the attributes you wish to copy.

4. Click **OK**.

5. With the **From** cursor, click on the text or object with the attributes you wish to copy.

Setting Default Conventional Attributes

Default conventional character attributes are the typeface, size, style, and placement CorelDRAW uses unless you specify otherwise. To set these defaults:

1. Make sure no artistic or paragraph text is selected.

2. Choose **Text ➤ Text Roll-Up** to display the Text roll-up.

3. In the roll-up, select the typeface, size, style, and placement.

4. Click **Apply** in the roll-up to display the Text Attributes dialog box.

5. As necessary, click the **Artistic Text** and **Paragraph Text** check boxes to check or uncheck them according to which type of text the defaults should apply.

NOTES Default character attributes set in this way are for the current session only.

You can use a similar method to set conventional defaults from the Character Attributes dialog box.

Setting Default Outline and Fill Attributes

Default outline and fill attributes are the outline and fill CorelDRAW uses unless you specify otherwise. To set these defaults:

1. Make sure no artistic or paragraph text is selected.

2. Follow steps 2 through 4 in "Setting Character Outline and Fill Attributes" above. In the **Outline Pen for New Object** or **Uniform Fill for New Object** dialog box, click the **Text Objects** option button.

CLEARING TRANSFORMATIONS

In one operation you can reset all rotation and skew transformations to zero; restore all scaling, stretching, and mirroring operations; and clear all envelope and perspective transformations made from the Effects menu.

1. Select one or more objects from which transformations are to be removed.

2. Choose **Effects ➤ Clear Transformations**.

NOTES This operation does not affect any changes you have made to an object's position. In the case of a group, transformations that apply to the group as a whole are cleared; transformations made to individual objects within the group are not affected.

CLIP ART

See "Using Mosaic to Import an Object" in *Importing an Object* for information about using clip art.

CLONES

A clone of an object is a duplicate that maintains a relationship with the master object, so that when you make changes to the master, the clone also changes. A master object can have many clones. You cannot create a clone of a clone.

new Creating a Clone

1. Select the master object with the **Pick** tool.

2. Choose **Edit ➤ Clone**. The clone appears above and to the right of the master.

NOTES When a clone is created, it inherits most of the master's attributes (including special effects such as blends, contours, extrusions, and powerlines). When you change many of the master's attributes (including special effects), the attributes of the clone also change; however, adding blends, contours, extrusions, and powerlines to a master object does not add those effects to existing clones.

You can change the attributes of a clone without affecting those of the master. After you have changed a clone attribute, a subsequent change of the same attribute for the master does not affect the clone.

new Identifying a Master Object's Clones

1. Right-click an object to display its Object menu. If the object has clones, the last item in the Object menu is Select Clones. This item is not present if the object does not have clones.

2. Click **Select Clones**. Handles appear around the clones. If the selected object has two or more clones, these are marquee-selected.

NOTES If handles surround one or two objects, these are both clones of the master. If handles surround more than two objects, all are not necessarily clones (some may be independent objects within the marquee-selected area). To confirm which objects are clones, use the procedure under "Identifying a Clone's Master" on each possible clone.

new Identifying a Clone's Master

1. Right-click a clone to display its Object menu.
2. Click **Select Master**. Handles appear around the clone's master.

CLOSING AN OPEN PATH

See "Joining Nodes to Create a Closed Path" in *Shaping and Reshaping an Object*.

COLOR

You can outline and fill objects with color. You can select outline colors from:

- The color palette at the bottom of the screen
- The Outline Color dialog box
- The Outline Pen dialog box

You can select fill colors from:

- The color palette at the bottom of the screen
- The Uniform Fill dialog box
- The Fill roll-up menu

You apply color to selected objects by clicking on a color in a palette. See *Outlining an Object* and *Filling an Object* for additional information.

You can use either process or spot colors. When using process colors, choose among CMYK, RGB, and HSB color models. With spot colors, choose specific colors in the PANTONE Matching System.

Displaying the Screen Color Palette

1. Choose **Display ➤ Color Palette** to display a secondary menu.

2. Click **Custom Palette, PANTONE Spot Colors, PANTONE Process Colors,** or **TRUMATCH Process Colors** to display a color palette at the bottom of the screen.

NOTES The palette displayed is the current default palette. See "Choosing a Color Palette" later in this entry for information about choosing a different palette.

To remove the color palette, click No Palette in Step 2 of the procedure above.

You can change the background and size of the color palette. Refer to CorelDRAW on-line Help: *color palette: changing the appearance of* for information.

Selecting a Color from the Screen Color Palette

1. Select one or more objects to be colored.

2. Point to the color you want to use in the palette at the bottom of the screen.

3. Click the left mouse button to apply a fill color to the selected objects, or click the right mouse button to apply an outline color to the selected objects. The right end of the status bar shows the current fill color.

NOTES Right-click the square marked with an X at the left end of the color palette to remove the outline color from the selected objects. Left-click the square to remove the fill.

Left-click one of the arrows at the ends of the palette to scroll the palette one color at a time. Right-click the arrows to scroll the palette one screen width at a time.

Selecting an Outline Color from the Outline Color Dialog Box

The Outline Color dialog box allows you to choose among colors in three color models, three industry-standard sets of colors, and colors in a custom palette. You can also create your own colors.

1. Select one or more objects to be colored.

2. Click the **Outline** tool to display the Outline flyout shown in Figure 1.6.

3. Click the **Colorwheel** icon to display the Outline Color dialog box, similar to that in Figure 1.7. This dialog box contains a color palette showing the colors available in the current color model or set, and the colors available in the current custom palette.

4. Open the **Show** list box and click the color model you want to use.

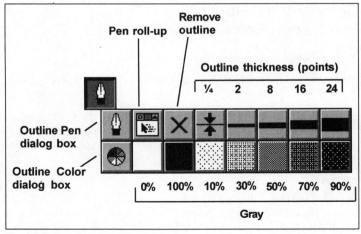

Figure 1.6: The Outline flyout

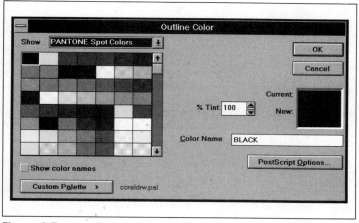

Figure 1.7: The Outline Color dialog box with PANTONE spot colors selected

5. Click the color you want to use either in the color model palette or in the custom palette. The square box at the right side of the dialog box shows the new color you have selected, together with a narrow stripe of the current outline color for comparison. In the case of PANTONE and TRUMATCH colors, the Color Name text box shows the name of the selected color. When you choose a color from the custom palette, the color's name is shown if the colors in that palette have names.

6. To lighten a spot color or modify a CMYK, RGB, or HSB color, change the value in the text boxes to the right of the palette. Whenever you select a color in the palette or modify a selected color, the preview box at the right side of the dialog box shows a sample of the new color.

7. Click **OK** to apply the color to the selected outlines.

NOTES   If you use PANTONE or TRUMATCH colors, you can click the Show Color Names check box to display lists of colors and color names instead of color palettes. When you do so, a

Search String text box replaces the Color Name text box. You can type color names into this box to select colors.

In the case of CMYK color model, the palette consists of a large square in which you adjust the amount of cyan and magenta, and a vertical rectangle in which you adjust yellow. The RGB and HSB palettes are similar.

If you use PostScript for printing and are using spot colors, click the PostScript Options button to display a dialog box in which you can specify halftone screens.

If you omit step 1 so that no object is selected, you can select a default outline color that is applied to new objects. You can choose whether the new default is applied to all new graphics objects, all new artistic text objects, or all new paragraph text objects, or to any combination of these types of objects.

See "Choosing a Color Palette" for additional information about custom color palettes.

Selecting an Outline Color
from the Outline Pen Dialog Box

1. Select one or more objects to be colored.

2. Click the **Outline** tool to display the Outline flyout.

3. Click the **Pen** icon to display the Outline Pen dialog box shown in Figure 1.8.

4. Click the **Color** button to display a small palette, scroll the palette to find the color you want, then click the color to return to the Outline Pen dialog box.

5. Click **OK** to apply the color to the selected objects.

NOTES After step 3 of the procedure above, you can click the More button to display the Outline Color dialog box.

See *Outlining an Object* for more information about using the Outline Pen dialog box.

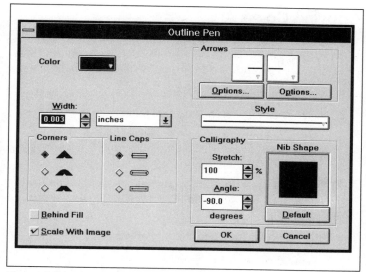

Figure 1.8: The Outline Pen dialog box

Selecting a Fill Color from the Uniform Fill Dialog Box

1. Select one or more objects to be colored.

2. Click the **Fill** tool to display the Fill flyout.

3. Click the **Colorwheel** icon to display the Uniform Fill dialog box, which is similar to the Outline Color dialog box shown in Figure 1.7.

4. Click the color you want to use as a fill, and then click **OK**.

NOTES   Use the same procedure to define a default fill color, but with no object selected. You can separately choose a default fill for graphic, artistic text, and paragraph text objects.

The information about the Outline Color dialog box in "Selecting an Outline Color from the Outline Color Dialog Box" above also applies to the Uniform Fill dialog box.

Copying Colors

You can copy an outline or fill color from one object to others. See *Styles and Templates* for additional information about coloring many objects. To copy an outline color from one object to others:

1. Select the objects to be colored.

2. In the Pen roll-up, click **Update From**.

3. With the **From** cursor, click the object having the outline color to be copied. The outline color sample in the roll-up changes to the new color.

4. In the Pen roll-up, click **Apply** to apply the outline attributes, including color, of the source object to the selected objects.

To copy the fill color from one object to others:

1. Select the objects to be colored.

2. In the Fill roll-up, click **Update From**.

3. With the **From** cursor, click the object having the fill to be copied. The fill sample in the roll-up changes to the new color.

4. In the Fill roll-up, click **Apply** to apply the fill attributes, including color, of the source object to the selected objects.

NOTES You can also copy selected attributes from one object to others by selecting a source object, then choosing Edit ➤ Copy Attributes From. Then, in the Copy Attributes dialog box, check the class of attributes to be copied and click OK.

Choosing a Color Palette

CorelDRAW includes several process color palettes and one spot color palette. You can create custom palettes. To select a palette:

1. Open the **Outline Color** or **Uniform Fill** dialog box. The name of the current palette is shown at the right of the Custom Palette button.

2.   Click **Custom Palette** to display a secondary menu, and then click **Open** to display the Open Palette dialog box, which shows a list of available palettes.

3.   Click the name of the palette you want to use and then click **OK** to redisplay the Outline Color or Uniform Fill dialog box with the new palette's name displayed at the right of the Custom Palette button.

NOTES   CORELDRW.PAL is the default custom color palette. PURE100.PAL is identical to CORELDRW.PAL and is available in case you make changes to the default palette. Custom palettes created from the color models or sets have names with a .PAL extension. Custom palettes created by selecting spot colors have names with a .IPL extension.

Creating a Custom Color Palette

You can create a color palette by choosing or creating colors in the Outline Color or Uniform Fill dialog box.

1.   Open the **Outline Color** or **Uniform Fill** dialog box.

2.   Click **Custom Palette** to display the custom palette menu, and then click **Open** to display the Open Palette dialog box.

3.   Click the name of a process color palette if you are going to create a custom process color palette, or click the name of a spot color palette if you are going to create a custom process color palette. Click **OK** to accept your choice.

4.   Again, click **Custom Palette** to display the custom palette menu, then click **New** to display an empty custom palette.

5.   Open the **Show** list box and click the color model you want to use to specify a color for the new palette.

6.   Click a color in the palette, or specify the color components.

7.   If you are using the CMYK, RGB, or HSB color model, click an insertion marker in the Color Name text box and type a name for the color.

8.   Click **Custom Palette** and then click **Add Color**.

9. Repeat steps 6 through 8 to add more colors to the custom palette.

10. Open the **Show** list box and click **Custom Palette** to show the new custom palette with the added colors.

11. Click **Custom Palette** and then click **Save As** to display the Save Palette As dialog box.

12. Type a name for the new palette, and then click **OK**.

NOTES   Changes you make to a palette affect the palette displayed at the bottom of the screen.

Creating a Custom Process Color

1. Open the **Outline Color** or **Uniform Fill** dialog box.

2. Open the **Show** list box and choose the **CMYK**, **RGB**, or **HSB** color model.

3. Use the scroll bars to adjust the color components (or type values into the adjacent text boxes) to create a color.

COLOR SEPARATIONS

CorelDRAW 4 can print each spot color in a drawing separately and can print the four process color components separately.

The color separation process uses templates (known as color circuits) which prepare images for various media. You can choose one of the templates provided with CorelDRAW or create your own. This process is beyond the scope of this book; for more information, see *Mastering CorelDRAW 4* by Rick Altman (SYBEX, 1993).

COLORING A MONOCHROME BITMAP OBJECT

You can change the black pixels of a black-and-white bitmap to any outline color, and you can change the white pixels to another color. You cannot color a grayscale or color bitmap.

1. Use the **Pick** tool to select the bitmap object. Make sure the status bar indicates that a *monochrome* bitmap is selected.

2. In the Outline tool flyout, click the **Colorwheel** icon to display the Outline Color dialog box.

3. Click an outline color, then click **OK** to apply that color to the black pixels in the bitmap.

4. In the Fill tool flyout, click the **Colorwheel** icon to display the Uniform Fill dialog box.

5. Click a fill color, then click **OK** to apply that color to the white pixels in the bitmap.

COMBINING OBJECTS AND BREAKING OBJECTS APART

See *Grouping and Ungrouping Objects.*

CONSTRAINING AN OBJECT

In many cases you can constrain a CorelDRAW action by holding down the Ctrl key. For example, you can constrain straight lines to specific angles, constrain rectangles to squares, and constrain ellipses to circles. See *Drawing an Object* for specific information.

You can also place constraints on moving and applying effects to objects.

CONTOURING AN OBJECT

You can add contouring to an artistic text or graphic object to give it a three-dimensional appearance.

new Adding Contours to an Object

1. Use the **Pick** tool to select an object.

2. Choose **Effects ➤ Contour Roll-up** to display the Contour roll-up shown in Figure 1.9.

3. In the Contour roll-up, click the **To Center, Inside**, or **Outside** option button. Use To Center to draw a series of contour lines starting just inside the outline and continuing to the center of the object. Use Inside to draw a specific number of contour lines inside the outline. Use Outside to draw a specific number of contour lines outside the outline.

4. Choose or type the distance between contour lines in the **Offset** dialog box.

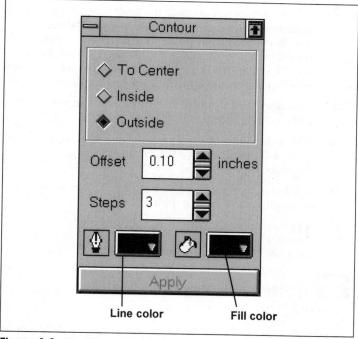

Figure 1.9: The Contour roll-up

5. If you chose the Inside or Outside option in step 3, choose or type the number of contour lines, up to a maximum of 50, in the **Steps** text box.

6. Click **Apply** to redraw the object with contours.

new Adding Filled Contours to an Object

1. Use the **Pick** tool to select an object having a uniform color fill.

2.   In the Contour roll-up, click the **To Center**, **Inside**, or **Outside** option button. Use To Center to draw a series of contour lines starting just inside the outline and continuing to the center of the object. Use Inside to draw a specific number of contour lines inside the outline. Use Outside to draw a specific number of contour lines outside the outline.

3.   Choose or type the distance between contour lines in the **Offset** dialog box.

4.   If you chose the Inside or Outside option in step 2, choose or type the number of contour lines, up to a maximum of 50, in the **Steps** text box.

5.   Click the color button adjacent to the Fill icon in the Contour roll-up to display a color palette.

6.   Click a color in the palette, and click **Apply** to redraw the object with filled contours progressing smoothly from the original fill color to the contour color.

NOTES   To remove contour lines, leaving only the fill colors, click X in the Outline flyout.

To color contour lines, click the color button adjacent to the Outline icon in the Contour roll-up to display a color palette, and then click a color.

CONVERTING AN OBJECT TO CURVES

You can convert rectangles, ellipses, and artistic text objects to curves so that you can reshape them (see *Shaping and Reshaping an Object* for more information).

Combining rectangles, ellipses, and artistic text also converts these objects into curves.

Converting a Rectangle, Ellipse, or Artistic Text Object to Curves

1. Select a rectangle, ellipse, or artistic text object.

2. Choose **Arrange ➤ Convert to Curves**.

NOTES For artistic text, these steps convert the text string to a curve object. You cannot edit curve objects as text. Use Undo to restore a converted text string, providing the number of commands since you converted the string does not exceed the available number of undo levels (see *Undoing, Redoing, and Repeating an Operation*).

You can convert curve objects to text characters. See *fonts: creating* in CorelDRAW on-line Help.

COPYING AN OBJECT

You can use the Clipboard to copy a graphic or text object within a drawing or from one drawing to another. See *Duplicating an Object* for other ways of copying an object.

Copying an Object within a Drawing

1. Select the object to be copied.

2. Choose **Edit ➤ Copy** to copy the object and its attributes to the Clipboard.

3. Choose **Edit ➤ Paste** to paste the copied object on top of the original.

4. Drag the object to another position so that you can see the original and copy separately.

NOTES   When you try to copy an object to the Clipboard, you may see a message indicating that the object is too large. To overcome this problem, break the object into parts and copy it part by part. Alternatively, you can save the object as a file and then import it into the drawing.

You can use the Clipboard to copy complete artistic or paragraph text objects. To copy individual characters from an artistic or paragraph text object, select those characters with the Text tool.

Copying an Object from One Drawing to Another

1. Use the **Pick** tool to select the object to be copied.

2. Choose **Edit ➤ Copy** to copy the object and its attributes to the Clipboard.

3. Open the drawing into which the object is to be copied.

4. Choose **Edit ➤ Paste** to place the copied object into the drawing.

Copying an Object between Another Windows Application and CorelDRAW

Use the procedure described in "Copying an Object from One Drawing to Another." The following formats may be cut or copied from CorelDRAW into the Clipboard:

*   CorelDRAW native format (CF_CORELDRW)
*   Windows Metafile

The following formats may be pasted from the Clipboard into CorelDRAW:

*   CorelDRAW native format (CF_CORELDRW)
*   Windows Metafile

- ASCII text

- Windows bitmaps

Objects containing PostScript textures, pattern fills, and bitmaps cannot be pasted into other applications.

Some applications cannot accept pasted objects larger than 64 kilobytes.

Certain Metafile features cut or copied from other applications cannot be pasted into CorelDRAW (see *Clipboard - General Pasting Limitations* in CorelDRAW on-line Help form more information).

CREATING TEXT

CorelDRAW allows you to create and edit artistic and paragraph text directly on your drawing or in a dialog box.

Artistic text consists of up to 250 characters that are not within a frame and can have special effects applied to them. Paragraph text consists of up to 4000 characters within a frame that can be as large as the printable page.

Creating Artistic Text

You can set default character attributes before you create text (as assumed here), or you can change the attributes after you have created the text.

1. Select a font and character attributes for the text to be created (see *Fonts* and *Character Attributes*).

2. Select the **Artistic Text** tool (see *Toolbox*).

3. Move the cursor to the place on your drawing where you want the text to begin and click the mouse button.

4. Type one or more lines of text.

5. When you have finished, click the **Pick** tool to display the text with the current outline and fill attributes.

Creating Paragraph Text

You can set default character attributes before you create text (as assumed here), or you can change the attributes after you have created the text.

1. Select font and character attributes for the text to be created (see *Fonts* and *Character Attributes*).

2. Select the **Paragraph Text** tool (see *Toolbox*).

3. Move the cursor to where the top left corner of the paragraph frame is to be.

4. Press the mouse button and drag down and to the right to create a frame for the text, then release the mouse button.

5. Type the text. Whenever the text reaches the right edge of the frame, it wraps to the next line.

6. When you have finished, click the **Pick** tool to display the text with the current outline and fill, showing the paragraph frame with handles.

NOTES To create a frame with one-inch margins in the printable page, in place of steps 2 and 3, just click anywhere on the page. To adjust the margins, drag the frame handles.

Only the text that fits within the frame shows on the screen. If you type more text than can fit into the frame, you can subsequently stretch the frame to make the extra text visible. See *Stretching and Shrinking an Object*.

new Creating Text in Linked Paragraph Frames

Text can flow between two or more linked frames on the same page or on different pages. Text flows between linked frames when the size of the frames changes, or when the text within the frames changes.

1. Use the tool to draw a paragraph text frame (see "Creating Paragraph Text" above).

2. Click the **Pick** tool to display the frame with its handles.

3. Click the empty handle at the center of the lower edge of the first frame to display the frame cursor.

4. Use the frame cursor to draw another paragraph next frame. Notice that a + appears in the handle at the center of the lower edge of the first frame, indicating the existence of a linked frame.

5. Click the **Paragraph Text** tool to display the two linked frames.

6. Type text. The text starts in the first frame, and when that frame is full, flows into the second frame.

NOTES If there is more text than fits in the first frame, the text automatically flows into the second frame. Similarly, if you add or delete text in either frame or change the size of a frame, text flows between the two.

When you use the Pick tool to select a frame, a + in the handle at the center of the top edge indicates the presence of a preceding linked frame; a + in the handle at the center of the bottom edge indicates the presence of a subsequent linked frame.

Breaking the Link between Frames

A text frame can be linked to a preceding frame, to a subsequent frame, or to both. You can select a frame and break its link to remove it from the linkage chain.

If a frame is only linked to a preceding frame and you break its link, text that was previously displayed in the frame remains attached to the preceding frame, even if there is more text than will fit. Similarly, if a frame is linked only to a subsequent frame and you break its link, the text remains attached to the subsequent frame.

If a frame is linked to a preceding and to a subsequent frame and you break its link, the preceding frame links directly to the subsequent frame and the text flows between those two frames.

To break all links between a frame and other frames:

1. Select the frame with the **Pick** tool.

2. Choose **Arrange ➤ Separate** to remove the frame from the linkage chain.

To break the link between frames, leaving the text in two separate frames:

1. Select both frames with the **Pick** tool or by marquee-selecting.

2. Choose **Arrange ➤ Separate** to split the text into two separate frames.

new **Creating a Bulleted List**

1. Create the list as paragraph text.

2. Use the **Text** tool to highlight the list.

3. Choose **Text ➤ Paragraph**, and click **Bullet** in the Category list.

4. Click the **Bullet On** check box.

5. Select the category of symbols and click a symbol within that category.

6. Choose **Size**, **Bullet Indent**, and **Vert Shift** parameters, and then click **OK** to place the bullet at the beginning of the highlighted list.

Pasting Text into a Drawing

You can create text in a Windows application, copy it to the Clipboard, and then paste it into your drawing as artistic or paragraph text. The text loses its original attributes and is pasted with the current default CorelDRAW attributes.

1. Create text in a Windows application.

2. Cut or copy the text to the Clipboard.

3. Open a CorelDRAW drawing.

4. To paste text as artistic text, click the **Artistic Text** tool, click where you want the text to appear, and choose **Edit ➤ Paste**. To paste text as paragraph text, click the **Paragraph Text** tool, click where you want the text to appear, and choose **Edit ➤ Paste**.

NOTES If the text in the Clipboard consists of more than 250 characters, it is always pasted as paragraph text.

Importing Text

You can create text in a word processor or text editor, including non-Windows applications, and then import it into your drawing as paragraph text, but not as artistic text.

1. Create text in a word processor or text editor and write the text to disk in a format for which you have installed CorelDRAW import filters (see step 3).

2. Open your CorelDRAW drawing and choose **File ➤ Import** to display the Import dialog box.

3. Open the **List Files Of Type** list box and choose the format of the file to be imported from the list of formats for which you have import filters.

4. Select the directory that contains the text file, click its name in the File Name list box, and click **OK**. A paragraph text frame the same size as the printable page is created and the text flows into it.

NOTES If the imported file contains more text than can fit on a page, a dialog box appears asking you to insert a page.

You can also import text into an existing frame, but the text must be unformatted ASCII text. To do this, create a paragraph text frame, and choose **Text ➤ Edit Text** to display the Paragraph Text dialog box. Then click **Import**, click the name of the file to import, and click **OK**.

Using Special Characters

CorelDRAW provides many special characters that you can display on your screen and print. All these characters are shown in the *Quick Reference Booklet* supplied with CorelDRAW.

To place a special character on your drawing or in a Artistic Text or Paragraph Text dialog box:

1. Find the special character in the *Quick Reference Booklet*.

2. Note the character's number in the column to the left of the symbol, and the font name at the top of the column containing the character.

3. Click the **Text** tool and place the text cursor where you want the special character to appear in the drawing or in the Artistic Text or Paragraph Text dialog box.

4. Select the font that contains the special character. Do this from the Text roll-up or from the Character Attributes dialog box.

5. Make sure that Num Lock is on, then press and hold down the **Alt** key.

6. Type the three- or four-digit number that identifies the special character. You must type the leading zero.

7. The special character appears on your screen when you release the **Alt** key.

NOTES If the special character's number is in the range 033 through 0126, you can access it by selecting the font and typing the equivalent keyboard character listed in the Windows column of the chart.

Some fonts do not contain certain special characters. If you choose a character that does not exist in the current font, you will see a black square or a different character.

CROPPING A BITMAP OBJECT

1. Use the **Shape** tool to select the bitmap object. The status bar shows that a bitmap is selected and how much it is currently cropped.

2. Drag each of the handles to crop the object.

NOTES You can uncrop a previously cropped object by dragging its handles out.

To minimize the size of a CorelDRAW file, import only slightly more of the original bitmap than you expect to use. In CorelDRAW, crop to adjust the final size of the bitmap.

CUSTOMIZING CORELDRAW

You can customize CorelDRAW by setting various preferences (see *Preferences*). You can also customize it by making changes to the WIN.INI, CORELDRW.INI, and CORELDRW.DOT files. The installation procedure makes necessary additions to your WIN.INI file and also creates a CORELDRW.INI file and a CORELDRW.DOT file. For information about these files and how you can modify them to customize the program, do the following:

1. Choose **Help ➤ Contents**.

2. Click the **Reference** icon.

3.   Click **Software-related Information**.

4.   Click on the name of the item you wish to reference.

You can also change many defaults. See *defaults* in CorelDRAW's on-line Help.

 NOTES   Always make a copy of your original WIN.INI, CORELDRW.INI, and CORELDRW.DOT files before editing them. Then, if you make a mistake, you can restore the originals.

DELETING AN OBJECT

1.   Select the object to be deleted.

2.   Choose **Edit ➤ Delete**. Alternatively, press the **Delete** key.

 NOTES   You can also choose Edit ➤ Cut to remove the selected object from a drawing and place it on the Clipboard.

DIMENSION LINES

You can add dimension lines to show the size of objects in a drawing.

new Adding a Dimension Line to an Object

1.   Choose **Layout ➤ Snap To ➤ Objects** to turn on snap-to objects so that you can accurately align dimension lines with objects.

2.   Select the vertical, horizontal, or angle **Pencil** tool, according to the direction in which you want to draw the dimension line (see *Toolbox*).

3.   Click where you want the dimension line to start, then double-click where you want it to end. The dimension line appears together with the dimension text that shows the size of the dimensioned object.

NOTES   The dimension text value appears in the same units as the horizontal grid, unless you specify otherwise in Preferences.

By default, the dimension text appears at the end of, and in line with, a dimension line. By setting preferences, you can change the position and alignment of the text.

new Editing a Dimension Line

Using the same methods as for other objects, you can separately edit the following:

- Color and other attributes of a dimension line

- Attributes of the dimension text

You can move the dimension line and text as a single object, and you can move the text independently.

DISPLAY VIEWS

You can create and edit drawings in two views: editable preview and wireframe view. Editable preview allows you to see the full effect of what you are doing, whereas wireframe view shows objects as skeleton outlines for faster screen redrawing.

Switching between
Editable Preview and Wireframe

Choose **Display ➤ Edit Wireframe** to change from the default editable preview to wireframe view, or vice-versa.

NOTES When you open the **Display** menu, a check mark adjacent to **Edit Wireframe** indicates that wireframe view is selected. The absence of a check mark indicates that editable preview is selected.

Previewing a Drawing

When Preview (distinct from editable preview) is selected, all menus, rulers, and tools are removed from the screen and you just see an enlarged view of your drawing or selected objects.

To preview your entire drawing:

1. Choose **Display ➤ Show Preview** to preview the entire drawing.

2. Press any key to leave Preview.

To preview only selected objects:

1. Select the objects you wish to preview.

2. Choose **Display ➤ Preview Selected Only**.

3. Choose **Display ➤ Show Preview**.

4. Press any key to leave Preview.

Displaying and Hiding Bitmap Objects

Bitmaps, particularly those that are complex and in color, can slow the process of redrawing the screen. In wireframe view, but not in editable preview, you can hide bitmaps to speed redrawing. Hidden bitmaps are displayed as empty boxes. Choose **Display ➤ Show Bitmaps** to switch between showing and not showing bitmaps in wireframe view.

DRAWING AN OBJECT

With CorelDRAW's tools you can draw rectangles, ellipses, and lines (straight or curved). The status bar displays information about the most recently drawn or currently selected object.

Drawing a Rectangle or Square

1. Select the **Rectangle** tool.

2. Point where you want to place a corner.

3. Press the mouse button and drag to the opposite corner, then release the mouse button. The rectangle is displayed with nodes at the four corners.

NOTES   To constrain the rectangle to a square, hold down the Ctrl key while you drag. Keep the Ctrl key pressed until you have released the mouse button.

Instead of drawing a rectangle from corner to corner, you can enlarge it from the center out by holding down the Shift key while you drag. Keep the Shift key pressed until you have released the mouse button.

To enlarge a square from the center out, hold down the Ctrl and Shift keys while you drag.

Drawing a Rounded Rectangle or Square

To draw a rectangle or square with rounded corners:

1. Draw a rectangle, following steps 1 through 3 in "Drawing Rectangles and Squares" above.

2. Use the **Shape** tool to select the rectangle.

3. Point to a corner node and press the mouse button.

4. Drag the node along an edge to achieve the rounding effect you want, then release the mouse button. The rounding applies to all four corners. As you drag, each corner
node becomes two nodes, one on each of the adjacent
edges.

NOTES   To adjust rounding, use the Shape tool to point
to one of the nodes and drag in either direction along an edge.

If you round the corners of a stretched rectangle, the corner rounding effect is elliptical.

Drawing an Ellipse or Circle

1. Select the **Ellipse** tool.

2. Point where you want a corner of the rectangular frame
that encloses the ellipse to be.

3. Press the mouse button and drag to the opposite corner of
the frame, then release the mouse button. The ellipse is
displayed with one node.

NOTES   Press the Ctrl key to constrain the ellipse as a
circle; press the Shift key to enlarge an ellipse from its center. See the
notes under "Drawing a Rectangle or Square" for more information.

Drawing an Arc or Wedge

You can draw an arc or a wedge by modifying an ellipse or circle.

1. First, create an ellipse or circle. Follow steps 1 through 3
under "Drawing Ellipses and Circles."

2. Using the **Shape** tool, select the ellipse.

3. Point to the node on the ellipse, then press and hold down
the mouse button.

4. Drag outside the ellipse to create an arc, or drag inside the
ellipse to create a wedge, then release the mouse button.

NOTES   Hold down the Ctrl key while you drag to constrain the angle of the arc or wedge to specific increments. See *Preferences* for information about setting this angle.

Selecting Freehand or Bézier Mode

CorelDRAW has two drawing modes: Freehand and Bézier. Freehand, which lets you draw by dragging the mouse, is ideal for making quick sketches. Bézier lets you draw smooth curves with precision by connecting points. The default is Freehand mode.

To switch between Freehand and Bézier modes:

1. Point to the **Pencil** tool.

2. Press and hold down the mouse button until a flyout menu with five pencil icons appears.

3. Click the left icon to select Freehand mode, or click the second-from-the-left icon to select Bézier mode.

NOTES   See *Dimension Lines* for information about the other three pencil tools.

The toolbox shows which of the pencil tools is currently available. Also, when you select the Pencil tool, the status bar tells you which pencil tool is available.

Drawing a Straight Line in Freehand Mode

You can draw a straight line in Freehand or Bézier mode. See above for information about selecting a drawing mode. To draw a straight line in Freehand mode:

1. In the PowerLine roll-up, make sure the **Apply when drawing lines** check box is not checked (see *Powerlines*).

2. Select the Freehand **Pencil** tool (see *Toolbox*). The status bar confirms that the current drawing mode is Freehand.

3. Point to where you want the line to begin, and click.

4.   Point to where you want the line to end, and click. You can see the line as you position the endpoint.

5.   If you want to draw a second straight line connected to the first, point to one end of the existing line, within the AutoJoin distance, and click (see *AutoJoin*). If you want to draw a second straight line that is not connected, point to a new position on the screen and click.

6.   Point to where you want the new line to end, and click.

7.   Repeat steps 5 and 6 to draw additional connected or unconnected lines.

8.   Terminate line drawing by selecting the **Pick** tool or any other tool.

Drawing a Straight Line in Bézier Mode

1.   In the PowerLine roll-up, make sure the **Apply when drawing lines** check box is not checked (see *Powerlines*).

2.   Select the Bézier **Pencil** tool (see *Toolbox*). The status bar confirms that the current drawing mode is Bézier.

3.   Point to where you want the line to begin, and click.

4.   Point to where you want the line to end, and click. The line appears after you click the endpoint.

5.   To draw a second straight line connected to the first, point to the endpoint of the second line, and click. The second line appears as soon as you click. To draw a second line not connected to the first, press the spacebar twice, then use steps 2 and 3 to draw the line.

6.   Repeat step 5 to draw additional connected or unconnected lines.

7.   Terminate line drawing by selecting the **Pick** tool.

NOTES   You can constrain a straight line drawn in Freehand mode, but not one drawn in Bézier mode, to be horizontal, vertical, or at a constraint angle by holding down the Ctrl key while you place the endpoint. See *Preferences* for information about setting the constraint angle.

Drawing a Curve in Freehand Mode

You can draw a curve in Freehand or Bézier mode. To draw a curve in Freehand mode:

1. In the PowerLine roll-up, make sure the **Apply when drawing lines** check box is not checked (see *Powerlines*).

2. Select the Freehand **Pencil** tool (see *Toolbox*).

3. Point where you want the curve to begin, then press and hold down the mouse button.

4. Drag the cursor to draw the curve, and release the mouse button when you have finished. Nodes are automatically created wherever the curve changes direction significantly.

5. To draw a second curve connected to the first, point within the AutoJoin distance of one end of the existing curve and repeat steps 3 and 4 (see *AutoJoin*). To draw a second curve not connected to the first, point to a new place on the screen and repeat steps 3 and 4.

6. Terminate drawing by selecting the **Pick** tool.

NOTES You can make corrections to your curve before you release the mouse button. At any time, with the mouse button still held down, press the Shift key and trace back along the curve you have just drawn. The curve is deleted portion by portion as you trace back. After deleting a portion, release the Shift key, and continue to draw the curve.

You can subsequently change the shape of a curve with the Shape tool (see *Shaping and Reshaping an Object*).

Drawing a Curved Line in Bézier Mode

Unlike Freehand mode, Bézier mode allows you to control where nodes are placed on a curve, so that you can produce smooth curves.

1. In the PowerLine roll-up, make sure the **Apply when drawing lines** check box is not checked (see *Powerlines*).

2. Select the Bézier **Pencil** tool (see *Toolbox*).

3. Point where you want a segment of a curve to begin, press and hold down the mouse button while you drag in the direction the curve is to be drawn, then release the mouse button. A node with control points appears.

4. Point where you want the segment to end, press and hold down the mouse button while you drag in the direction the curve should pass through (or end at) the node. Drag the mouse to create the curve you want, then release the mouse button.

5. Repeat step 4 to draw additional segments.

6. Terminate curve drawing by selecting the **Pick** tool.

NOTES   These steps produce connected curve segments. To draw disconnected segments, press the spacebar twice after completing one segment and before starting the next.

You can subsequently use the Shape tool to change the shape of the curve. See *Shaping and Reshaping an Object*.

You can constrain the position of control points relative to a node by holding down the Ctrl key while you drag. See *Preferences* for information about setting the constraint angle.

Drawing a Powerline

See *Powerlines*.

Drawing a Dimension Line

See *Dimension Lines*.

DUPLICATING AN OBJECT

1. Select the object, or group of objects, to be duplicated.

2. Tap + on the numeric keypad to create a duplicate on top of the original object, or choose **Edit ➤ Duplicate** to create a duplicate slightly above and to the right of the original object.

NOTES   See *Clones* and *Copying an Object* for other ways of duplicating an object.

See *Preferences* for information about setting the position of the duplicate.

EDITING TEXT

You can edit paragraph text and most artistic text in three ways: directly on a drawing, in a text dialog box, or as extracted text. Artistic text to which you have applied special effects (with the exception of blend) cannot be edited directly in a drawing.

Editing Text in a Drawing

1. Use the **Zoom** tool to magnify the text so that you can see each character clearly (see *Viewing an Object at Different Magnifications*).

2. Select the **Text** tool.

3. Point to the position in the text where you want to edit and click to create an insertion point.

4. Press **Backspace** to delete characters to the left of the insertion point, or press **Delete** to delete characters to the right.
Alternatively, use the **Text** tool to highlight a number of
characters, and press **Delete** to delete them all.

5. Type characters to insert them at the insertion point.

Editing Text in a Dialog Box

1. Use the **Pick** tool to select artistic or paragraph text.

2. Choose **Text ➤ Edit Text**.

3. In the Artistic Text or Paragraph Text dialog box, use the
techniques in "Editing Text on a Drawing" to delete or insert text.

4. Click **OK** to return to the drawing.

NOTES   You can change character attributes in the Artistic Text and Paragraph Text dialog boxes.

Editing Extracted Text

You can edit artistic or paragraph text in a drawing by saving it as a
text file, editing the text file with a word processor or text editor,
and subsequently merging the edited text back into your drawing.
Some, but not all, attributes of the original text are applied to the
merged-back text.

You do not need to select the text you wish to extract because the
procedure extracts all the text in your drawing.

To extract, edit, and merge back text:

1. Save your current drawing (see *File Management*). This
step is necessary because you must have saved the drawing as a file before you can use the Merge Back command.

2. Choose **Special ➤ Extract** to display the Extract dialog box.

3. Either accept the file name for the extracted text that Corel-DRAW proposes by clicking **OK**, or type a new name and then click **OK**. Unless you specify otherwise, the file is written into your COREL40\DRAW subdirectory.

4. Minimize CorelDRAW and open a word processor or text editor such as Windows Notepad.

5. Open the file containing the extracted text, edit it (see the notes below), and save the edited text.

6. Restore CorelDRAW.

7. Choose **Special ➤ Merge Back** to display the Merge Back dialog box.

8. If necessary, select the edited text file.

9. Click **OK** and the edited text appears in your drawing.

NOTES   It is very important that you change only the text, not the surrounding codes, in the text file. CorelDRAW needs these codes to identify the file from which the text was extracted and the position of the text in the file.

The text strings in the text file are shown in the reverse order to that in which you placed them into your drawing. Each text string starts with an identifying code and ends with the <CDR> delimiter.

Edit only the text strings. If you use a word processor, make sure you save the file as a text file so that it does not include any word processing codes.

EMBEDDING AN OBJECT

See *Linking and Embedding an Object*.

EXPORTING AN OBJECT

You can export CorelDRAW drawings and objects in many file formats so that you can import them into applications such as word processors, desktop publishing programs, presentation programs, and other graphics programs running on PC (MS-DOS and OS/2), Macintosh, and UNIX platforms. See the Appendix for a list of file formats supported by CorelDRAW.

You can either export to a file, or if you are going to use your drawing in another Windows application, you can copy it to the Clipboard.

Exporting to a File

1. If you want to export individual objects, use the **Pick** tool to select those objects.

2. Choose **File ➤ Export** to display the Export dialog box.

3. Select an export format in the **List Files of Type** box.

4. In the **Directories** list box, select a destination disk and directory.

5. Choose a name for the exported file from those in the File Name list box, or type a name in the text box. If you type a new name, do not add an extension; CorelDRAW automatically adds an extension appropriate for the type of file.

6. To export only selected objects, click the **Selected Only** check box to place a check mark in it. With no check mark there, the entire drawing is exported.

7. Click **OK** to write the drawing, or selected objects, to a file.

8. Open the target application and import the file into it. See the target application's documentation for information about using the exported objects.

Exporting by Way of the Clipboard

You can use the Clipboard to copy objects from one CorelDRAW drawing to another, from a CorelDRAW drawing to another Windows application, or from another Windows application to a CorelDRAW drawing.

To copy from one CorelDRAW drawing to another:

1. Select the object or objects you want to export.

2. Choose **Edit ➤ Copy**.

3. Open the file into which you want to import the object.

4. Choose **Edit ➤ Paste**.

NOTES You use almost the same procedure as that just given to copy objects from one application to another. The only difference is that steps 1 and 2 apply to the application you are copying from, and steps 3 and 4 apply to the application to which you are copying.

If your object is too large for the Clipboard, you will see an error message. In this case you should export the object as a file and subsequently import the file into the other application.

Various Windows applications handle the Clipboard in different ways. Therefore, your CorelDRAW objects may look different in those applications. See the Reference section of CorelDRAW's online Help for information.

EXTRUDING AN OBJECT

You can extrude objects to give an illusion of depth. Figure 1.10 shows an orthogonal extrusion on the left and a perspective extrusion on the right. See *Perspective* for information about making one-point and two-point perspective views of objects.

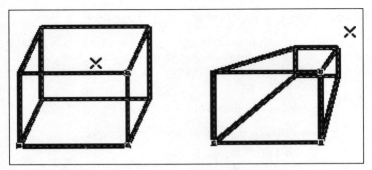

Figure 1.10: An orthogonal extrusion (left) and a perspective
extrusion (right)

Drawing an Extrusion

To draw a basic extrusion:

1.   Use the **Pick** tool to select the object you wish to extrude.

2.   Choose **Effects ➤ Extrude Roll-Up** to display the Extrude
roll-up shown in Figure 1.11 (top left), and to create an extrusion defined by the initial conditions in the roll-up.

3.   Open the list box in the roll-up and click one of the six
options.

4.   Choose or type a value in the **Depth** text box.

5.   Click **Apply** and then click the **Pick** tool.

NOTES   The first four options in the list box allow you to
choose perspective extrusions; the other two options provide orthogonal extrusions. In each case, the extrusion may extend behind
or in front of the object.

The value in the Depth box is a percentage that determines how far
a perspective extrusion extends towards the vanishing point.

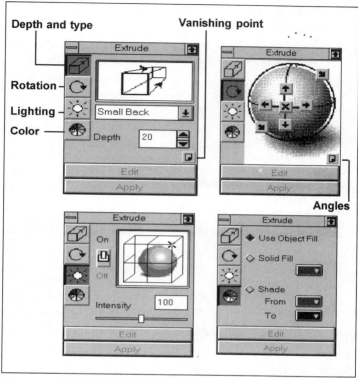

Figure 1.11: The four forms of the Extrude roll-up: format (top left), rotation (top right), lighting (bottom left), and color (bottom right)

Placing the Vanishing Point

By default, the vanishing point, shown as an X on a drawing, is at the center of the page. After you have created an extrusion, you can move the vanishing point by dragging it. To place the vanishing point with precision:

1. Select an extrusion.

2. Click the small icon at the bottom right of the Extrude roll-up to display the current coordinates of the vanishing

point. By default, these coordinates are relative to the
page origin.

3. To display the vanishing-point origin relative to the center of
the extruded object, click the **Object Center** option button.

4. Choose or type a new horizontal coordinate value in the
H text box and a new vertical coordinate value in the **V**
text box, then click **Apply**.

5. Click the small icon at the bottom right of the roll-up to
return to the original roll-up.

Rotating an Extrusion

1. Select an extrusion.

2. Click the **Rotation** icon in the Extrude roll-up to display
rotation, as shown in Figure 1.11 (top right).

3. Either click the arrows in the roll-up to rotate the extrusion interactively in five-degree increments, or click the
small icon at the bottom right of the roll-up and choose
or type rotation values in the three text boxes.

4. Click **Apply** to redraw the extruded object.

NOTES   Click the X at the center of the rotation model to
remove rotation from the extruded object.

Lighting an Extrusion

1. Select an extrusion.

2. Click the **Lighting** icon in the Extrude roll-up to display
lighting as shown in Figure 1.11 (bottom left).

3. Click the **Switch** icon to turn the light on.

4. Click one of the 16 intersections around the lighting model
to place the light source.

5. Set the light intensity by typing a value in the text box or by dragging the marker on the intensity line.

6. Click **Apply** to redraw the extruded object.

Coloring an Extrusion

1. Select an extrusion.

2. Click the **Colorwheel** icon in the Extrude roll-up to display color choices as shown in Figure 1.11 (bottom right).

3. Click the **Object Fill**, **Solid Fill**, or **Shade** option button to choose a fill for the extruded surfaces. In each case, the original object has the current fill. Object Fill applies the current fill to the extruded surfaces. Solid Fill applies a different solid fill to the extruded surfaces. Shade applies a shaded fill to the extruded surfaces.

4. If you have chosen Solid Fill or Shade, click the appropriate color button and choose colors for the extruded surfaces.

5. Click **Apply** to redraw the extruded object.

Removing an Extrusion

1. Use the **Pick** tool to select the extruded object.

2. Choose **Effects ➤ Clear Extrude** to display the object without an extrusion.

FILE MANAGEMENT

See the Appendix for a list of file types compatible with CorelDRAW.

Opening a New CorelDRAW File

1. Choose **File ➤ New** to open a new editing window. By default, the page parameters are the same as those in the most recent CorelDRAW session.

2. Choose **Layout ➤ Page Setup** and specify the page parameters, as described in *Page Setup*.

new Opening a New CorelDRAW File Based on a Specific Template

To open a new file based on a template other than the default:

1. Choose **File ➤ New From Template** to open the New From Template dialog box, which lists available templates.

2. Click the name of the template you want to use to display a thumbnail.

3. As needed, click the **With Contents** option box. With this box unchecked, the new file opens without the template's contents. With the box checked, the file opens with the template's contents in place.

4. Click **OK** to open the new drawing based on the specified template.

NOTES If a template includes fonts that are not installed, a dialog box appears listing those fonts. Click OK to allow font substitution, or click Cancel, install the missing fonts, and then repeat the procedure.

See *Styles and Templates* for more information about Templates.

Opening an Existing File

1. Choose **File ➤ Open** to display the Open Drawing dialog box.

2. Select the appropriate directory, and if necessary, open the **List Files of Type** box and select the file type.

3. From the list of file names, select the one you want to open. If Preview is enabled (see below), you see a miniature view of the selected file in the window at the right side of the Open Drawing dialog box.

4. Click **OK**.

At any time before you click OK, you can click the options button to:

- Display file names sorted by name or date
- Find a file by searching for keywords
- Use CorelMOSAIC to help you find a file
- See any keywords or notes you have attached to files
- Display the size of a file and its date

Saving a File with Its Existing Name

To save a previously saved file, choose **File ➤ Save**.

NOTES When you use this command to save a file you have previously named, the file is saved immediately, overwriting the existing file with the same name. When you use the Save command with a file you have not previously saved, the command acts as a Save As command (see below).

Saving a File with a Specified Name

When you use the Save As command, the file is saved by default as a CorelDRAW drawing in the directory most recently accessed in a CorelDRAW session. You can save a complete drawing or document, or you can save selected objects only.

To save a drawing, or selected objects on a drawing, with a specified name:

1. Choose **File ➤ Save As** to display the Save Drawing dialog box. The File Name list box shows the names of files with a .CDR extension in the default directory.

2. To save the file in other than the proposed directory, select that directory in the Directories list box.

3. Replace the name proposed in the File Name text box with the name you wish to give your file. Do not type an extension unless you want it to be different from the extension CorelDRAW automatically supplies.

4. If you wish, add keywords and notes in the appropriate boxes.

5. To save the file in a format compatible with CorelDRAW version 3, click the **Version 3.0** check box.

6. To save the entire document or drawing, leave the **Selected Only** check box unchecked. Check this box to save selected objects only.

7. If you wish, you can change the image header from the default by opening the **Image Header** list box and clicking your choice. See the note below.

8. Click **OK** to save the drawing, document, or selected objects.

NOTES The image header, a miniature representation of your drawing, is displayed when you open an existing file or when you search for files with CorelMOSAIC. The detail shown in this miniature depends on the size of the image header. Reduce the size of the image header if you want to conserve disk space and can accept less detail in the header.

If you try to save a file to a directory that already contains a file with the same name, CorelDRAW warns you that you are about to write over an existing file.

Closing a File

There is no Close command in the File menu. When you open a new or existing file, CorelDRAW automatically closes the current one. CorelDRAW warns you if you are about to close a file you have not saved since you changed it, and gives you the opportunity to save it before you close it.

Importing and Exporting a File

See *Importing an Object* and *Exporting an Object*.

Inserting an Object into a CorelDRAW File

See *Embedding and Linking an Object* and *Inserting an Object*.

Backing Up a File

CorelDRAW has two ways of creating backup files, Automatic and Normal:

- Automatic backups, by default, are made every ten minutes and are written as .ABK files in your COREL40\AUTO-BACK subdirectory. Each new backup file writes over the previous one.

- Normal backup files, by default, are made every time you save a file with the Save or Save As command and are written as .BAK files in the subdirectory in which you are currently saving files. These files are automatically deleted when you exit CorelDRAW. However, these files are not deleted if CorelDRAW terminates abnormally, such as when you experience a power failure.

NOTES   Both backup methods are controlled by entries in your CORELDRW.INI file, which by default is in your COREL40\CONFIG directory. You can change the time interval at which automatic backups occur and the directory into which .ABK files are written. You can also disable either or both forms of backup. See *Specifying Backup File Creation Options* in the CorelDRAW on-line Help for more information.

Opening a Backup File

1. Choose **File ➤ Open** to display the Open Drawing dialog box.

2. Change the file-name extension to .ABK or .BAK.

3. Proceed with steps 2 through 4 above under "Opening an Existing File" above.

4. After opening a backup file, save it with a .CDR extension.

NOTES In step 2, you can specify several extensions. For example, to list all .CDR, .ABK, and .BAK files, the text box would contain *.CDR,*.ABK,*BAK. Note the commas that separate the terms.

Printing a File

See *Printing a Drawing*.

Temporary Files

CorelDRAW creates temporary files while it is running. These files start with ~WAL and have the .TMP extension. Some of these files can be quite large, so you should make sure that you have several megabytes of free space on your hard disk before using CorelDRAW.

Under normal circumstances, CorelDRAW automatically erases all temporary files at the end of each session. However, if CorelDRAW terminates abnormally—for example, when a power outage occurs—you may be left with temporary files on your disk. Check your hard disk from time to time and delete any unnecessary temporary files.

FILLING AN OBJECT

You can fill closed objects with solid colors or shades of gray, and with patterns, fountains, and textures. If you use PostScript for printing, you can also fill objects with PostScript textures and halftone screens. In addition to the fill patterns and textures supplied with CorelDRAW, you can create your own.

With the exception of PostScript textures and halftone screens, fills appear on your screen when you are working in editable preview, but not when you are working in wireframe view. The status line displays the current fill when a single object is selected, but not when more than one object is selected.

When you fill two overlapping closed objects, only the non-overlapping parts of the object are filled. The overlapped region remains unfilled and is transparent.

If you combine closed and open objects with the Combine command in the Arrange menu and subsequently fill the combined object:

- Each closed object is filled as normal.

- Each open object is filled as if a straight line joined its ends.

You can fill objects either from the color palette at the bottom of the screen, from the Fill flyout shown in Figure 1.12, or from the Fill roll-up shown in Figure 1.13.

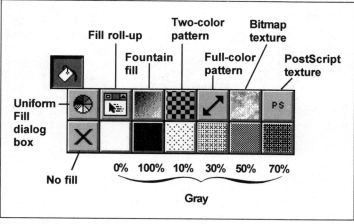

Figure 1.12: The Fill flyout

66 CorelDRAW

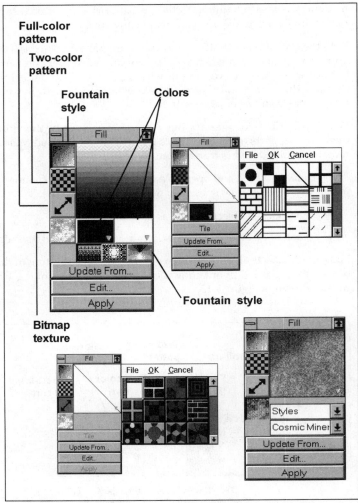

Figure 1.13: The four forms of the Fill roll-up: fountain fills (top left), two-color pattern fills (top right), full-color pattern fills (bottom left), and bitmap textures (bottom right)

Filling an Object with
White, Black, or a Shade of Gray

You can fill an object with white, black, or one of the four grays in the Fill flyout, or you can choose a shade of gray from the color palette at the bottom of the screen. Also, see "Filling an Object with a Tint of Gray" below to select from a wider range of grays.

To fill an object from the Fill flyout:

1. Select the object to be filled.

2. Click the **Fill** tool to display the Fill flyout.

3. Click one of the seven squares in the bottom row of the flyout. From left to right the squares represent no fill (transparent), white, black, and four shades of gray.

NOTES   An object on your screen filled with white appears the same as an object with no fill. However, an object filled with white is opaque and hides anything behind it, whereas an object with no fill is transparent. Also, an object filled with white can be selected anywhere on the outline or within the object, whereas an object with no fill can only be selected on the outline.

Filling an Object with a Tint of Gray

You can fill an object with gray by choosing a tint of gray from the PANTONE spot color palette or by choosing a shade of gray from another palette. To choose a PANTONE tint of gray:

1. Select the object to be filled.

2. Click the **Fill** tool to display the Fill flyout.

3. Click the **Colorwheel** icon to display the Uniform Fill dialog box (similar to the Outline Color dialog box shown in Figure 1.7).

4. If the PANTONE palette is not selected, open the **Show** list and click **PANTONE Spot Colors**.

5.   Click the black color sample at the top, left of the palette, then choose a **Tint** percentage to produce a shade of gray. The New sample box shows the tint of gray.

6.   Click **OK** to apply the tint of gray to the selected objects.

NOTES   The CORELDRW.PAL color palette contains various grays at 10 percent intervals. The SMALL.PAL custom color palette contains grays at 5 percent intervals.

Filling an Object with a Uniform Color

See "Selecting a Fill Color from the Uniform Fill Dialog Box" in *Color*.

Filling an Object with a Pattern

You can fill an object with a two-color or full-color pattern from various sources:

- The patterns provided with CorelDRAW

- Patterns you create with a paint program such as CorelDRAW's Two-color Pattern Editor or CorelPHOTO-PAINT

- Drawings you create with CorelDRAW and save as patterns

To fill an object with a pattern supplied with CorelDRAW, use the steps necessary to achieve your objective in the following procedure:

1.   Select the object to be filled.

2.   Click the **Fill** tool to display the Fill flyout.

3.   Click the **Two-color Pattern** icon to display the Two-color Pattern dialog box, or click the **Full-color Pattern** icon to display the Full-color Pattern dialog box.

4.   Click the pattern preview in the dialog box to display a palette of available patterns, click the pattern you want to use, then click **OK** to select the pattern and display it in the preview box.

5. Choose a size for the pattern by clicking the **Small**, **Medium**, or **Large** option button.

6. In the case of a two-color pattern, choose background and foreground colors by clicking the **Back** and **Front** buttons and choosing from a color palette.

7. To adjust the pattern tiling, click the **Tiling** button to extend the dialog box. Then choose values for **Width** and **Height**, for **X** and **Y First Tile Offset**, for **Row** or **Column Offset**, and for percentage offset.

8. Click **OK** to fill the selected object with the pattern.

NOTES To create a pattern from an imported graphic, click the Import button in the Two-color Pattern or Full-color Pattern dialog box, locate the pattern, click its name, and click OK to display it in the pattern preview box.

The Full-color Pattern dialog box initially provides access to a palette of 35 patterns supplied with CorelDRAW. To add a pattern to this palette, click Load to display the Load Full-color Pattern dialog box, locate the new pattern, click its name, and click OK.

The Two-color Pattern dialog box initially provides access to a palette of 49 patterns supplied with CorelDRAW. To create a pattern and add it to this palette, click Create in the Two-color Pattern dialog box to display the Two-color Pattern Editor dialog box. Point to cells and click the mouse button to create a pattern, then click OK to add the new pattern to the palette.

If you use PostScript for printing, you can fill objects with halftone screens. Click the PostScript Options button in the Two-color Pattern dialog box to access this capability.

You can also use the Fill roll-up to choose two-color and full-color patterns. Click the Two-color icon to choose from a palette of two-color patterns, as shown in Figure 1.13 (top right), or click the Full-color icon to choose from a palette of full-color patterns, as shown in Figure 1.13 (bottom left). In the case of two-color patterns, click buttons to choose the background and foreground colors. Click Edit in the roll-up to display the Two-color or Full-color dialog box.

Filling an Object with
a Two-Color Fountain Fill

A fountain fills an object with a blend of two or more colors. After
you have created a fountain fill, you can save it and subsequently
apply it to other objects.

To fountain-fill an object with a blend of two colors, use only those
steps in the following procedure necessary to achieve your objective:

1. Select the object to be filled.

2. Click the **Fill** tool to display the Fill flyout.

3. Click the **Fountain** icon to display the Fountain Fill dialog box.

4. Click one of the **Type** option buttons to select Linear, Radial, or Conical. The sample box at the right shows the current fountain, and continues to do so as you make
selections in the following steps.

5. Click the **From** color button and select the start color from
the current custom color palette.

6. Click the **To** color button to select the end color from the
current custom color palette.

7. In the **Angle** text box, type or choose an angle for a linear
or conical fill. You can also change the angle interactively
by pointing into the sample box, pressing the right mouse
button, and dragging the angle line.

8. For radial and conical fills, you can move the focus of the
fill by typing or selecting percentages in the Horizontal
and Vertical text boxes, or by pointing into the sample
box, pressing the left mouse button, and dragging.

9. To increase the amount of edge padding in the object,
type or select a percentage in the Edge Pad dialog box.
Edge padding improves the appearance of fountains in
circles and irregularly shaped objects by moving the beginning of the color transitions away from the edges of
the object.

10. To define the number of stripes the printer will use to print the fountain, click the Lock icon, and then type or choose the number of stripes in the Steps text box.

11. If you are using spot colors and will use PostScript to print, click the **PostScript** options button to display a dialog box in which you can specify a halftone screen.

12. Click **OK** to apply the fountain fill to the selected object.

NOTES In steps 5 and 6, you can click the More button to select colors in the same way that you do in the Uniform Fill dialog box.

If you are using spot colors and will make color separations, select only tints of the same color.

You can also specify a fountain fill from the Fill roll-up shown in Figure 1.13 (top left), which allows you to specify colors and the type of fill. Clicking Edit in the roll-up displays the Fountain Fill dialog box.

new Filling an Object with a Multicolor Fill

As an alternative to a two-color fountain fill, you can create three types of multicolor fills:

- Direct: The fountain colors progress in a direct line across the color wheel.

- Rainbow: The fountain colors progress around the color wheel.

- Custom: The fountain colors progress in the order you specify.

To fill an object with a multicolor fountain fill:

1. Follow steps 1 through 4 in the preceding procedure.

2. Click **Options** in the Fountain Fill dialog box to display the Fountain Fill Color Options dialog box.

3. Click one of the Blend option buttons: **Direct**, **Rainbow**, or **Custom**.

4. Click the **From** button and choose a start color.

5. Click the **To** button and choose an end color. In the case of a Direct fill, a straight line through the color wheel shows the progression of colors.

6. If you chose a Rainbow fill, a line around the color wheel shows the progression of colors. Click one of the direction option buttons to switch between clockwise and counter-clockwise progression.

7. If you chose a Custom fill, a horizontal sample bar shows the progression of colors. To place a color into the bar, drag one of the location markers under the sample bar to the position where you want the new color to peak, then click the color in the palette. You can place up to 99 colors in this way.

8. Click **OK** to return to the Fountain Fill dialog box.

9. Follow steps 7 through 12 in the preceding procedure.

Saving a Fountain Fill

1. With a sample fountain fill displayed in the Fountain Fill dialog box, click the **Presets** text box to place an insertion point.

2. Type a name (up to 32 characters) for the fountain fill, then click **Save**. The named fill is saved in the file CORELDRW.CFG and can be used in the present and future CorelDRAW sessions.

Applying a Saved Fountain Fill to an Object

1. Select the object to be filled.

2. Open the **Fountain Fill** dialog box, as described earlier in this entry.

3. Open the **Presets** list box and click on the name of the fountain fill you want to display the fill in the sample box.

4.   Click **OK** to apply the fountain fill to the selected object.

Filling an Object with a PostScript Texture

You can only fill an object with a PostScript texture if you use Post-Script for printing. To fill an object with a PostScript texture:

1.   Select the object to be filled.

2.   Click the **Fill** tool to display the Fill flyout.

3.   Click the **PS** icon to display the PostScript Texture screen.

4.   Select a texture and its parameters.

5.   Click **OK** to apply the texture to the selected objects.

NOTES   CorelDRAW allows you to select PostScript textures even if you do not have PostScript. Even if you have Postscript, textures are not displayed on screen because they are created during printing. If you use a texture and then print without PostScript, the texture is printed as a shade of gray.

new Filling an Object with a Bitmap Texture

CorelDRAW provides over 100 bitmap modifiable textures that can be displayed on screen and do not require PostScript for printing.

To fill an object with a bitmap texture:

1.   Select the object to be filled.

2.   Click the **Fill** tool to display the Fill flyout.

3.   Click the **Texture Fill** icon to display the Texture Fill dialog box.

4.   Open the **Texture Library** list box and click the name of a library.

5.   Scroll the **Texture List** and click the name of a texture to display it in the Preview box.

6. Vary the texture parameters to modify its appearance. After you change parameters, click **Preview** to display the texture in the Preview box. Each texture has a set of appropriate parameters (see the note below).

7. Click **OK** to fill the selected object with the texture.

NOTES You can also select bitmap textures from the Fill roll-up shown in Figure 1.13 (bottom right). Click the sample box to display a palette of textures from which you can choose.

Copying a Fill from One Object to Another

1. Select the objects you want to fill.

2. Choose **Edit ➤ Copy Attributes From** to display the Copy Attributes dialog box.

3. Click the **Fill** check box, then click **OK**.

4. With the **Fill** arrow, point onto the fill you want to copy and click. The selected objects become filled.

NOTES You can also copy fills using the Fill roll-up. After step 1, click Update From in the roll-up, point onto the fill you want to copy, then click Apply.

Removing the Fill from an Object

1. Select the object or objects from which you want to remove the fill.

2. Click the **Fill** tool to display the Fill roll-up.

3. Click the **X** icon in the Fill flyout.

Setting Default Fills

To set a default fill to be applied to newly created objects, use any of the procedures for applying fills, but without having an object selected. You have the choice of setting a default fill for graphic, artistic text, or paragraph text, or any combination of them.

FINDING AND REPLACING TEXT

You can find words and phrases within a block of paragraph text and replace them with other words and phrases.

Finding Text

1. Use the **Paragraph Text** tool to place an insertion marker in a block of paragraph text at the position you want to start.

2. Choose **Text ➤ Find** to display the Find dialog box.

3. Type the character string you want to find in the **Find What** text box.

4. To find only a text string that matches the case (upper- and lowercase letters) in the text box, click the **Match Case** check box.

5. Click **Find Next** to find the next occurrence of the string.

6. Repeat step 5 to find subsequent occurrences.

7. Click **Close** to leave the dialog box with the most recent found string highlighted.

Replacing Text

1. Use the **Paragraph Text** tool to place an insertion marker in a block of paragraph text at the position you want to start.

2. Choose **Text ➤ Replace** to display the Replace dialog box.

3.   Type the character string you want to find in the **Find What** text box.

4.   Type the character string you want to replace the found string with in the **Replace With** text box.

5.   To find only a text string that matches the case (upper- and lowercase letters) in the text box, click the **Match Case** check box.

6.   Click **Find Next** to find the next occurrence of the string and click **Replace** to replace the currently found text string (repeat this as often as necessary), or click **Replace All** to replace all occurrences of the text string.

FONTS

CorelDRAW is compatible with TrueType, Adobe Type 1, and WFN fonts. You can choose from the 153 fonts Corel provides on disk or more than 750 supplied on CD-ROM. You can also purchase additional fonts, and you can use CorelDRAW to add special characters to existing fonts and to create your own fonts. You can use the fonts supplied with CorelDRAW in other Windows applications.

Setting the Default Font

When you open a new drawing, CorelDRAW uses the default styles template CORELDRW.CDT unless you specify otherwise. This and other templates include a default font. See *Styles and Templates* for information about creating, editing, and using fonts.

Choosing a Font

See *Character Attributes* for information about choosing fonts for artistic and paragraph text.

Using a Custom Symbol

See *Symbols*.

FORMATTING TEXT

You can control various attributes of artistic and paragraph text, including horizontal and vertical spacing, horizontal alignment, and
shaping within an envelope. You can format paragraph text in
columns and activate automatic hyphenation.

You have additional control over artistic text, including fitting it to
a path.

See *Creating Text* for general information about artistic and
paragraph text.

Spacing Text Horizontally and Vertically

To change the horizontal or vertical spacing of artistic or
paragraph text:

1. Use the **Pick** tool to select the text.

2. Choose **Text ➤ Paragraph** to display the Paragraph
dialog box.

3. Click **Spacing** in the list of Categories.

4. Choose or type percentage values to change the default
values of character, word, line, before paragraph, and after
paragraph spacing.

NOTES   If you omit step 1 so that no text is selected, you
can specify default spacing that applies to artistic text, paragraph
text, or both.

Select zero or negative paragraph spacing to make paragraphs
overlap, or zero line spacing to make lines overlap. Select zero

word spacing to eliminate space between words. Select negative character spacing to bring characters closer together than normal.

Spacing selected in this way affects all the characters in a text object. See *Kerning Text* for information about controlling the space between individual characters.

Shifting Characters Horizontally and Vertically

This method of adjusting spacing allows you to select specific characters and move them in any direction.

1. Use the **Shape** tool to select text, then select the nodes of those characters you want to shift.

2. Choose **Text ➤ Character** to display the Character Attributes dialog box.

3. Choose or type a value for the **Horizontal Shift** and **Vertical Shift** (a percentage of the character size), then click **OK**.

Rotating Characters

1. Use the **Shape** tool to select text, then select the nodes of the characters you want to shift.

2. Choose **Text ➤ Character** to display the Character Attributes dialog box.

3. Choose or type a value for the **Character Angle**, then click **OK**.

Aligning Artistic Text

Artistic text normally extends to the right from the insertion point. To center the text or extend it to the left:

1. Use the **Pick** tool to select artistic text.

2.   At the top of the Text roll-up, click one of the alignment icons, then click **Apply**.

Aligning Paragraph Text within a Frame

You can choose among five ways of aligning paragraph text within a frame.

1.   Use the **Pick** tool to select the text.

2.   Choose **Text ➤ Edit Text**.

3.   In the Paragraph Text dialog box, click one of the five buttons in the Alignment option group, then click **OK**.

Button	Alignment
Left	Left-aligned with a ragged right margin.
Center	Centered within the frame.
Right	Right-aligned with a ragged left margin.
Justify	All lines except the last line aligned on both margins, inserting extra space between words if necessary.
None	Current alignment retained. Allows you to use the Shape tool to change the position and size of individual characters.

NOTES   You can also change text alignment from the Text roll-up shown in Figure 1.5.

Aligning Characters to the Baseline

If you have moved individual characters out of vertical alignment, do this to realign characters to the baseline:

1.   Use the **Pick** tool to select misaligned text characters.

2.   Choose **Text ➤ Align To Baseline**.

80 CorelDRAW

Fitting Artistic Text to a Path

You can fit artistic text, but not paragraph text, to a closed or open path. If you want to fit text to the shape of a text character, you must first convert that character to curves.

1. Use the **Pick** tool to select the text and the path.

2. Choose **Text ➤ Fit Text To Path** to display the Fit Text To Path Roll-up shown in Figure 1.14.

3. In the Fit Text To Path roll-up, select a character orientation and a position relative to the path. Also click **Place on other side**, if appropriate.

4. Click **Edit** if you want to specify the **Horizontal Offset** or **Distance From Path**, choose or type values for these parameters, and click **OK**.

5. Click **Apply**.

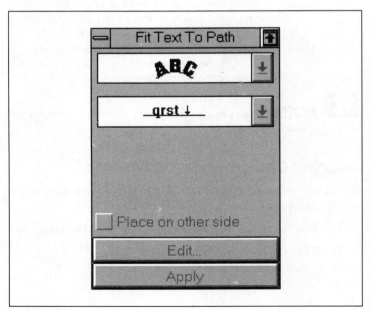

Figure 1.14: The Fit Text To Path roll-up

NOTES   To remove a path, select the text and the path, and choose Arrange ➤ Separate. Then, with just the path selected, choose Edit ➤ Delete.

Fitting Text within an Envelope

You can fit text within a closed shape. See *Shaping and Reshaping an Object*.

Formatting Paragraph Text in Columns

1. Use the **Pick** tool to select paragraph text.

2. Choose **Text** ➤ **Frame** to display the Frame Attributes dialog box.

3. Choose or type the number of columns and the gutter width (the space between columns).

4. Click **OK**.

new Setting Tabs for Paragraph Text

By default, paragraph text has no tabs set. To set tabs at intervals or to set tabs at specific positions:

1. With the **Paragraph Text** tool, click anywhere within a paragraph.

2. Choose **Text** ➤ **Paragraph** to display the Paragraph dialog box.

3. Click the **Tabs** icon in the Category list.

4. To set tabs at intervals, choose or type the interval, and then click **Apply Tabs Every** to display the tab positions in the list box.

5. To set a tab at a specific position, type the position in the box above the list box, and then click **Set**.

6. To clear a tab, highlight it in the list, then click **Clear**. To clear all tabs, click **Clear All**.

7. Click **OK** to apply the tabs to the selected paragraph text.

 NOTES By default, all tabs are left-alignment tabs. To change a tab to right alignment, center alignment, or decimal alignment, click the tab value in the dialog box to highlight it, then click an alignment option button.

The ruler in the dialog box shows tab positions. You can click in the ruler to create new tabs or drag existing tabs to change their position. To change tab alignment in the ruler, click the tab, click an alignment option button, and click Set.

new Setting Indents for Paragraph Text

1. With the **Paragraph Text** tool, click anywhere within a paragraph.

2. Choose **Text ➤ Paragraph** to display the Paragraph dialog box.

3. Click the **Indent** icon in the Category list.

4. Choose or type values for **First Line**, **Rest Of Lines**, **Left Frame Margin**, and **Right Frame Margin** indents, then click **OK** to apply the indents to the paragraph text.

NOTES You can specify positive and negative indents.

Using Automatic Hyphenation

1. Use the **Pick** tool to select paragraph text.

2. Choose **Text ➤ Paragraph** to display the Paragraph dialog box.

3. Click the **Automatic Hyphenation** check box to turn on hyphenation.

4. Choose or type a value in the **Hot Zone** text box to specify the hot zone, then click **OK**.

NOTES   A word that starts within the hot zone and is too long to fit within the right margin wraps to the next line. A word that starts to the left of the hot zone and is too long to fit within the right margin is automatically hyphenated, if possible.

GRAPHICS DATABASE

You can create a database containing information about graphics objects. The database consists of one record for each object, each record containing several fields. The steps involved in creating a database are as follows:

1. Select the objects to be included in the database.

2. Create the database structure, defining each field's name and format.

3. Add the empty field structure to the selected objects.

4. For each object, provide data for the fields.

5. Format and print the database.

These steps are covered in detail below.

Creating a Database Structure

Creating a structure consists of defining the fields to be used for every record.

1. Select the objects for which you want to create a database.

2. Right-click one of the objects to open the Object menu, click **Data Roll-Up** to open the Object Data roll-up, and click the right-pointing arrow to display the object data menu.

3. Click **Field Editor** to display the Object Data Field Editor dialog box.

4. Delete or add fields as described in the next two procedures.

5. Click **Close** to close the Object Data Field Editor.

Deleting Fields from a Database Structure

The Object Data Field Editor dialog box first appears with three default fields: Name, Cost, and Comments. You can use these default fields, or delete any of them. To delete a field:

1. Click the name of the first field to be deleted.

2. Hold down the **Ctrl** key and click the name of another field to be deleted.

3. Repeat step 2 to select additional fields for deletion.

4. Click **Delete Field(s)** to display the Object Data dialog box.

5. Click **OK** to delete the selected fields.

Adding a Field to a Database Structure

1. Click **Create New Field** to create a new field that is automatically given the name "Field0."

2. Type the name you want to use for this field, and press **Enter** to place this name in the list of fields.

NOTES In the Object Data Field Editor dialog box, you can change the order of field names by dragging.

You can change the name of any field by selecting a name and then typing a new name.

Changing the Format of a Field

You can format fields for:

- General (alphanumeric) data
- Date/Time (date and times in various formats) data

- Linear (measurement) data
- Numeric (numbers in various formats) data

To format a field:

1. Click the name of a field.
2. Click **Change** to display the Format Definition dialog box.
3. Click one of the four Format Type buttons and the variation of that format.
4. Click **OK** to return to the Object Data Field Editor dialog box.

Adding Fields to an Object

After you have defined the fields, you can apply these fields to objects. To add fields to an object:

1. Select the objects to which you want to attach data.
2. Click the top field name in the list of fields, then hold down the **Shift** key and click the bottom name to select all fields.
3. Click **Add Selected Fields** to attach the fields to the selected object.

Attaching Data to Individual Objects

To attach data to an object and place it in the database:

1. Open the **Object Data** roll-up.
2. Select the object to which data is to be attached. Any data already attached to the object appears in the roll-up.
3. In the roll-up select a field, type the value for the field, and press **Enter**.
4. Repeat step 3 to supply data for other fields.
5. Repeat steps 2 through 4 to attach data to other objects.

Attaching Data to a Group of Objects

1. Select all the objects and open the **Object Data** roll-up.

2. Click the object data manager icon at the top left of the roll-up to display the Object Data Manager dialog box. The dialog box shows data already attached to objects, and empty cells or default values for objects to which data is not attached.

3. To place data in a cell, select the cell, type the data, and press **Enter**.

NOTES When you select a cell in the Object Data Manager, the corresponding object is selected in the drawing.

Formatting and Printing Object Data

You can divide the object data into groups and you can use menu at the top of the Object Data Manager to format and print object data.

To divide the object data into groups, close the Object Data Manager, then select the objects to be grouped and choose **Arrange ➤ Group**. Repeat this to create other groups. Reopen the Object Data Manager to display the grouped data.

To format or print object data:

Menu	Operation
File	Set up a page and print object data.
Edit	Undo and redo operations on object data, and also cut or copy data to the Clipboard and paste data from the Clipboard.
Field Operations	Change field formats or field names; show group or column totals for numeric fields; indent fields to show hierarchy.
Preferences	Set preferences.

GRID

Every page of a CorelDRAW document has an underlying grid you can choose to display or not. You can align objects by turning on snap-to-grid so that new objects created and object moved align to grid positions.

If you are drawing an object to scale, set the grid according to that scale. Otherwise, set the grid to units of your choice.

Setting Up the Grid

Setting up the grid also sets the scales for the horizontal and vertical rulers.

To set up the grid for a scaled drawing:

1. Choose **Layout ➤ Grid Setup** to display the Grid Setup dialog box.

2. If there is no check mark in the Set for Global Units check box in the Scale section at the top of the dialog box, click to place a check mark there.

3. Choose or type the scale in the three text boxes on the next line. For example, to set a scale in which one foot on the object is represented by one inch in your drawing, choose **1** in the first box, **Feet** in the second, and **inch** in the third.

4. In the Grid Frequency section of the dialog box, you cannot change the dimensions because these are automatically set to correspond to the object dimensions you specified in step 3. You can change the number of grid dots within each unit of the chosen dimension. For example, having selected a scale in which one foot on the object is represented by one inch in the drawing, you can set the vertical and horizontal frequency to **12** to have grid points representing one inch.

5. See "Changing the Grid Origin" if you need to change the grid origin.

6. Click **OK**.

To set up the grid for a non-scaled drawing:

1. Choose **Layout ➤ Grid Setup** to display the Grid Setup dialog box.

2. If there is a check mark in the Set for Global Units check box in the Scale section at the top of the dialog box, click to remove the check mark.

3. In the Grid Frequency section of the dialog box, choose Horizontal and Vertical units. You can separately choose between inch, millimeter, pica, and point for each axis.

4. Type or choose the number of grid points between each measurement unit for each axis.

5. See "Setting the Grid Origin" if you need to change the grid origin.

6. Click **OK**.

Setting the Grid Origin

By default, CorelDRAW measures from the grid origin at the bottom-left corner of the printable page. The zero point on the horizontal ruler corresponds to the left edge of the printable page and the zero point on the vertical ruler corresponds to the bottom edge of the printable page.

To position the grid point by dragging:

1. If you want to place the new origin exactly on a current grid point, make sure that snap-to-grid is on. If you want to place the new origin at a position other than a current grid point, make sure snap-to-grid is off.

2. With the rulers displayed, point into the small square at the intersection of the horizontal and vertical rulers.

3. Press the mouse button, drag to the new origin position, and release the mouse button.

To position the grid point numerically:

1. Choose **Layout ➤ Grid Setup** to display the Grid Setup dialog box.

2. In the Grid Origin section of the dialog box, choose or type the position of the new grid origin relative to the bottom left corner of the printable page (right page if two pages are displayed).

3. Click **OK** to redisplay the page with the rulers (if displayed) showing the new origin, grid (if displayed) spaced from the new origin, and object positions shown in the status line shown with respect to the new origin.

GROUPING AND UNGROUPING OBJECTS

CorelDRAW provides two ways to bind objects together: combining and grouping. Group objects when you want to manipulate them as a single object. Combine objects when you want to perform certain specific operations (see "Combining Objects" below for details).

Grouping Objects

Group objects when you want to manipulate them as a group, doing such operations as copying, duplicating, moving, or changing attributes. After you have grouped objects, they remain grouped until you ungroup them.

1. Select the objects you want to group.

2. Choose **Arrange ➤ Group**.

NOTES You can group individual objects and you can group groups of objects up to ten levels of grouping.

Ungrouping Grouped Objects

1. Select the group.

2. Choose **Arrange ➤ Ungroup**.

NOTES When you ungroup groups of objects, the last group you made is ungrouped first, then the next to last, and so on.

Combining Objects

Combine objects in order to:

- Speed screen drawing for objects that contain many lines and curves, all with the same attributes

- Join line or curve segments together

- Create clipping holes or masks

- Align nodes of separate objects

When you combine rectangle, ellipse, or text objects, those objects are converted into curves as they are combined.

To combine objects:

1. Select the objects to be combined.

2. Choose **Arrange ➤ Combine**.

Breaking Combined Objects Apart

1. Select the combined object.

2. Choose **Arrange ➤ Break Apart**.

NOTES Objects that were rectangles, ellipses, or text remain as curves after they are broken apart.

HALFTONE SCREENS

If you use PostScript for printing, you can fill objects with halftone screens. See the information about filling objects with a two-color pattern in *Filling an Object*.

HELP

CorelDRAW has various Help facilities, which are similar to those in many other Windows applications. You can access context-sensitive Help, indexed Help, and reference information.

There is a wealth of information in Help, some of which is not in the *User's Manual*. The following summarizes some of the more significant aspects of using Help. See your Windows *User's Guide* for more information.

To print information displayed in a Help screen, choose **File** in the CorelDRAW! - Help menu, and then click **Print Topic**.

To exit from Help, choose **File ➤ Exit**.

Using Context-Sensitive Help

There are two kinds of context-sensitive Help. One is available when a dialog box is open or you have highlighted an item under one of the Main menu commands. To access this:

1. Open a dialog box or highlight an item under one of the Main menu commands.

2.   Press **F1**. A Help screen appears with information relating to the dialog box or menu item.

The second kind of context-sensitive Help is available when no dialog boxes are open and no menu items are highlighted. To access this:

1.   Press **Shift+F1**. The cursor changes to an arrow with a question mark.

2.   Point to the subject you want information about, such as a tool or a roll-up, and click. A Help screen appears with relevant information.

Using the Help Menu

1.   Click **Help** in the menu bar.

2.   Choose **Contents, Screen/Menu Help, How To Use Help, Search for Help On**, or **About CorelDRAW!**.

NOTES   If you choose Contents, you can select information about using Help, the CorelDRAW screen, commands, tools, or the keyboard. You can also select a section of Help about how to perform certain tasks, a glossary, or reference material.

HYPHENATING PARAGRAPH TEXT

See "Using Automatic Hyphenation" in *Formatting Paragraph Text*.

IMPORTING AN OBJECT

You can use the following methods to use objects created in other applications:

- Copy the object from another application into the Clipboard and then paste it into your drawing. See *Copying an Object*.

- Use an object from another application by linking or embedding. See *Linking and Embedding Objects* and *Inserting an Object*.

- Use Mosaic to locate and then import an object. See "Using Mosaic to Import an Object" below.

- Import the file through a CorelDRAW input filter. See "Installing an Input Filter" and "Importing an Object from Another Application" below.

For information about importing text, see *Creating Text*.

Installing an Input Filter

You must have the appropriate input filters installed before you can import files. See the *Import File Formats* topic in on-line Help for information about file formats available and specific information about how CorelDRAW handles each type of file.

If CorelDRAW was fully installed on your computer, all the filters will be available. If CorelDRAW was only partially installed, the filters you need may not be present. To verify which filters are present:

1. Choose **File ➤ Import**.

2. In the Import dialog box, open the **List Files of Type** list box.

3. Scroll through the list of file types to see which filters are installed.

If the filters you need are not installed, do the following to install filters from your CorelDRAW distribution disks:

1. Minimize CorelDRAW and display the Windows Program Manager dialog box.

2. Choose **File ➤ Run**.

3. Insert your CorelDRAW distribution disk 1 in a floppy disk drive, type either **A:SETUP** or **B:SETUP**, according to which disk drive you are using, and click **OK**.

4. When the CorelDRAW! Setup dialog box appears, click **Continue** to display the CorelDRAW! Installation Options dialog box, then click **Custom Install** to display the Set Destination Path dialog box.

5. Make sure the path is correct, then click **Continue** to display the CorelDRAW! Custom Installation dialog box.

6. Click the **CorelDRAW! Some** button to display the Installation Options for CorelDRAW! dialog box.

7. Click each button except **Filters** so that only that one is checked, then click **Continue** to return to the CorelDRAW! Custom Installation dialog box.

8. Click the **None** buttons for all applications except CorelDRAW, then click **Continue** to display the Set Program Manager Group dialog box; verify that the correct group is identified, then click **Continue** to display the CorelDRAW! dialog box.

9. Click **Install** to start the installation process.

10. Replace the CorelDRAW disk when a message on the screen asks you to do so.

11. When the CorelDRAW! Setup Exit dialog box appears, click **Continue**.

12. Maximize CorelDRAW.

Importing an Object from Another Application

If you know the name and location of the file you want to import, you can import it directly. If you want to search for an image to import, use Mosaic to import files. See "Using Mosaic to Import an Object" below.

To import an object created in another application:

1. Choose **File ➤ Import** to display the Import dialog box.

2. Open the **List Files of Type** list box and select the type of file you want to import.

3. In the Directories list box, select the drive and directory that contains the file to be imported. A list of files of the type you specified appears in the File Name list box.

4. Click the name of the file to be imported.

5. Click the **For Tracing** check box, if necessary, to place a check mark in it if you are importing a bitmap object that will be traced. There should be no check mark in this box if the imported object is not going to be traced.

6. Click **OK**. After a few seconds, the object appears in the drawing.

Using Mosaic to Import an Object

With Mosaic you see a thumbnail image of an object before you import it.

1. Choose **File ➤ Import**.

2. In the Import dialog box, click **Mosaic** to display the Corel-Mosaic dialog box.

3. Choose **File ➤ View Directory** to display the View Directory dialog box.

4. Select the directory that contains the object you want to import.

5. In the **List Files of Type** list box, select the type of file you want to import. The names of all files of the selected type in the directory are displayed in the **File Name** list box.

6. Click **OK** to display thumbnail images of files in the selected directory appear, if those files have image headers.

7. Scroll through the thumbnails and click the image you want to import into your drawing.

8. Choose **Edit ➤ Import into CorelDRAW!**. After a few moments Mosaic disappears and the selected image appears in your drawing.

Using Mosaic to Import a Photo CD Image

CorelMOSAIC can open and import Kodak Photo CD images.

1. In the CorelMOSAIC Main Menu, choose **PhotoCD ➤ View Photo CD** to display the Select CD-ROM Drive dialog box.

2. Open the list box to show the CD-ROM drives installed and click the one from which you want to import an image. Then click **OK** to display the Open Photo CD dialog box, which appears with OVERVIEW.PCD in the File Name text box.

3. Click **OK**. Thumbnails of images on the CD-ROM appear.

4. Scroll if necessary and click the image you want to use.

5. Click **OK** to import the image into your drawing.

You can also use CorelMOSAIC to convert Kodak Photo CD images into BMP, EPS, PCX, and TIF formats. To do this, choose PhotoCD ➤ Convert Images, select the images you want to convert, the format you want to convert them into, and the directory into which you want to write the converted files, and then click OK.

INSERTING AN OBJECT FROM AN OLE APPLICATION

You can insert objects from OLE-compliant applications into a drawing. You can choose to create new objects or use already-existing objects.

Creating a New Drawing with an Inserted Object

1. Choose **File ➤ Insert Object** to display the Insert Object dialog box which shows a list of OLE-compliant applications available on your computer.

2. In the **Object Type** list box, click the type of object to use.

3. Click the **Create New** option button, then click **OK**. After a few seconds, the OLE application you chose in step 2 is displayed.

4. Create the object to be inserted.

5. Choose **File ➤ Update <filename>** to insert the object into your drawing.

6. Choose **File ➤ Exit & Return to <filename>** to return to your drawing, which now includes the inserted object.

NOTES In steps 5 and 6, <filename> is the name of the CorelDRAW file into which you are inserting the object.

Inserting an Object into an Existing Drawing

To insert an existing file from an OLE-compliant application:

1. Choose **File ➤ Insert Object** to display the Insert Object dialog box which shows a list of OLE-compliant applications available on your computer.

2. In the **Object Type** list box, click the type of object to use.

3. Click the **Create From File** option button.

4. In the File text box, type the complete path name of the file to be inserted, then click **OK**. After a few seconds, the OLE object is displayed in your drawing.

 NOTES In step 4, you can use Browse to locate the file.

KERNING TEXT

Kerning is the process of adjusting the space between text characters to improve their appearance and legibility. You can adjust the spacing between characters interactively, as described here, or from the Paragraph dialog box. See "Spacing Text Horizontally and Vertically" in *Formatting Text*.

Changing Character, Word, Line, and Paragraph Spacing

1. Use the **Shape** tool to select artistic or paragraph text. Nodes appear next to each character, and spacing-control handles appear below the text, as shown in Figure 1.15.

2. To decrease or increase the spacing between characters, point to the spacing-control handle at the right end of the block and press the mouse button, then drag the spacing-control handle to the left or right.

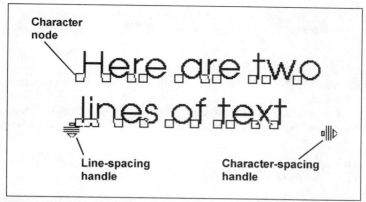

Figure 1.15: A selected block of text with nodes and
spacing-control handles

3. To decrease or increase the spacing between words, point
to the spacing-control handle at the right end of the block,
hold down the **Ctrl** key and press the mouse button, then
drag the spacing-control handle to the left or right.

4. To decrease or increase the spacing between lines, point to
the spacing-control handle at the left end of the block and
press the mouse button, then drag the spacing-control handle up or down.

5. To decrease or increase the spacing between paragraphs,
point to the spacing-control handle at the left end of the
block, hold down the **Ctrl** key and press the mouse button, then drag the spacing-control handle up or down.

Changing the Spacing
between Individual Characters

1. Make sure all snap options are disabled.

2. Use the **Shape** tool to select the text. Nodes appear next to
each character, and spacing-control handles appear below
the block.

3. Holding down the **Ctrl** key, point to the node just to the
left of the character to be moved, then drag the character
horizontally.

NOTES Holding down the Ctrl key while you drag a
node constrains the selected character so that it only moves horizontally. If you accidentally move a character out of horizontal alignment, use the Align to Baseline command to restore its alignment
(see *Formatting Text*).

Having a snap option enabled may interfere with your ability to
place characters exactly where you want.

To move two or more characters simultaneously, select those characters and drag the node of any one of the selected characters.

You can also change character spacing by nudging. Use the Shape
tool to select one or more character nodes, and press one of the arrow keys to move the characters left or right. The distance the character moves depends on the setting in the Preferences dialog box
(see *Preferences*).

You can change character spacing with numerical precision by using the Character Attributes dialog box (see *Formatting Text*).

LAYERING A DRAWING

You can organize a drawing on as many layers as you wish. Although
you can simultaneously view and edit objects on any number of layers, you create objects on only one layer at a time. You can choose
which layers to display and which layers to print.

Displaying the Layers Roll-up

To display the Layers roll-up, choose **Layout ➤ Layers Roll-Up** to
display the Layers roll-up, as shown in Figure 1.16.

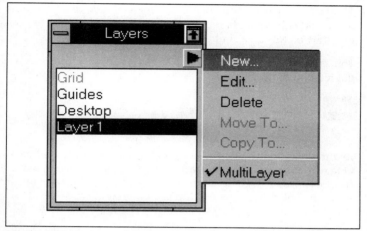

Figure 1.16: The Layers roll-up with layers for the grid, guides, desktop, and a drawing

Selecting a Layer

By default, a drawing has four layers:

- Grid, which contains the grid
- Guides, which contains guidelines and guides
- Desktop, which contains objects outside the printable page
- Layer 1, in which you draw objects, the default active layer

To make a layer active:

1. Point to a layer in the **Layers** roll-up.

2. Click the mouse button.

NOTES Guidelines and guide objects exist in their own layer. You can hide this layer to remove and subsequently replace guidelines and guides. You can draw on and print this layer.

The grid also exists in its own layer. You can hide this layer to re-move and subsequently replace the grid on your screen. You can-not draw on this layer, but you can print it.

You can snap objects on any drawing layer to guidelines and guides, and to the grid.

new ## Using Layers to Move Objects between Pages

In a multilayer drawing the desktop layer exists behind all pages. One way to move an object from one page to another is to move it from its current page to the desktop layer, go to a new page, and move the object from the desktop layer onto that page.

Adding a Layer

1.   Click the right-pointing arrow in the **Layers** roll-up to dis-play a secondary menu.

2.   Click **New** to display the Layer Options dialog box.

3.   Click the four check boxes as appropriate to make the layer visible or invisible, printable or not printable, locked or unlocked, or to have a color override or not. See the notes below.

4.   If you want to name the layer, rather than using the de-fault name, type a name in the text box.

5.   Click **OK** to redisplay the Layers roll-up with the new layer in the list of layers.

NOTES   If you make a layer visible, you can see objects on it even if it is not selected as the active layer. Making a layer visible or invisible does not affect printing.

If you make a layer printable, it will be included when you print your drawing. Making a layer printable or not printable does not affect its visibility on the screen.

If you lock a layer you cannot subsequently access objects on it unless that layer is active.

If you choose Color Override, you can click on a color palette to choose a color. Subsequently, all objects on that layer will appear as wireframes in the color you have chosen, even if you have are using editable preview. This allows you to easily identify which objects are on each layer.

new Creating a Master Layer for Multipage Documents

Follow the procedure in "Adding a Layer" directly above. Between steps 4 and 5, click the Master Layer check box. All objects on this layer appear on every page of a multipage document. Margins and other page setup options specified for a master layer apply to every page. More than one layer can be a master.

Editing a Layer's Attributes and Name

1. In the Layers roll-up, click on the layer you want to edit, then click the right-pointing arrow to display a secondary menu.

2. Click **Edit** to display the Layer Options dialog box.

3. Click the four buttons to select attributes, and if required, change the layer's name. See "Adding a Layer" above for information.

Deleting a Layer

1. In the Layers Roll-up, click on the layer you want to delete, then click the right-pointing arrow to display a secondary menu.

2. Click **Delete** to delete the layer together with all objects on it.

Changing Layer Stacking Order

Objects drawn in layers are stacked in the order shown in the Layers roll-up, the top layer in the list being the top layer in the stack. You can change the order in the list to change the stacking order in the drawing.

1. In the Layers roll-up, point to the name of the layer you want to move.

2. Press the mouse button and drag the name up or down to the layer that will be immediately below its new position on the list, then release the mouse button.

NOTES   Within each layer, objects are stacked in the order they are created, or the order set by the use of the Order command in the Arrange menu.

Activating and Deactivating Multilayering

Multilayering affects your ability to select and manipulate objects on inactive layers. Whether multilayering is active or not, you can draw only on the active layer. When multilayering is active, you can select and manipulate objects on all layers. When multilayering is inactive, you can select and manipulate objects on the active layer only.

When multilayering is active, the status line indicates which layer a selected object is on.

1. Click the arrow in the Layers roll-up.

2. Click **Multilayer** to change multilayering from active to inactive or vice-versa.

NOTES   Even when multilayering is inactive, you can still create and move guidelines on the guides layer from another layer.

Copying and Moving an Object from One Layer to Another

1. Make sure multilayering is active. See "Activating and Deactivating Multilayering" above.

2. Select the object you want to copy or move.

3. Look at the status bar to see which layer the object is on. In the Layers roll-up, select that layer.

4. Click the arrow in the **Layers** roll-up to display the secondary menu, and click **Copy To** or **Move To**.

5. Point with the **To** arrow to the name of the layer on which you want to place the object, and click.

Grouping and Combining Objects on Different Layers

You can group or combine objects in different layers, provided multilayering is activated. When you select objects on different layers, all the grouped or combined objects move to the currently active layer. If you subsequently ungroup or break apart the objects, they all remain on the layer in which there were grouped or combined. See *Grouping and Ungrouping Objects*.

NOTES   Group across layers to collect objects from various layers and move them all to a new layer.

When you combine objects, the combined object takes on the fill and outline attributes of the last selected object.

LINKING AND EMBEDDING OBJECTS

CorelDRAW allows you to exchange information with files containing objects created in Windows applications that support Object Linking and Embedding (OLE). For general information about OLE refer to your Windows *User's Guide*.

CorelDRAW can act as an OLE server and as an OLE client.

Embedding an Object into a Drawing

You can embed (insert) an object created in another Windows application into a CorelDRAW drawing. The exact procedure varies from application to application. The following steps assume you are embedding an application created in CorelPHOTO-PAINT. If you use a different application to create the object, consult its documentation for precise information.

1. Open CorelDRAW and choose **File ➤ Insert Object** to open the Insert Object dialog box.

2. Select **CorelPhoto-Paint! 4.0 Picture** from the list of object types.

3. Click **Create New** and then click **OK** to open CorelPHOTO-PAINT and create the new object (see Part 3 of this book).

4. Choose **File ➤ Exit & Return** to return to the CorelDRAW drawing with the new object embedded.

NOTES You can embed an object that already exists as a file. In this case, click Create from File in step 3, and then click Browse to locate the file in the Browse dialog box. Click the file name, and then click OK to return to the Insert Object dialog box. Click OK to

open CorelPHOTO-PAINT with the object displayed. Do step 4 to
return to CorelDRAW with the object embedded.

Editing an Embedded Object

You can move and resize an embedded object within a CorelDRAW
drawing. These operations do not change the fundamental object,
they just affect the way CorelDRAW acts on the object.

From within CorelDRAW, you can use the application in which you
created the object to perform other editing operations. The following steps apply specifically to an object created in CorelPHOTO-
PAINT. Objects created in other applications may require slightly
different procedures.

1. Within CorelDRAW, select the embedded object.

2. Choose **Edit ➤ Edit CorelPHOTO-PAINT! Object**.

3. Edit the object using CorelPHOTO-PAINT tools.

4. In the CorelPHOTO-PAINT File menu, choose **Update**.

5. Again in the CorelPHOTO-PAINT File menu, choose **Exit
& Return** to return to CorelDRAW with the edited object
displayed.

NOTES With these steps, your changes affect only the object embedded in CorelDRAW, not the original object in CorelPHOTO-
PAINT. If you use CorelPHOTO-PAINT to make changes directly to the
original object, the object embedded in your CorelDRAW drawing will
not be affected. Contrast this with what happens with linked objects,
where the changes to the original object do affect the linked copy.

Linking an Object into a Drawing

You can link an object created in another application into a
CorelDRAW drawing. The exact procedure varies slightly from application to application. The following steps assume you are linking an object created in CorelPHOTO-PAINT (see Part 3 of this
book). If you use a different application to create the object, consult
its documentation for precise information about linking.

1. Create and save an object in CorelPHOTO-PAINT.

2. If necessary, open the CorelPHOTO-PAINT file that contains the object you want to link into your CorelDRAW drawing.

3. Select the object you wish to link.

4. Choose **Edit ➤ Copy** to copy the object to the Clipboard.

5. Minimize or close CorelPHOTO-PAINT.

6. Open CorelDRAW.

7. Choose **Edit ➤ Paste Special** to display the Paste Special dialog box.

8. Select **CorelPhoto-Paint! 4.0 Picture** to confirm the source of the object, click **Paste Link**, and click **OK** to display the object as part of your drawing.

Editing a Linked Object

You can move and resize an object linked into a CorelDRAW drawing. These operations do not affect the fundamental object, just the way CorelDRAW acts on it.

Also, from within CorelDRAW, you can use the application in which you created the object to perform other editing operations. The following steps apply specifically to an object created in CorelPHOTO-PAINT. Objects created in other applications may require slightly different procedures.

1. Within CorelDRAW, select the linked object.

2. Choose **Edit ➤ Edit CorelPHOTO-PAINT! Link** to display the object in CorelPHOTO-PAINT.

3. Edit the object using CorelPHOTO-PAINT tools.

4. In CorelPHOTO-PAINT, choose **File ➤ Save** to save the edited object.

5. In CorelPHOTO-PAINT, choose **File ➤ Exit** to return to CorelDRAW with the edited object displayed.

NOTES   With these steps, your changes affect the object in CorelPHOTO-PAINT. Moreover, if you have linked the object to other CorelDRAW files or to files in another application, the changes you make here will affect those files as well. Also, if you use CorelPHOTO-PAINT to make changes directly to the original object, your changes will affect not just your CorelDRAW drawing, but any other CorelDRAW drawings or other application files to which the Corel-PAINT object is linked. By contrast, with embedded objects, changes made to the original object do not affect the embedded one.

Automatic and Manual Link Updating

When you enable automatic update for the link between your CorelDRAW file and the linked file, changes made to the linked file immediately affect the CorelDRAW drawing. With manual update enabled, you must manually update your CorelDRAW drawing after making changes to the linked file.

To change a link from manual to automatic, or from automatic to manual:

1.   Choose **Edit ➤ Links** to display the Links dialog box containing a list of linked images.

2.   Click the linked image you want to change.

3.   Click **Manual** to change from automatic to manual updating, or click **Automatic** to change from manual to automatic updating.

4.   Repeat steps 2 and 3 to change the linking for other objects.

NOTES   To update an object that has a manual link to a source, use steps 1 and 2 in this procedure, and then click Update Now in the dialog box.

Changing from manual to automatic updating does not affect previously made changes to the linked object.

Canceling a Link

When you cancel a link to an object, the object remains in your CorelDRAW drawing in the form it was when you last updated it, but there is no longer any link to the application in which the object was created. The effect is the same as if you had copied the object to the Clipboard and then pasted it into your drawing.

1. Use the **Pick** tool to select the object in your CorelDRAW drawing for which you want to cancel the link.

2. Choose **Edit ➤ Links** to open the Links dialog box.

3. Select the link you want to cancel and click **Cancel Link**.

Changing and Updating a Link

When you link an object to a CorelDRAW drawing, you establish a link between your CorelDRAW file and an object created in another application. CorelDRAW accesses the object by way of this link. You should leave the linked object in place on disk so that CorelDRAW can access it. If you move the object to another directory or change its name, you must update the link. Use the steps below to do this. You can use the same steps to replace one linked object in a drawing with another.

1. Use the **Pick** tool to select the object in your CorelDRAW drawing for which you want to change or update the link.

2. Choose **Edit ➤ Links** to open the Links dialog box.

3. Select the link you want to change and click **Change Source** to display the Change Source dialog box.

4. Select the file you want to link instead of the existing one and click **OK**.

MAIN MENU BAR

The CorelDRAW Main menu bar provides access to nine individual menus. Refer to *Menus* in the CorelDRAW on-line Help for information about each menu and a general description of the items on it. See *Screen* for an illustration of the Main menu bar.

MARQUEE-SELECTING OBJECTS

See *Selecting and Deselecting Objects* and *Shaping and Reshaping an Object*.

MASKS AND CLIPPING HOLES

You can create a transparent hole in a filled object and make anything behind the filled object visible.

Creating a Mask

The following steps create a circular hole in a filled rectangle. You can use these steps with other shapes.

1. Create a filled rectangle.
2. Create a circle, smaller than the rectangle, with no fill.

3. Move the circle on top of the rectangle.

4. Marquee-select both objects.

5. Choose **Arrange ➤ Combine**. A circular hole appears in the rectangle. Now you have a mask.

6. Move the mask over another object.

7. If necessary, select the mask and then choose **Arrange ➤ Order ➤ To Front**.

8. The object, or part of it, is visible through the mask.

NOTES All the characters in the typefaces provided with CorelDRAW have transparent counters (the holes in such characters as a, e, and o).

If you use PostScript for printing, a mask can have no more than about 125 nodes.

MIRRORING AN OBJECT

See *Scaling and Stretching an Object*.

MOVING AN OBJECT

You can move an object to a different position in your drawing by dragging it with your mouse, you can move it with precision under keyboard control, or you can nudge it with the arrow keys.

Moving an Object with the Mouse

1.   Enable or disable snap-to options as appropriate (see *Alignment and Placement Aids*).

2.   Select the object or group of objects to be moved.

3.   Point onto the object's outline (or anywhere within it if it is filled), and press and hold down the mouse button while you drag to a new position. A dashed rectangle shows the object's new position. The status line shows how far the object has moved.

4.   Release the mouse button.

NOTES   To constrain the object to move in a horizontal or vertical direction only, hold down the Ctrl key while you drag. Release the mouse button before you release the Ctrl key.

To move a copy of an object and leave the original in place, tap the + key on the numeric keypad or click the right mouse button before you release the left mouse button.

See *Copying an Object* for information about moving an object between layers.

To move an object between pages of a multipage document, move it from its original page to the desktop, select the new page, then move the object from the desktop onto that page.

Moving an Object a Specific Distance or to a Specific Position

1.   Select the object, or group of objects, to be moved.

2.   Choose **Arrange ➤ Move** to display the Move dialog box.

3.   In the Move dialog box, leave the **Absolute Coordinates** check box unchecked to move the object a specific distance or check the box to move the object to a specific position.

4. If you checked Absolute Coordinates, click one of the handles in the dialog box to indicate which point of the object is to move to the specified position.

5. Select or type the **Horizontal** and **Vertical** coordinates representing the distance of the move or the final location of the object. Positive values are up and to the right.

6. Leave the **Leave Original** check box unchecked if you do not want to leave a copy of the original object in place; check the box if you do want to leave a copy of the original.

7. Click **OK** to move the object.

Nudging an Object

1. Select the object, or group of objects, to be moved.

2. Tap one or more of the arrow keys to move the object.

NOTES See *Preferences* for information about setting the nudge distance.

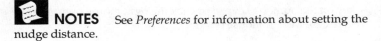

MULTIPAGE DOCUMENTS

Multipage documents are new in CorelDRAW 4.0. See *Page Setup* for information about adding pages. See *Layering a Drawing* for information about creating objects which appear on every page. See *Printing a Drawing* for information about printing specific pages. See *Creating Text* for information about linking text between pages.

When you work with a multipage document, the left end of the horizontal scroll bar shows the number of the current page and has arrow buttons you can click to move from page to page. You can also choose Layout ➤ Go To Page to jump to a specific page.

NODES

Nodes are dimensionless points that define the position of objects. There are nodes at the beginning and end of each line and curve segment of a curve object, at the corners of each rectangle object, at one point on each ellipse object, and at the beginning of each character in a text object.

See *Shaping and Reshaping an Object* for information about manipulating nodes.

OBJECT LINKING AND EMBEDDING

See *Linking and Embedding Objects*.

OUTLINING AN OBJECT

You create an object by drawing an outline.

When you are working in wireframe view, you see only thin black lines. When you work in editable preview, you see lines with their attributes of thickness, color, and style and, in the case of closed objects, you also see the fill. See *Display Views* for information about selecting wireframe view or editable preview.

You can select line attributes from:

- The on-screen color palette
- The Outline flyout

- The Pen roll-up
- The Outline Pen dialog box
- The Outline Color dialog boxes

If you change a line attribute without having an object selected, you change the default attribute for graphic objects, artistic text, or paragraph text, or for any combination of the three.

Creating an Outline

See *Drawing an Object* for information about creating lines and outlines.

Changing Line Thickness

To use the Outline tool shown in Figure 1.6 to change line thickness:

1. Select the object.

2. Click the **Outline** tool to display the Outline flyout.

3. Click one of the line-thickness icons to choose among ¼-, 2-, 8-, 16-, or 24-point thicknesses.

To use the Pen roll-up shown in Figure 1.17 to change line thickness:

1. Select the object.

2. Click the **Outline** tool to display the Outline flyout.

3. Click the **Pen** roll-up icon (the second from the left in the top row) to display the Pen roll-up.

4. Click the arrows next to the thickness sample box to change the line thickness. Each click changes the thickness by 0.01 inch, and the thickness is displayed in the roll-up.

5. Click **Apply**.

To use the Outline Pen dialog box to change line thickness:

1. Select the object.

2. Select the **Outline** tool to display the Outline flyout.

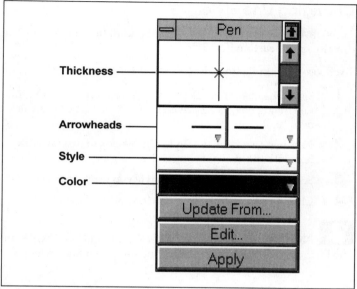

Figure 1.17: The Pen roll-up

3. Click the **Pen** icon (the leftmost icon in the top row) to display the Outline Pen dialog box, in which the Width text box shows the current line width.

4. Change the width by clicking on the arrows next to the Width text box or by typing a width value.

5. Click **OK**.

Changing Line Color

The fastest way to select a line color is to right-click a color in the on-screen color palette. See *Color* for additional information about applying colors.

Changing Line Style

CorelDRAW offers a variety of dashed and dotted line styles. You can also create custom line styles.

To choose a line style from the Pen roll-up:

1.   Select the object and display the Pen roll-up or the Outline Pen dialog box, as described under "Changing Line Thickness" earlier in this entry.

2.   In either case, click the **Style** sample box to display a list box with the available line styles.

3.   Scroll if necessary to show the style you want, and click on it.

4.   Click **Apply** in the roll-up, or click **OK** in the dialog box.

NOTES   Refer to *CorelDRW.DOT File* in CorelDRAW on-line Help for information about creating your own line styles.

Changing Line-ending Shape

To select butt flat, round, or square line endings:

1.   Select the object and display the Outline Pen dialog box, as described under "Changing Line Thickness" earlier in this entry.

2.   Click one of the **Line Caps** option buttons.

3.   Click **OK**.

NOTES   See the Outline Pen dialog box for illustrations of the three line-ending shapes.

Adding an Arrowhead to a Line

1.   Select the object and display the Pen roll-up or the Outline Pen dialog box, as described under "Changing Line Thickness" earlier in this entry.

2. Click one of the two arrow boxes to display an arrow list box. Use the left-arrow box to choose an arrowhead for the beginning (not necessarily the left end) of the line, and the right-arrow box to choose an arrowhead for the ending (not necessarily the right end) of the line.

3. Click the arrowhead you want to use. It appears in the arrow box.

4. If necessary, click the second arrow box and choose an arrowhead.

5. Click **Apply** in the roll-up, or click **OK** in the dialog box.

NOTES Arrowheads are automatically created at a size proportional to line thickness. If you have a thin line and are displaying it without magnification, the arrowhead might be invisible. To see the arrowhead, magnify the screen image or make the line thicker.

You can control the arrowhead size independently of the line width by using the arrowhead editor. You can also use the arrowhead editor to adjust the arrowhead's position relative to the end of the line. See *Editing an Arrowhead or Line Ending Shape* in the CorelDRAW on-line Help system.

To create a new arrowhead and add it to the arrowhead palette, draw it as a normal object, choose Special ➤ Create Arrow, and click OK in the Create Arrow dialog box. You can have up to one hundred arrowheads in the palette, including those supplied with CorelDRAW.

Changing Corner Style

To select miter (pointed), round, or bevel (clipped) corners where two lines meet:

1. Select the object and display the Outline Pen dialog box, as described under "Changing Line Thickness" earlier in this entry.

2. Click one of the **Corners** option buttons.

3. Click **OK**.

NOTES See the Outline Pen dialog box for illustrations of the three corner styles.

CorelDRAW squares a corner when two lines meet at less than a specified miter angle. See *Preferences* for information about specifying the miter angle.

Changing Pen Shape

By default, CorelDRAW creates outlines with a square pen so that horizontal and vertical lines have the same width.

To change the pen size and shape for a calligraphic effect:

1. Select the object and display the Outline Pen dialog box, as described under "Changing Line Thickness" earlier in this entry.

2. Click one of the arrows by the Stretch text box under Calligraphy to change the pen from a square to a rectangle, or type a percentage value for the width-to-height proportion. The shape is displayed in the Nib Shape box.

3. Click one of the arrows by the Angle text box under Calligraphy to change the angle of the pen, or type a value for the angle. The angle is displayed in the Nib Shape box.

4. Click the rounded-corner option button in the Corners group to change from a rectangular pen shape to an elliptical shape.

5. Click **OK** to apply the new pen shape to the selected object.

NOTES Be prepared to experiment to see the effect of various pen shapes.

You can also point into the Nib Shape sample box and drag to change the pen shape and angle.

To restore the default pen shape, click Default in the Calligraphy box.

Copying Outline Attributes

To copy the attributes of an outline to another object:

1. Select the object or objects with the outline you want to change.

2. Choose **Edit ➤ Copy Attributes From**.

3. In the Copy Attributes dialog box, click the **Outline Pen** button if you wish to copy the pen attributes with the exception of color. Click the **Outline Color** button if you wish to copy the pen color.

4. Click **OK**.

5. Point with the **From** arrow to the outline having the attributes to be copied. Click to copy the attributes to the selected object.

Alternatively:

1. Select the object with the outline you want to change and display the Pen roll-up, as described under "Changing Line Thickness" earlier in this entry.

2. Click **Update From** in the Pen roll-up.

3. Point with the **From** cursor to the object that has attributes to be copied, then click.

4. Click **Apply** in the roll-up.

Removing an Object's Visible Outline

Do the following to make an outline invisible:

1. Select the object and display the Pen roll-up or the Outline flyout, as described under "Changing Line Thickness" earlier in this entry.

2. Reduce the line thickness to X in the Pen roll-up, then click **Apply**, or click **X** in the flyout.

NOTES If the object is filled, the fill is still visible after the outline becomes invisible. However, if the object you select is not filled (or is filled with the background color) you will not see it in editable preview once the outline becomes invisible.

You can make an outline visible again by switching to wireframe view, selecting the outline, and changing its width attribute to a non-zero value.

Placing an Outline behind a Fill

By default, a fill is behind an outline. To reverse this:

1. Select a filled outline.

2. Display the Outline Pen dialog box.

3. Click the **Behind Fill** check box to insert a check mark, then click **OK**.

Scaling an Outline

By default the thickness of an outline changes in proportion when you enlarge or reduce an object. To keep the outline thickness unchanged:

1. Select a filled outline.

2. Display the Outline Pen dialog box.

3. Click the **Scale With Image** check box to remove the check mark, then click **OK**.

OVERPRINTING COLORS

When you print overlapping, uniformly filled objects, CorelDRAW by default knocks out underlying colors so that they do not interfere with the top color. You can choose to allow overprinting to create trap and other effects.

Enabling Overprinting

To allow one uniform fill to print on top of another:

1. Display two objects with uniform fill, one overlapping the other.

2. Right-click the top object to display its Object menu.

3. Click **Overprint Fill**.

Subsequently, when you print, the top color is printed on top of the bottom color.

NOTES You can also overprint with an outline. In step 3, click Overprint Outline.

By default, when you open an object's Object menu, Overprint Fill and Overprint Outline are not checked. If you open an object's Object menu after you have previously clicked one of these, that item is checked.

Creating Trap

When printing color-separated material, there is some small mis-alignment between the colors. To avoid paper color showing between adjacent colors, a small amount of color overlap, known as trap, is allowed.

To create trap between two objects, you slightly enlarge one them. You can create a spread trap in which a foreground object spreads slightly over the background, or a choke trap in which the background extends into the foreground. The amount of trap required depends on many aspects of the printing process and can only be determined by experiment or previous experience.

With CorelDRAW, you can create trap manually or automatically.

To create trap manually for filled objects with no outline:

1. Select the filled object that is to provide trap.

2. Add an outline to that object and make the outline the same color as the fill.

3. Set the outline width to twice the size of the desired trap. Because the outline is centered on the path that defines the object's shape, the trap is half the width of the outline.

4. Right-click the object to display its Object menu, and click **Overprint Outline**.

To create trap for an object with an outline but no fill:

1. Select the unfilled object that is to provide trap.

2. Copy the object to the Clipboard and paste it onto the drawing. This places a duplicate exactly on top of the original, with the duplicate selected.

3. Increase the thickness of the duplicate by twice the size of the desired trap.

4. Right-click the duplicate to select its Object menu, and click **Overprint Outline**.

5. If the line is open, use the **Line Caps** option to provide trap at the ends of the line.

NOTES Use the Outline Pen dialog box to set the outline width exactly. If you are experimenting, try an initial width of 0.004 inches (to give a trap of 0.002 inches).

Using Autotrap

Instead of creating trap manually you can, in some situations, use CorelDRAW's autotrapping feature, which you enable in the Print Options dialog box.

When autotrap is enabled, CorelDRAW automatically creates trap for objects that:

- Have no outline

- Are filled with a uniform fill

- Do not have Overprint Fill or Overprint Outline enabled

PAGE SETUP

The Page Setup command lets you establish page size, orientation, and background color. You can also add a printable background pattern or texture to the page.

Setting the Page Size, Orientation, and Background

1. Choose **Layout** ➤ **Page Setup**.

2. To use a page orientation and size that corresponds with your current printer setting, click **Set From Printer**, then proceed to step 6. Otherwise go to step 3.

3. Click the **Portrait** or **Landscape** button. This affects only the displayed page. You must set the printer orientation separately. See *Printing a Drawing*.

4. Open the Paper Size list box and choose one of the 18 pre-set sizes, or choose **Custom**.

5. If you chose Custom paper size, select the Width and Height (up to a maximum of 30 inches), otherwise CorelDRAW sets the page dimensions automatically.

6. Open the Page Layout list box and choose one of the six page layouts. After you click a page layout, a description appears in the dialog box.

7. Click the **Paper Color** button and choose a paper color from the palette. The color you choose is displayed, but does not print.

8. Click the **Show Page Border** check box to switch between showing and not showing the page border on screen.

9. Click the **Add Page Frame** button if you want to add a printable frame. By default, the frame is the same size as the page, but you can change its size (see *Scaling and Rescaling an Object*).

10. Click **Facing Pages** if you want to switch between displaying and not displaying facing pages. Then click the **Left First** or **Right First** option button, according to how you want facing pages to be displayed.

11. Click **OK** to accept your page setup.

Adding a Background to a Page

You can use a pattern, texture, fountain fill, or another object as a page background.

1. Choose **Layout ➤ Page Setup**.

2. Click the **Add Page Frame** button.

3. Click **OK**.

This draws a rectangle the same size as the page and places it behind all objects on the screen. You can fill the rectangle the same way you fill any other object. See *Filling an Object*.

`new` Adding Pages to a Document

You can create documents with up to 999 pages. To add pages:

1. Choose **Layout ➤ Insert Page** to display the Insert Page dialog box.

2. Type or select the number of pages you want to insert.

3. Click the **Before** or **After** option button to specify whether to insert the pages before or after the current page. The number of the current page is shown in the Page text box. You can change this number.

4. Click **OK**.

NOTES   When you work with a multipage document, the left end of the horizontal scroll bar shows the current page number and contains buttons you can click to move from page to page.

`new` Deleting Pages from a Multipage Document

1. Choose **Layout ➤ Delete Page** to display the Delete Page dialog box.

2. Specify the range of pages to delete. By default, the current page is selected.

3. Click **OK** to deleted the selected pages.

`new` Selecting a Page in a Multipage Document

1. Choose **Layout ➤ Go To Page** to display the Go To Page dialog box.

2. Type or select the page number to display, then click **OK**.

NOTES You can also move between pages by clicking the arrow buttons at the left end of the horizontal scroll bar.

PATTERNS

You can use two-color or full-color patterns to fill objects. See *Filling an Object*.

Creating a Pattern

To create a pattern and add it to the two-color or full-color pattern palette:

1. Open a new CorelDRAW drawing and create the object you want to use as a pattern.

2. Choose **Special ➤ Create Pattern** to display the Create Pattern dialog box.

3. To create a two-color pattern, click the **Two Color** option button and then click one of the **Resolution** buttons. To create a full-color pattern, click the **Full Color** option button.

4. Click **OK** to show the object with the crosshair cursor activated.

5. Use the crosshair cursor to marquee-select the area to be used as a pattern.

6. Click **OK** to accept the defined area. If you are creating a two-color pattern, the pattern is added to the two-color pattern palette so that you can use it to fill objects. If you are creating a full-color pattern, the Save Full Color Pattern dialog box is displayed, allowing you to name the pattern and save it.

NOTES You can also create two-color patterns using the Two-color Pattern Editor (see *Filling an Object*).

Creating a Pattern from a Symbol

You can use any of the symbols supplied with CorelDRAW to create a pattern. To do this:

1. Display with Symbols roll-up (see *Symbols*).

2. Select the symbol category and find the symbol you want to use.

3. Click the **Tile** check box, then click **Options** to display the Tile dialog box.

4. Choose or type numbers in the Horizontal and Vertical Grid Size text boxes to specify how many times the symbol repeats on the page, then click **OK** to create the pattern.

5. Save the page as a pattern file (see *File Management*).

PERSPECTIVE

You can create one-point and two-point perspective views of an object. Figure 1.18 shows a rectangle containing text without perspective, with one-point perspective, and with two-point perspective. These perspective views are different from those made as a perspective extrusion of an object (see *Extruding an Object*).

Creating a Perspective

See the Glossary in on-line Help for information about one-point and two-point perspective.

To create a perspective view of an object:

1. Use the **Pick** tool to select an object.

2. Choose **Effects ➤ Add Perspective** to outline the object with a rectangular dashed frame having handles at each corner. The cursor changes to an arrowhead.

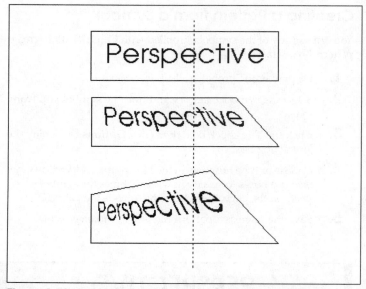

Figure 1.18: The same object without perspective (top), with one-point perspective (center), and with two-point perspective (bottom)

3. Point onto one of the handles and the cursor changes to a cross.

4. To create a one-point perspective, hold down the **Ctrl** key, and drag the handle vertically or horizontally. To create a two-point perspective, drag the handle diagonally. An X shows the vanishing point of a one-point perspective; two X's show the vanishing points of a two-point perspective.

5. Release the mouse button and select the **Pick** tool.

NOTES If you hold down the Shift key while you drag a handle horizontally or vertically, the opposite handle moves the same distance, but in the opposite direction.

After you have added perspective to an object, you can restore a rectangular frame so that you can again add perspective. Do this by selecting the object and then choosing Effects ➤ Add Perspective.

Moving a Vanishing Point

1. Use the **Shape** tool to select the object and show the vanishing points.

2. If the vanishing points are not visible, scroll the image to find them.

3. Drag the vanishing point to a new position.

Copying an Object's Perspective

1. Use the **Pick** tool to select the object to which you want to apply perspective.

2. Choose **Effects** ➤ **Copy Effect From,** and in the secondary menu, choose **Copy Perspective From**.

3. Point with the **From** arrow onto the object from which you want to copy perspective.

4. Click the mouse button.

Clearing an Object's Perspective

1. Use the **Pick** tool to select the object from which you want to clear perspective.

2. Choose **Effects** ➤ **Clear Perspective**.

PLACING AN OBJECT

See *Aligning and Shaping Text* and *Alignment and Placement Aids*.

POWERLINES

Powerlines are lines with a variable weight that give a drawing a hand-drawn look. Powerlines have outlines that can be filled.

The procedures that follow show how to use powerlines. However, because so many effects are available, you should take time to experiment in order to fully appreciate the possibilities.

new Creating a Powerline

You can create a line as a powerline, or you can convert an existing line into a powerline.

To create a line as a powerline:

1. Choose **Effects ➤ PowerLine Roll-Up** to display the Powerline roll-up shown in Figure 1.19 (left).

2. Click the topmost icon at the left of the roll-up to access powerline effects.

3. Scroll the powerline list box and double-click on one of the effects. The sample at the top of the roll-up shows the effect.

4. Choose or type a maximum width for the line in the Max Width text box.

5. If necessary, click the check box to turn on Apply when drawing lines.

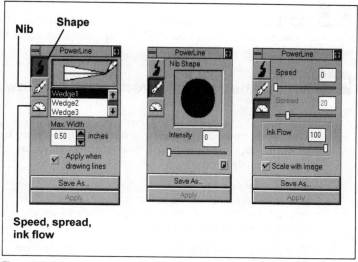

Figure 1.19: The PowerLine roll-up used to define style (left),
pen shape (center), and characteristics (right)

6. Draw a line and the line appears with the effect you chose
in step 3 and the maximum width you chose in step 4.

NOTES   After you have checked the Apply When Drawing Lines check box, all lines you subsequently draw will have the
current powerline effect. You should uncheck this box after you have
finished using it.

new Adjusting the Powerline Nib Shape

1. Click the second icon at the top left of the powerline roll-
up to access nib shapes as shown in Figure 1.19 (center).

2. Point into the Nib Shape sample at the top of the roll-up
and drag to change the nib shape.

3. Adjust the Intensity by dragging the slider or by typing a
value in the text box.

134   CorelDRAW

NOTES   Click the page icon at the bottom right of the roll-up to set the nib shape numerically. Click the page icon again to return to the graphic display.

new **Setting the Speed, Spread, and Ink Flow**

To adjust the powerline characteristics:

1.   Click the bottom icon at the left of the powerline roll-up to access speed, spread, and ink flow controls as shown in Figure 1.19 (right).

2.   Vary the **Speed** setting to control the pen speed. At low speed, the pen draws a powerline closely following the original line; at higher speeds, the pen tends to smooth out sudden changes of direction.

3.   Vary the **Spread** setting to control how much the power-line spreads.

4.   Vary the **Ink Flow** setting to create an effect varying between that of a pen that is almost out of ink to one that is full.

5.   Click the **Scale with image** check box if necessary. When the box is checked, powerline effects stay in proportion as an object size changes. When the box is not checked, powerline effects remain the same when an object size changes.

new **Drawing a Pressure-Sensitive Powerline**

A pressure-sensitive powerline is a line that varies in thickness according to the pressure you apply while you draw with a pressure-sensitive stylus. If you are drawing with a device that is not pressure sensitive, press ↓ while you draw to give the effect of increased pressure and produce a thicker line, or press ↑ while you draw to give the effect of reduced pressure and produce a thinner line. Be prepared to spend some time practicing to get the effect you want with this technique.

To draw a line with controlled thickness, using the arrow keys to control pressure:

1. Choose **Effects ➤ PowerLine Roll-Up** to display the roll-up shown in Figure 1.19 (left).

2. Scroll the powerline list box and double-click **Pressure**.

3. In the Max Width text box, choose or type a normal width value. This is the width of a line created without added or decreased pressure.

4. If necessary, click **Apply when drawing lines**.

5. Use the Pencil tool to draw a line. As you draw, press ↓ to increase the thickness of the line, or press ↑ to decrease its thickness.

new Editing a Powerline

You can edit the nodes in a powerline just as you can edit nodes of ordinary lines (see *Shaping and Reshaping an Object*). In addition, you can use pressure-editing to change the thickness of the powerline.

To change the shape of a powerline:

1. Use the **Shape** tool to select a powerline and display its nodes.

2. Use the techniques described in *Shaping and Reshaping an Object* to change the shape of the powerline.

To pressure-edit a powerline:

1. Use the **Shape** tool to select a powerline and display its nodes.

2. Double-click a node to display the Node Edit roll-up, which, in these circumstances, has a Pressure Edit check box.

3. Click the **Pressure Edit** check box to display pressure-edit nodes which control the thickness of the powerline.

4. Drag one or more pressure-edit nodes to alter the thickness of the powerline, effectively changing the pen pressure.

5. Click the **Pressure Edit** check box again in the Node Edit roll-up to restore the normal nodes.

NOTES You cannot pressure-edit a pressure-sensitive powerline.

new Saving a Powerline

After you have established all the settings for a powerline, you can save those settings with a name. The new name appears subsequently in the powerline list box.

1. In the PowerLine roll-up, click **Save As** to display the PowerLine Presets dialog box.

2. Type a name for the new settings and click **OK** to save them.

PREFERENCES

You can alter many of the ways in which CorelDRAW works by changing values and making choices in the Preferences dialog box, and changing, adding, or deleting entries in the CORELDRW.INI file.

You can also add files that in some cases enhance the performance of your monitor and printer.

Setting Preferences

To set preferences:

1. Choose **Special** ➤ **Preferences**.

2. Select or type new values for the Place Duplicate and Clones **Horizontal** and **Vertical** values, the **Nudge** value, the **Constrain Angle**, the **Miter Limit** angle, and the number of **Undo Levels** allowed.

3. Click buttons to enable or disable **Auto-Panning, Inter-ruptible Display**, the **Cross Hair Cursor**, and the **3.x Compatibility Message** features.

4. Click the **Curves** button to display the Preferences - Curves dialog box. Here, you can set preferences for **Freehand Tracking, Autotrace Tracking, Corner Threshold, Straight Line Threshold, AutoJoin**, and **Auto-Reduce**. Click **OK** to accept changes and return to the Preferences menu.

5. Click the **Display** button to display the Preferences - Display dialog box. Here, you can set the **Preview Fountain Steps** value, the **Greek Text Below** pixel value, the way colors are shown on your screen, and the flatness of curves. Click **OK** to accept changes and return to the Preferences menu.

6. Click the **Mouse** button to display the Preferences - Mouse dialog box in which you can assign functions to the right mouse button. Click **OK** to accept changes and return to the Preferences menu.

7. Click the **Roll-Ups** button to display the Preferences - Roll-Ups dialog box to choose how roll-ups are displayed when you start CorelDRAW. Click **OK** to accept changes and return to the Preferences menu.

8. Click the **Dimension** button to display the Preferences - Dimension dialog box in which you can set a default format for the display of labels in drawings. Click **OK** to accept changes and return to the Preferences menu.

9. Click **OK** to retain the new preferences.

NOTES   CorelDRAW on-line Help provides extensive information on the many preference choices available. Access Help information by displaying the appropriate Preferences dialog box and pressing F1.

Editing the CORELDRW.INI File

You can also change many defaults by editing the CORELDRW.INI file. For information, see *Software-related Information* in the Reference section of on-line Help.

Enhancing Monitor and Printer Performance

Corel provides some files that enhance the performance of some monitors and printers. For information about these files, see *Hardware-related Information* in the Reference section of on-line Help.

PRINTING A DRAWING

CorelDRAW can print a drawing on any Windows-supported printer, using the same commands as most Windows applications. Refer to your Windows documentation for information about installing printers and printing files.

Setting Up the Printer

Check, and if necessary modify, the Print Setup dialog box before printing a drawing. To do this:

1. Choose **File ➤ Print Setup** to display the Print Setup dialog box.

2. In the Printer box, verify that the correct printer is selected.

3. In the Orientation box, click the **Portrait** or **Landscape** button to correspond with the page orientation. See the information about setting the page size, orientation, and color in *Page Setup*.

4. In the **Paper** box, select the paper size and source.

5. Click the **Options** button to display the Options dialog box.

6. Modify the options as necessary. See your Windows and printer documentation for information about these options.

7. Click **OK** to return to the Print Setup dialog box.

8. Click **OK** to make your printer setup information effective.

NOTES   If you are going to print to a file, the printer selected should be the one on which the drawing will eventually be printed, not the printer connected to the computer you are using.

new Printing a Drawing

You can choose to print a drawing directly, or you can print to a file.

1. Choose **File ➤ Print** to display the Print dialog box. The left side of the dialog box shows a preview of what will be printed. If the current document has two or more pages, you can click the arrows at the bottom of the dialog box to preview specific pages.

2. To use other than the default printer, open the printer list box at the top right of the dialog box and click on the name of the printer to use.

3. To display information about the selected printer, click the **?** button.

4. To print to a file, click the **Print to File** check box to place a check mark in it. If you print to a file that will be printed on a Macintosh, click the **For Mac** check box.

5. Choose or type the number of copies to be printed in the **Copies** text box.

6. If the document has two or more pages, click the **All** check box to print all pages, or specify the range of pages to be printed in the **From** and **To** text boxes.

7. Click the **Selected Objects Only** check box if you want to print only selected objects in the drawing.

8. Click **Options** to display the Options dialog box, in which you can select various printing options appropriate to the printer.

9. Click **Color** to define how colors in the drawing are to be printed.

10. Click **Printer** to change settings defined in Printer Setup (see "Setting Up the Printer" above).

11. Select choices and set values in the Position and Size section of the dialog box to control the position and size of the printed objects. You can also drag the preview image in the left side of the dialog box to change its position and size.

12. Click **OK** to start printing.

Merge Printing

Merge printing in CorelDRAW is similar to merge printing in many word processors. You can create a master document, in this case a drawing, and print many copies of it with each copy having different text in specific places.

You can use merge print, for example, to print multiple copies of certificates or diplomas in which people's names and other information differ from one copy to another.

Merged text has the same attributes and transformations as the text it replaces, unless the original text has been blended, extruded, or fitted to a path. However, the attributes of individual characters are not transferred to the merged text.

There are three steps in producing a merged drawing:

1. Prepare a master drawing containing all objects common to every printed drawing and with labels to mark the place and attributes of text that will be merged into the master drawing.

2. Prepare a merge file containing text that replaces the labels in each drawing.

3. Use Print Merge to print the merged drawings.

These three steps are described in detail below.

To prepare a master drawing for use with print merge:

1. Prepare a CorelDRAW drawing (such as a diploma) using any tools to draw objects that will appear on every drawing, but using only artistic text for the text that will be different on each drawing. Each text object to be replaced must be a separate artistic text object.

2. Print the drawing as usual to verify that it is satisfactory.

3. Replace each artistic text object that will be different on from one drawing to another with a unique label (Corel calls a label "secondary text"). A label can be any text string and should have the text attributes that the merged text will have on the printed drawing. Typical labels are *Name*, *Address*, *Date*, and so on.

4. Save the drawing.

To prepare a merge file containing the text that will replace labels in the master drawing:

1. Open a new file in a text editor, such as Windows Notepad, or a word processor.

2. On the first line, type the number of labels in your drawing.

3. On the second line, type a backslash (\), followed by the first label, and then another backslash. The text here must be exactly the same as the label in the drawing (see the note below).

4. On the next line, type the next label preceded and followed by a backslash.

5. Repeat step 4 until you have typed all the labels.

6. On the next line, type a backslash, the text that will replace the first label on the first printed drawing, and another backslash.

7. Repeat step 6 until you have typed text that corresponds with each label on the first printed drawing.

8. Repeat steps 6 and 7 to type the text that replaces labels on another printed version of your drawing.

9. Repeat step 8 for each drawing you want to print. You can have replacement text for as many printed drawings as necessary.

10. Save your text as an ASCII file with a .TXT extension.

NOTES Labels in the merge document must be exactly the same as those in the drawing. Specifically, capitalization and line breaks must be the same. Also, there must be no spaces between the two backslashes other than those in the labels on the drawing.

Each set of replacement text must contain text to replace every label. If there is no text to replace a label, use two backslashes to represent an empty text string.

If the master drawing has two labels, *Name* and *City*, and you want to print three drawings each with different replacement text, a typical merge document might be

```
2
\Name\
\City\
\John Brown\
\New York\
\Mary Smith\
\Los Angeles\
\Carlo Spinoza\
\Los Alamos\
```

Printing a Merged Drawing

1. Open the drawing with which you want to merge text.

2. Choose **File ➤ Print Merge** to display the Print Merge dialog box.

3. Select the merge text file, then click **OK** to display the Print dialog box.

4. Select the appropriate print options (see note below) and click **OK**.

NOTES   Set the number of copies in the Print Options dialog box to 1 if you want to print one copy of each drawing for which a set of replacement text exists in the merge document. If you specify more than one, you will print multiple copies of each drawing.

Printing Specific Layers

See *Layering a Drawing* for information about selecting layers to be printed.

REFRESHING A WINDOW

Sometimes, after making changes to a drawing, remnants of the original are left behind. To clear these remnants, choose **Display ➤ Refresh Window**.

RESIZING AN OBJECT

See *Scaling or Stretching an Object*.

ROLL-UPS

A roll-up is a small dialog box that remains on screen after you have used it. You can choose which roll-ups you want to display, and whether to display each one in full or just as a title bar. You can move roll-ups anywhere on your screen.

You can use roll-ups to control many CorelDRAW operations more conveniently than by using menu commands.

The information in this entry applies to roll-ups in general. Specific information about each roll-up, together with an illustration, is included in entries that describe tasks in which roll-ups are used.

Selecting Default Roll-ups

Default roll-ups are those that are displayed as title bars when you start CorelDRAW. The choice you make here does not affect your current CorelDRAW session.

To choose how roll-ups are initially displayed:

1. Choose **Special ➤ Preferences**.

2. Click **Roll-Ups**.

3. Click one of the four options. You can choose to display no roll-ups, all roll-ups, the roll-ups as they currently appear, or the roll-ups as they appear when you exit CorelDRAW.

4. Click **OK** to return to the Preferences dialog box, and then click **OK** to accept your preferences.

Displaying a Roll-up

Some roll-ups are displayed by menu commands, others from the toolbox, and one by double-clicking:

- The Layout, Effects, and Text menus all contain commands that display roll-ups. To display one of these roll-ups, choose the menu and click on the appropriate command.

- The Outline and Fill tools display icons that you can click to display the Pen and Fill roll-ups.

- The Node Edit roll-up is displayed by double-clicking an object node.

Minimizing and Restoring a Roll-up

1. To minimize a roll-up to its title bar, click the arrow at the right end of the title bar.

2. To restore a roll-up that you previously minimized, click on the arrow at the right end of the title bar.

Closing a Roll-up

To close a roll-up, double-click on the **Control-menu** box at the left end of its title bar.

NOTES If you click just once on a roll-up's Control-menu box, you can choose to:

- Roll down the roll-up

- Roll up the roll-up

- Arrange the roll-up—that is, minimize it and move the title bar to a corner of the drawing area

- Arrange all—that is, minimize all roll-ups and move all the title bars to the corners of the screen

- Access on-line Help for information about using the roll-up

- Close the roll-up

ROTATING OR SKEWING AN OBJECT

You can rotate and skew objects, including bitmap objects, to any angle.

Rotating or Skewing an Object Interactively

1. Select the object to be rotated or skewed.

2. Click again on the object to replace the normal selection handles with rotation and skew handles, as shown in Figure 1.20.

3. To rotate the object, point onto one of the curved rotation handles at a corner of the object's frame. To skew the object, point onto one of the skew handles along an edge of the frame. In either case, the cursor changes to a cross.

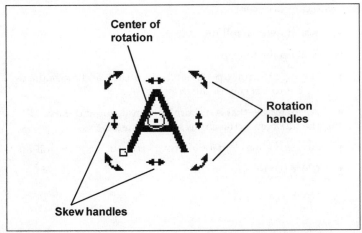

Figure 1.20: Rotation handles, skew handles, and the center of rotation

4. Press the mouse button and drag the cursor. As you drag, a dashed rectangle shows the amount of rotation or skew, and the status line shows the angle of rotation or skew.

5. Release the mouse button.

NOTES Tap the right mouse button or + on the numeric keypad before releasing the mouse button if you want to leave an original unrotated and unskewed copy of the object.

Hold down the Ctrl key until after you have released the mouse button to constrain the rotation or skew to specific angles. See *Preferences* for information about setting the constrain angle.

Rotating or Skewing an Object with Precision

1. Select the object to be rotated or skewed.

2. Choose **Effects ➤ Rotate & Skew**.

3. In the Rotate & Skew dialog box, select or type the **Rotation Angle**, or select or type the **Skew Horizontally** angle and the **Skew Vertically** angle.

4. Click the **Leave Original** check box to rotate or skew a copy of the object, leaving the original unchanged.

5. Click **OK**.

Moving an Object's Center of Rotation

1. Select the object to be rotated.

2. Click again on the object to replace the normal selection handles with rotation and skew handles and to show the center of rotation. By default, the center of rotation is at the center of the object's frame.

3. Point onto the center of rotation and press the mouse button.

4. Drag the center of rotation to a new position, then release the mouse button.

NOTES   The new center of rotation applies to subsequent rotation of the object made with the mouse or from the Rotate & Skew command.

Restoring an Object's Rotation and Skew

See *Clearing Transformations*.

Rotating Text

1. Use the **Text** tool to select one or more characters.

2. Choose **Text ➤ Character** to display the Character Attributes dialog box.

3. Choose or type an angle in the **Character Angle** text box, then click **OK**.

SCALING OR STRETCHING AN OBJECT

You can scale an object, keeping its height and width in proportion, or you can stretch it, independently changing its height and width. You can also create a mirror image of an object.

When you scale an object, you can choose between keeping the outline thickness unchanged or changing the outline thickness in proportion (see "Scaling an Outline" in the *Outlining an Object* entry). When you stretch an object, the outline thickness always changes in proportion to the amount of stretch.

You can scale and stretch artistic text just as you can other objects. When you scale or stretch paragraph text, the size of the frame changes, but the characters within the frame do not change size.

The procedures in this entry apply to entire objects. You can also scale and stretch an individual segment of a curve object (see *Shaping and Reshaping an Object*).

Scaling or Stretching an Object Interactively

1. Select the object.

2. Point onto one of the corner handles to scale the object, to a center handle on a vertical edge of the object's frame to stretch it horizontally, or to a center handle on a horizontal edge of the frame to stretch it vertically.

3. Press the mouse button and drag the handle to a new position. A dashed rectangle on the screen shows the new size, and the status line shows the percentage change.

4. Release the mouse button.

NOTES   Tap the right mouse button or + on the numeric keypad before releasing the mouse button if you wish to retain an original-size copy of the object.

Hold down the Ctrl key until you have released the mouse button to scale or stretch the object to an exact multiple of its original size.

Hold down the Shift key until you have released the mouse button to scale or stretch the object in equal amounts from the center.

Scaling or Stretching an Object with Precision

1. Select the object.

2. Choose **Effects** ➤ **Stretch & Mirror**.

3. In the Stretch & Mirror dialog box, select or type horizontal and vertical percentages. Use equal percentages to scale the object, unequal percentages to stretch it.

4. Click **Leave Original** if you want to keep an original-size copy of the object.

5. Click **OK**.

Mirroring an Object Interactively

Use the procedure "Stretching or Shrinking an Object Interactively." In step 3, drag a handle across the object and beyond its opposite edge or corner.

Mirroring an Object with Precision

Use the procedure "Stretching or Shrinking an Object with Precision". Use a negative value in the Stretch Horizontally or Stretch Vertically text box. You can convert a positive number to a negative number by clicking the **Horz Mirror** or **Vert Mirror** button.

Restoring a Scaled, Stretched, or Mirrored Object

See *Clearing Transformations*.

SCREEN

Figure 1.21 shows the screen components described in the table below. You can choose to display or hide certain screen components.

Component	Purpose
Color palette	Contains colors from which you can select outline and fill colors.
Control-menu box	Provides conventional Windows commands.
Cursor	Selects a specific point on the screen. The cursor changes shape according to the current operation.
Editing window	The area in which you create your drawing.

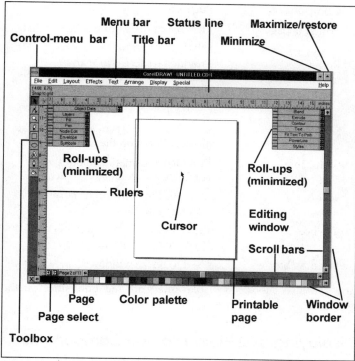

Figure 1.21: The CorelDRAW screen

Component	Purpose
Menu bar	Provides access to nine pull-down menus.
Maximize/Restore button	Expands a window to fill the entire screen, or contracts the window to occupy only part of the screen.
Minimize button	Shrinks a window to an icon at the bottom of the screen.
Page indicator	Shows the number of the current page of a multipage document.
Page section buttons	Select the next or previous page.

Component	Purpose
Printable page	The area of the editing window that can be printed.
Roll-ups (minimized)	Provide fast access to many CorelDRAW operations.
Rulers	Used for sizing and positioning objects.
Scroll bars	Used to view parts of a drawing that are not shown on the current screen.
Status line	Provides information about the currently selected object or action.
Title bar	Displays the name of the current program and file.
Toolbox	Provides rapid access to tools used to create and edit drawings.
Window border	Used to resize windows.

You can also choose to display the grid and guidelines on the screen.

Displaying and Hiding Screen Components

You can choose to display or hide rulers, the status line, the color palette, the toolbox, and the roll-ups.

1. Choose **Display**. The top four items in the Display menu allow you to display or hide screen components. A check mark by the item indicates that the item is displayed; the absence of a check mark indicates that the item is hidden.

2. Click one of the top four items in the menu to switch between display and hide.

NOTES See *Roll-ups* for information about displaying roll-ups.

Showing a Full-Screen View

1. Choose **Display ➤ Show Preview** to display only the objects in a drawing.

2. Press any key to return to the original view.

SELECTING AND DESELECTING OBJECTS

You must select an object before you can make any changes to it. You know an object is selected by the eight small boxes (handles) around it. The status bar identifies selected objects.

Selecting and Deselecting the Most Recently Drawn Object

To select the object you have just drawn, press the **spacebar**.

Selecting Any Object

1. Use the **Pick** tool to point anywhere onto the outline of the object, or within the object if it is filled.

2. Click the mouse button.

Selecting Multiple Objects

You can select any or all objects on a page. You cannot select objects on more than one page.

1. Use the **Pick** tool to point anywhere onto the first object.

2. Click the mouse button.

3. Point anywhere onto another object.

4.   Hold down the **Shift** key while you click the mouse button.

5.   Repeat steps 3 and 4 to select additional objects.

Selecting an Object within a Group

An object within a group is known as a child object. To select a child object:

1.   Use the **Pick** tool to point anywhere on the outline of the child object, or within it if it is filled.

2.   Hold down the **Ctrl** key and click the mouse button.

NOTES   If you have nested groups—that is, groups within groups—you may have to click several times with the Ctrl key pressed to reach the object you want.

Selecting All Objects within a Rectangular Area

To marquee-select all objects within a rectangular area:

1.   Use the **Pick** tool to point onto an unoccupied space in the drawing window above and to the left of all objects to be selected.

2.   Press and hold down the mouse button while you drag down and to the right. Drag until a dotted rectangle encloses all the objects.

3.   Release the mouse button. Handles appear around the selected group of objects.

NOTES   Marquee-selection temporarily groups objects only as long as the group remains selected. See *Grouping and Ungrouping Objects* for information about permanent grouping.

The same technique is used, using the Shape tool, to select multiple nodes (see *Shaping and Reshaping an Object*).

Selecting All Objects in a Drawing

To select all objects in a single-page drawing, or all objects on the current page of a multipage drawing, choose **Edit ➤ Select All**.

Selecting the Next or Previous Object in a Drawing

This technique is particularly useful when you want to select from several superimposed objects. Do the following:

1. Select an object.

2. Press the **Tab** key to select the next object, or press **Shift+Tab** to select the previous object.

Deselecting All Selected Objects

To deselect all objects, press **Esc**, or press the **spacebar**, or point with the **Pick** tool onto an unoccupied space in the editing window and click the mouse button.

Deselecting One of Many Selected Objects

1. Use the **Pick** tool to point onto the outline of the object to be deselected, or within the object if it is filled.

2. While holding down the **Shift** key, click the mouse button.

Reselecting Previously Selected Objects

To select the object or objects you have just deselected, press the **spacebar**.

NOTES Use this to reselect a single object or a group of objects that have just been deselected. If you have deselected one object from a group of selected objects, you cannot reselect that object as part of the group by this method. Instead, hold down the Shift key and click the object.

SHAPING AND RESHAPING AN OBJECT

You can use the Shape tool to change the shape of lines or curves. You can also change the shape of a rectangle, ellipse, or text object, but you must first convert it to curves. See *Converting an Object to Curves*.

The following terms are used to describe CorelDRAW objects and their shape:

- Control point: A point, associated with a node of a curve object, that controls the direction in which the curve object passes through the node and the curvature at the node

- Curve object: An object consisting of one or more curve or line segments

- Curve segment: An object with a node at each end, each having a control point

- Cusp node: A node at which the direction of a curve may change abruptly

- Line segment: A straight line with a node at each end, neither node having a control point

- Node: A point through which a curve passes and at which the curvature may change

- Path: A set of straight lines or curves, not necessarily connected, that defines the shape of an open or closed object

- Segment: A line or curve between adjacent nodes in a curve object

- Smooth node: A node at which the direction of a curve may change smoothly, rather than abruptly

- Subpath: A path that has been combined with other curves or paths to form a larger path

- Symmetrical node: A node at which a curve arrives and leaves at the same angle, a special case of a smooth node

Most of the following procedures are defined in terms of commands selected from menus and the Node Edit roll-up. See Table 1.3 in the *Shortcut Keys* for shortcut keys you can use when shaping and reshaping objects.

Selecting a Node on a Line or Curve

1.   Point onto an object with the **Shape** tool.

2.   Click the mouse button. The nodes on the object appear as small open squares. The status line indicates the type of object selected, and in the case of a line or curve, the number of nodes it has.

3.   Point onto the node you want to use, click the mouse button and the node turns black, as shown in Figure 1.22. The status line shows the position of the node and its type. If the object is a curve, dashed lines extend to control points.

4.   To select an additional node, point to that node, and hold down the Shift key while you click the mouse button. The status line shows how many nodes are selected. Control points are not shown if more than one node is selected.

5.   Repeat step 4 to select more nodes.

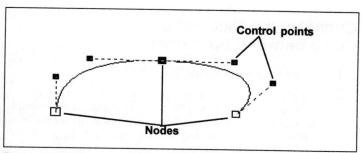

Figure 1.22: Selected nodes with control points

NOTES   It is often easier to work with nodes in wireframe view rather in editable preview.

You can use marquee-selection to select one or multiple nodes with the Shape tool in the same way that you use the Pick tool to select objects (see *Selecting and Deselecting an Object*). With a node selected, you can press Tab to select the next node, or Shift+Tab to select the previous node.

When you select a node, you also select the segment that precedes it. When you select a segment, a round marker appears to show the point selected on the segment and the node at the end of the segment is also selected.

With a curve selected, you can press Home to select the first node or End to select the last node.

After you have selected two or more nodes, you can move or edit them together.

Deselecting Nodes

Using the **Shape** tool, click on an unselected node to select that node and, at the same time, to deselect all other nodes.

To deselect all nodes without selecting another, point with the **Shape** tool onto an unoccupied place in the drawing area and click the mouse button. The curve remains selected.

Changing the Shape of a Curve between Two Nodes

1.   Select the curve with the **Shape** tool.

2.   Point onto the curve at any place other than on a node, and drag the curve. As you drag, the curve changes shape between the two nodes, while those nodes do not move. The status line shows the distance moved. Release the mouse button to accept the change.

Moving a Control Point

1. Select the curve with the **Shape** tool.

2. Point onto a node and drag it to a new position. The curve changes shape so that it continues to pass through the node. The status line shows the distance moved. Release the mouse button to accept the change.

NOTES   To move two or more nodes simultaneously, first select them, and then drag one of them. All selected nodes move the same distance, unless elastic mode is selected (see "Using Elastic Mode").

Hold down the Ctrl key until you have released the mouse button to move nodes horizontally or vertically only.

Changing Curvature Close to a Node

1. Select the curve with the **Shape** tool.

2. Select a node.

3. Point onto a control point.

4. Press and hold down the mouse button while you drag the control point to change the curvature close to the node. The status line shows the distance moved.

5. Release the mouse button.

NOTES   Angular movement of a control point changes the angle at which the curve passes through a node. Moving the control point further from, or nearer to, a node increases or decreases the effect on the curvature close to the node.

Displaying the Node Edit Roll-up

Apart from the basic curve-shaping operations described above, nodes are controlled from the Node Edit roll-up shown in Figure 1.23.

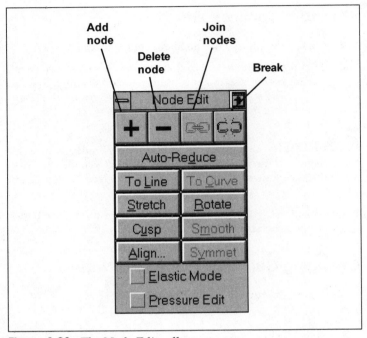

Figure 1.23: The Node Edit roll-up

1. Select the curve with the **Shape** tool.

2. Double-click on the curve with the Shape tool.

NOTES The Pressure Edit option at the bottom of the roll-up is present only if the selected curve is a powerline.

Adding a Node to a Curve

1. Select the curve with the **Shape** tool.

2. Point with the **Shape** tool onto the curve at the point where you want to add a node and click.

3.   Click + in the **Node Edit** roll-up or press + on the numeric
keypad. The new node with its control points appears on
the curve.

NOTES   If, in step 2, you click an existing node other than
the first, the new node is created at the mid-point of the preceding
segment. If you select two or more nodes, new nodes are created at
the mid-points of each selected segment.

When you press + on the numeric keypad to add a node, one node
is added. If you press + again, two addition nodes are added. Each
subsequent time you press +, twice the preceding number of nodes
are added.

Deleting a Node from a Curve

To delete specific nodes:

1.   Using the **Shape** tool, click on the node, or nodes, you
want to delete.

2.   Click– in the Node Edit roll-up, press **Delete**, or press –
on the numeric keypad.

To delete nodes automatically:

1.   Select the curve with the **Shape** tool.

2.   Click **Auto-Reduce** in the Node Edit roll-up. Any nodes
closer than five pixels to another node are deleted.

NOTES   You can set the Auto-Reduce distance to any value
up to ten pixels (see *Preferences*). The default value is five pixels.

Aligning Nodes and Control Points

1.   Use the **Shape** tool to select the node you want to align.

2.   Hold down **Shift** while you select the node to which you
want to align the first.

3. Click **Align** in the Node Edit roll-up to display the Node Align dialog box with Align Horizontal, Align Vertical, and Align Control Point check boxes all checked.

4. Leave all three check boxes checked if you want to align the shape of a curve as well as its nodes. Otherwise, click whichever check box you want to deselect, then click **OK**.

NOTES You can align nodes on the same path or on different subpaths in the same object.

If you need to align nodes in different objects, first combine the objects, align the nodes, and then break the object apart.

You can use the same technique to align control points.

Joining Nodes to Create a Closed Path

You can join the two end nodes of an open path to create a closed path.

1. Select the open path with the **Shape** tool. The open path must have at least one node between the end nodes.

2. Select the two end nodes of the open path with the **Shape** tool, and check that the status line indicates two nodes are selected.

3. Click the **Join Nodes** button in the Node Edit roll-up. The two nodes disappear and are replaced by a single node half-way between the original two, and the status line indicates the object is a closed curve.

Joining Nodes to Form a Single Curve from Separate Curves

1. Using the **Pick** tool, select the two separate paths to be joined.

2.   Choose **Arrange ➤ Combine** to combine the two paths into a single discontinuous path consisting of two subpaths.

3.   Using the **Shape** tool, select the two nodes to be joined.

4.   Click the **Join Nodes** button in the Node Edit roll-up. The two nodes disappear and are replaced by a single node half way between the original two, and the curve becomes continuous.

NOTES   The curves to be combined must be combined into a single object before you can form a single curve from them. If the curves are already a single object (as reported in the status bar), omit steps 1 and 2.

After you select the Pick tool, the status line tells you how many subpaths (unconnected paths) exist in the selected object.

Breaking a Curve into Separate Subpaths

1.   With the **Shape** tool, select the curve and then click at the node, or other place on the curve, where you want to break the curve.

2.   Click the **Break-apart** icon in the Node Edit roll-up. Two superimposed nodes are created at the break point.

3.   Move either subpath to make the two discontinuous.

NOTES   You can break a curve at several nodes simultaneously. Select the nodes, and then click the Break-apart icon.

Using Smooth, Symmetrical, and Cusp Nodes

CorelDRAW has three types of nodes—smooth, symmetrical, and cusp:

• Smooth nodes are those in which the node and its two control points lie on a straight line. When you move one control point, the other moves to maintain the linear relationship. Curves are continuous at a smooth node.

- Symmetrical nodes are smooth nodes with the added property that the two control points are the same distance from the node. Curvature is the same on both sides of a symmetrical node.

- Cusp nodes have two independent control points. The node and its two control points are not necessarily on a straight line, and the two control points can be at different distances from the node. Curves are discontinuous at a cusp node.

When a single node is selected, the status line shows what type of node it is. The status line does not show node type when two or more nodes are selected.

There are two types of segments that can exist between each pair of nodes:

- A curve segment, which has two control points associated with it, one for the node at each end

- A line segment, which has no control points associated with it

Changing a Node's Type

1. Use the **Shape** tool to select the node or nodes you want to change.

2. Click **Smooth**, **Symmet**, or **Cusp** in the Node Edit roll-up. The curve is redrawn with the new type of node and the status line shows the node's new type.

Changing between Curve and Line Segments

1. With the **Shape** tool, select one or more segments, or the nodes that follow them.

2. Click **to Line** in the Node Edit roll-up to change curve segments to line segments, or click **to Curve** to change line segments to curve segments.

`new` Scaling or Stretching a Segment

1. With the **Shape** tool, select the first and last node of the segment or segments to be scaled or stretched.

2. Click **Stretch** in the Node Edit roll-up to display handles around the selected segment or segments.

3. Scale or stretch the selected region using the normal method (see *Scaling and Stretching an Object*).

`new` Rotating or Skewing a Segment

1. With the **Shape** tool, select the first and last node of the segment or segments to be rotated or skewed.

2. Click **Rotate** in the Node Edit roll-up to display handles around the selected segment or segments.

3. Rotate or skew the selected region using the normal method (see *Rotating and Skewing an Object*).

`new` Using Elastic Mode

Activate or deactivate elastic mode according to the effect you want when you drag multiple nodes. With elastic mode deactivated, all nodes other than end nodes move the same distance. With elastic mode activated, nodes move in proportion to their distance from the node you drag, giving an elastic effect.

To activate or deactivate elastic mode, click the **Elastic Mode** check box in the Node Edit roll-up.

Shaping an Object with an Envelope

You can shape a text or graphics object to fit within another object (an envelope) as shown in Figure 1.24. You can use this to wrap paragraph text around an object.

To fit an object into an envelope:

1.   Use the **Pick** tool to select the object to be shaped.

2.   Choose **Effects ➤ Envelope Roll-up** to display the Envelope roll-up shown in Figure 1.25.

3.   Click **Add New** in the roll-up to draw a dashed rectangle with nodes around the object.

4.   Click one of the four envelope modes (see the notes below for explanations of these modes).

5.   Drag any of the nodes to shape the envelope.

6.   Click **Apply** in the roll-up to shape the object.

NOTES   From left to right in the roll-up, the four envelope modes allow you to create envelopes with:

• Straight sides

• Single-curve sides

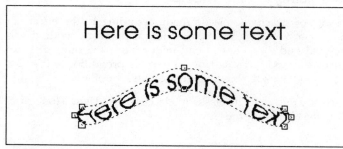

Figure 1.24:   An artistic text object before being shaped by an envelope (top) and after being shaped (bottom)

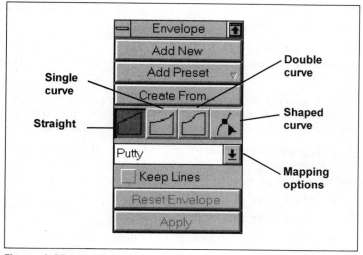

Figure 1.25: The Envelope roll-up

- Double-curve sides
- Sides that can be shaped using Node Edit roll-up functions

In the first three envelope nodes, hold down the Ctrl key while you drag to make a node and the one opposite it move in the same direction. Hold down the Shift key while you drag to make a node and the one opposite it move in opposite directions. To expand or contract the object, hold down the Ctrl and Shift keys while you drag a corner node to make all four corner nodes move, or hold down the Ctrl and Shift keys while you drag a center node to make all four center nodes move.

If you click the Keep Lines check box, straight lines in the object will remain straight and the object may not exactly conform to the envelope.

You can create an envelope around an object already shaped in an envelope, and you can shape this outer envelope as you shaped the first.

Text shaped within an envelope can be edited as text within an Artistic Text or Paragraph Text dialog box.

Instead of starting with a rectangular envelope, you can select from preset shapes. In step 3, click Add Preset, and choose from a palette of shapes.

You can create a shape and use it as an envelope. If you create the shape with the Rectangle, Ellipse, or Text tool, you must convert it into curves. In step 3, click Create From and then click on the shape.

Mapping options allow you to modify how the object is shaped. To choose a mapping option, open the list in the lower part of the roll-up and click on an option. The effects of these options are

- Original: Provides compatibility with objects shaped in CorelDRAW version 3.

- Putty: Provides less exaggerated distortion than Original

- Vertical: Squeezes or stretches objects vertically

- Horizontal: Squeezes or stretches objects horizontally

- Text: Used to shape paragraph text

Copying an Envelope from One Object to Another

1. Use the **Pick** tool to select the object to which you want to copy an envelope.

2. Choose **Effects ➤ Copy Effect From** and then click **Copy Envelope From**. The From arrow appears.

3. Point onto the envelope you want to copy, click the mouse button to apply the envelope to the selected object.

Clearing an Envelope

1. Use the **Pick** tool to select an object enclosed within an envelope.

2.   Choose **Effects ➤ Clear Envelope**. The object returns to
the shape it had before the envelope was applied.

NOTES   If you shaped an object with two or more envelopes, each time you choose Effects ➤ Clear Envelope, you remove the topmost envelope. To remove all envelopes surrounding an object in one step, choose Effects ➤ Clear Transformations.

SHORTCUT KEYS

Most procedures in this book are described in terms of selecting from menus. However, CorelDRAW provides shortcuts to speed certain actions. These are listed in Tables 1.1, 1.2, 1.3, and 1.4.

Table 1.1: Function Key Shortcuts

Key	Use
F1	Displays help on the currently selected command or the currently open dialog box
Shift+F1	Displays the help cursor with which you point at the part of the screen on which you want help
Ctrl+F1	Opens the Help Search dialog box
F2	Displays the Zoom-in cursor
Ctrl+F2	Opens the Text roll-up
F3	Zooms out by a factor of two
Ctrl+F3	Opens the Layers roll-up
F4	Changes the magnification so that all objects fit within the editing window
Alt+F4	Exits from CorelDRAW
F5	Selects the Pencil tool

Table 1.1: Function Key Shortcuts (continued)

Key	Use
Ctrl+F5	Opens the Styles roll-up
F6	Selects the Rectangle tool
F7	Selects the Ellipse tool
Ctrl+F7	Opens the Envelope roll-up
Alt+F7	Opens the Move dialog box
F8	Selects the Text tool
Ctrl+F8	Opens the PowerLine roll-up
Alt+F8	Opens the Rotate & Skew dialog box
F9	Toggles between the Normal and Preview display modes
Shift+F9	Toggles between editable preview and wireframe view
Ctrl+F9	Opens the Contour roll-up
Alt+F9	Opens the Stretch & Mirror dialog box
F10	Selects the Shape tool
Ctrl+F10	Opens the Node Edit roll-up
Alt+F10	Aligns selected text to baseline
F11	Opens the Fountain Fill dialog box
Shift+F11	Opens the Uniform Fill dialog box
F12	Opens the Outline Pen dialog box
Shift+F12	Opens the Outline Color dialog box
Ctrl+F12	Opens the Object Data roll-up

Table 1.2: Speed Key Shortcuts

Key	Use
Ctrl+<0–9>	Applies style to paragraph text
Ctrl+A	Opens the Align dialog box
Ctrl+B	Opens the Blend roll-up
Ctrl+C	Executes the Copy command
Ctrl+D	Executes the Duplicate command
Ctrl+E	Opens the Extrude roll-up
Ctrl+F	Opens the Fit Text To Path dialog box
Ctrl+G	Executes the Group command
Ctrl+J	Opens the Preferences dialog box
Ctrl+K	Executes the Break Apart command
Ctrl+L	Executes the Combine command
Ctrl+N	Opens a new drawing
Ctrl+O	Opens the Open Drawing dialog box
Ctrl+P	Opens the Print dialog box
Ctrl+Q	Executes the Convert To Curves command
Ctrl+R	Executes the most Repeat command
Ctrl+S	Executes the Save command
Ctrl+T	Opens the Edit Text dialog box
Ctrl+U	Executes the Ungroup command
Ctrl+V	Executes the Paste command
Ctrl+W	Executes the Refresh Window command
Ctrl+X	Executes the Cut command
Ctrl+Y	Toggles snap-to grid on and off
Ctrl+Z	Executes the Undo command
Alt+Enter	Negates the most recent Undo command
Shift+Insert	Executes the Paste command
Ctrl+Insert	Executes the Copy command
Del	Executes the Delete command
Shift+Del	Executes the Cut command

Table 1.2: Speed Key Shortcuts (continued)

Key	Use
Alt+Backspace	Executes the Undo command
PgDn	Executes the Back One command
Shift+PgDn	Executes the To Back command
PgUp	Executes the Forward One command
Shift+PgUp	Executes the To Front command

Table 1.3: Node Editing Shortcuts

Key	Use
+	Adds a node at the selected place on a curve object
-	Deletes selected nodes
Tab	Selects the node ahead of the currently selected node
Shift+Tab	Selects the node behind the currently selected node
Home	Selects the first node of the selected curve object
Shift+Home	Toggles selection of the first node of the currently selected curve object on and off
Ctrl+Home	Selects the first subpath in the currently selected curve object
Shift+Ctrl+Home	Toggles selection of the first subpath in the currently selected curve object on and off
End	Selects the last node on the selected curve object

Table 1.3: Node Editing Shortcuts (continued)

Key	Use
Shift+End	Toggles selection of the first node of the currently selected curve object on and off
Ctrl+End	Selects the last subpath in the currently selected curve object
Shift+Ctrl+End	Toggles selection of the last subpath in the currently selected object on and off
→, ←, ↑, ↓	Nudges the selected node or nodes in the direction of the arrow

Table 1.4: Other Shortcuts

Action	Result
Double-click on the border of printable page	Opens the Page Setup dialog box
Double-click on a guideline	Opens the Guidelines dialog box
Double-click on a ruler	Opens the Grid Setup dialog box
Double-click on a character node	Opens the Character Attributes dialog box.
Spacebar	Selects the most recently selected (or drawn) object, or deselects the currently selected object; also switchesbetween the Pick tool and the most recently used drawing tool
Esc	Deselects all selected objects

SPELL CHECKING

You can check the spelling of individual words before you place them into a drawing, and of words in artistic or paragraph text. In addition to using CorelDRAW's built-in spelling dictionary, you can create your own dictionary.

Spell Checking Artistic and Paragraph Text

1. Use the **Pick** tool to highlight an entire artistic or paragraph tool object, or use the **Text** tool to highlight individual words you wish to check.

2. Choose **Text ➤ Spell Checker** to display the Spelling Checker dialog box.

3. If you want to compare words with those in a personal dictionary as well as with those in the CorelDRAW dictionary, open the **Personal Dictionary** list box and click on the name of the dictionary to use.

4. Click **Check Text**. CorelDRAW compares the selected text with words in the standard dictionary and in a personal dictionary, if you are using one. When the spell checker finds a word in the selected text that is not in the dictionary or dictionaries, it displays that word in the Word Not Found box.

5. If you selected a personal dictionary, you can click **Add** to add the word in the Word Not Found text box to that dictionary. You cannot add words to the standard dictionary.

6. If you are satisfied your word is correct even though it is not in the dictionary, click **Ignore** to accept your spelling of the word, or click **Ignore All** to make CorelDRAW ignore all occurrences of the word in the selected text.

7. If you want to correct the spelling, click in the **Replace With** text box to create an insertion point, and then type the correctly spelled word. Alternatively, click the **Suggest** box and CorelDRAW will display a list of similar words.

Click the correct word and it appears in the **Replace With** text box.

8. Click **Replace** to replace the incorrect word with the correct word. Alternatively, click **Replace All** to replace every occurrence of the incorrect word with the correct word.

9. Repeat steps 3 through 8 until the **CorelDraw!** dialog box displays the message "Spelling check finished."

10. Click **OK**.

NOTES If you prefer CorelDRAW to always provide suggestions for correct spelling, click the Always Suggest button.

Spell Checking Individual Words

1. Choose **Text ➤ Spell Checker**. The Spelling Checker dialog box appears.

2. Type the word you want to check in the **Word To Check** text box.

3. Click **Check Word**. The CorelDRAW! dialog box appears and displays either the message "Word Not Found" or "Word OK."

4. Click **OK**.

5. Type another word you want to check and repeat steps 3 and 4, or click **Cancel**.

NOTES See the previous procedure for information about comparing the spellings with those in a personal dictionary and adding the word to a personal dictionary.

Creating a Personal Dictionary

1. Choose **Text ➤ Spell Checker**.

2. Type a name for your dictionary in the **Create a personal dictionary** text box.

3. Click **Create**. The name of your personal dictionary appears in the Personal Dictionary text box.

NOTES The name you choose for a personal dictionary becomes a file name with the extension .DIC.

You can create as many personal dictionaries as you wish. However, you can only use the standard dictionary and one personal dictionary at a time to check spelling.

STACKING ORDER

Filled objects are opaque. When they overlap, the more recently created object in a layer obscures part or all of the objects previously created in the same layer.

Changing Object Stacking Order

1. Select the object to be moved.
2. Choose **Arrange ➤ Order** to display a flyout menu.
3. In the flyout menu, click **To Front**, **To Back**, **Forward One**, or **Back One**.

Reversing the Stacking Order of Two Objects

1. Select the two objects to be reversed.
2. Choose **Arrange ➤ Order** to display a flyout menu.
3. In the flyout menu, click **Reverse Order**.

STARTING A NEW DRAWING

See the explanation of opening a new file in *File Management*.

STARTING CORELDRAW

1. Start Windows and display the Program Manager window.

2. Double-click the **Corel4** icon to display the Corel4 window.

3. Double-click the **CorelDRAW!** icon to display the CorelDRAW screen.

 NOTES   See *Screen* for information about the CorelDRAW screen.

Closing CorelDRAW

1. Choose **File ➤ Exit**. If you have already saved your current drawing, CorelDRAW immediately closes. Otherwise, a dialog box provides the opportunity to save your drawing before CorelDRAW closes

2. Click **Yes** to save your drawing, click **No** to close CorelDRAW without saving your drawing, or click **Cancel** if you do not want to close CorelDRAW.

STRETCHING AND SHRINKING AN OBJECT

See *Scaling and Stretching an Object*.

STYLES AND TEMPLATES

A style is a definition of an object's attributes. By defining an object's attributes as a style, you can easily create other objects with the same attributes. You can assemble a set of styles into a template with one template for each type of project, thus maintaining consistency in your work. The Styles roll-up shown in Figure 1.26 provides access to styles and templates.

Templates are stored as files with the extension .CDT. By default, a new drawing uses the CORELDRAW.CDT template which contains a graphics style, an artistic text style, and four paragraph text styles. You can base a new drawing on a different template (see *File Management*).

new **Displaying the Styles Roll-up**

To display the Styles roll-up, choose **Layout ➤ Styles Roll-up**.

NOTES   When you first display the Styles roll-up it lists the styles in the default template file CORELDRW.CDT as shown in Figure 1.26. By clicking the icons near the top of the roll-up, you can choose to see any combination of artistic text, paragraph text, or graphic styles.

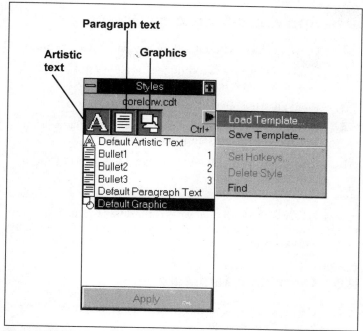

Figure 1.26: The Styles roll-up with its secondary menu

Creating a New Style

1. Draw an object and set its attributes, such as outline width, outline color, and fill color.

2. Right-click on the object to display its Object menu.

3. In the Object menu, click **Save As Style** to display the **Save Style As** dialog box.

4. Type a name for the style.

5. In the Include section of the dialog box, click on the check boxes to check only those attributes you want included in the style, then click **OK** to add the style name to the list in the Styles roll-up.

`new` Applying a Style to an Object

1.   Draw an object without setting any particular attributes.

2.   Load the template that contains the style you want to use (see "Selecting a Template" later in this entry).

3.   Right-click the object to display its Object menu.

4.   In the Object menu, click **Apply Style** to display a list of styles in the current template.

5.   Click the name of the style you want to use to redraw the object with that style.

NOTES   Alternatively, select the object to which you want to apply the style, click the name of the style in the Styles roll-up, and then click Apply.

`new` Creating a Template

1.   Click the arrowhead close to the top of the Styles roll-up to display a secondary menu.

2.   Click **Save Template** to display the Save Template dialog box.

3.   In the dialog box, type a name for the new template, then click **OK**. The template is saved with the new name and an extension .CDT.

NOTES   Every template has the same six default styles which you cannot delete, although you can change their contents.

`new` Selecting a Template

1.   Click the arrowhead close to the top of the Styles roll-up to display a secondary menu.

2.   Click **Load Template** to display the Load Template dialog box.

3. In the File Name list, click the name of the template you want to use, then click **OK** to display the list of that template's styles in the Styles roll-up.

new Deleting a Style from a Template

1. Load the template from which you want to delete a style.
2. In the Styles roll-up, delete the name of the style to be deleted.
3. Click the arrowhead close to the top of the Styles roll-up to display a secondary menu.
4. Click **Delete Style** to delete that style from the template.

new Finding Objects Using a Style

1. Load the template that contains the style and click on that style to highlight it.
2. Click the arrowhead close to the top of the Styles roll-up to display a secondary menu.
3. Click **Find** in the secondary menu to select one object that uses the style.
4. To find other objects using the style, repeat step 2 and then click on **Find Next**.

SYMBOLS

CorelDRAW has a large number of symbols you can use in drawings. If you have installed the CD-ROM version of CorelDRAW, you have access to many thousands of symbols. Otherwise you can use only those supplied on disk. Refer to the *Corel Libraries Catalog* to see what symbols are available.

Symbols are in vector, not bitmapped, format. You can manipulate symbols just as you can manipulate any other curve object.

Placing Symbols in a Drawing

1. Point to the **Text** tool.

2. Press and hold down the mouse button until a flyout menu appears, and then release the mouse button.

3. Click on the **Star** icon to display the Symbols roll-up shown in Figure 1.27.

4. Open the categories list box in the roll-up, and choose a symbol category to display the symbols within that category.

5. To see additional symbols in the category, click one of the arrow buttons near the bottom of the roll-up.

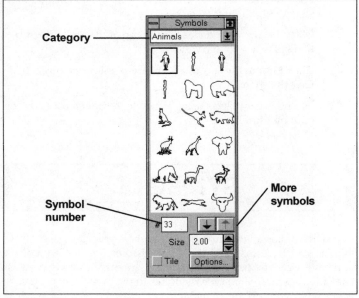

Figure 1.27: The Symbols roll-up

6. Choose or type a size for the symbol in the **Size** text box.

7. Point onto the symbol you want to use, drag it into your drawing, and release the mouse button.

NOTES Each symbol has a number within its category. This number appears in the # text box. If you know the number of the symbol you want, you can type the number in the text box instead of scrolling through the list box to find it.

You can drag the roll-up frame to change its size.

For information about using a symbol in a pattern, see *Patterns*.

TEMPLATES

A template is a set of styles. See *Styles*.

THESAURUS

CorelDRAW's Thesaurus allows you to look up the meaning of words and to find words with similar meanings.

Looking Up Words in Artistic and Paragraph Text

1. Use the **Text** tool to highlight a word in your drawing.

2. Choose **Text ➤ Thesaurus** to display the Thesaurus dialog box. If the word is in the CorelDRAW dictionary, the dialog box displays the word's part of speech and one or more definitions, one of which is highlighted. One or more synonyms for the highlighted definition are also listed.

3. If there are two or more definitions, click one to see a list of appropriate synonyms.

4. If you want to replace the original word with a synonym, click the synonym and click **Replace**. Otherwise, click **Cancel**.

Looking Up Other Words

1. With no words selected on your drawing, choose **Text ➤ Thesaurus** to display the Thesaurus dialog box.

2. Type the word you want to look up in the Synonym for dialog box.

3. Click **Lookup** to see definitions and synonyms for the word.

TOOLBOX

The CorelDRAW toolbox, shown in Figure 1.21, contains nine tools, two of which exist in alternative forms.

Changing the Size of the Toolbox

You can edit the CORELDRW.INI file to enlarge the toolbox and color palette. See *Toolbox* in on-line Help for information.

Ellipse Tool

Use the Ellipse tool to draw ellipses and circles. You can subsequently use the Shape tool to change ellipses and circles into arcs and wedges (see *Drawing an Object*).

Fill Tool

When you select the Fill tool, the flyout shown in Figure 1.12 appears.

Outline Tool

When you select the Outline tool, the flyout shown in Figure 1.6 appears.

Pencil Tool

When you select the Pencil tool and hold down the mouse button, the flyout shown in Figure 1.28 appears. When you click one of the five tools in the flyout, the flyout disappears and that tool appears in the toolbox.

Use the Freehand tool to draw lines and curves by a click and drag technique. Use the Bézier tool to draw with a connect-the-dots style. Use one of the dimension tools to draw dimension lines (see *Drawing an Object*).

Pick Tool

Use the **Pick** tool to select individual objects or groups of objects. You can also use this tool to move, rotate, scale, skew, and stretch objects.

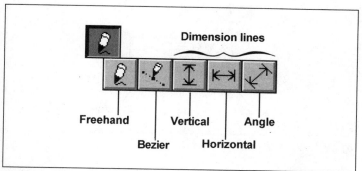

Figure 1.28: The Pencil tool flyout

Rectangle Tool

Use the Rectangle tool to draw rectangles and squares.

Shape Tool

Use the Shape tool to:

- Change the shape of lines and curves by manipulating nodes
- Edit character attributes and kern text
- Crop bitmaps
- Round the corners of rectangles
- Create arcs and wedges from ellipses

Text Tool

When you select the Text tool and hold down the mouse button, the flyout shown in Figure 1.29 appears.

When you click the artistic or paragraph tool, the flyout disappears and that tool appears in the toolbox. When you click the Symbols icon, the Symbols roll-up is displayed.

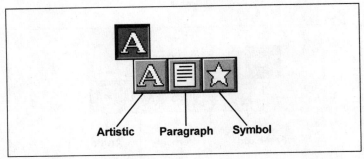

Figure 1.29: The Text tool flyout

Zoom Tool

When you click the Zoom tool you get the flyout menu shown in Figure 1.30. See *Viewing an Object at Different Magnifications.*

TRACING A BITMAP IMAGE

Tracing a bitmap image converts it into an object-based drawing you can manipulate with CorelDRAW.

CorelDRAW has two methods of tracing bitmaps: built-in AutoTrace and the more powerful CorelTRACE program. The built-in method is described here. See Part 5 of this book for information about CorelTRACE.

Using AutoTrace to Trace a Black-and-White Bitmap

AutoTrace is intended for tracing black-and-white bitmaps. It cannot be used satisfactorily to trace color or grayscale bitmaps. To trace an object:

1. Choose **File ➤ Import** to display the Import dialog box.
2. Open the directory that contains the file to import and click on the file name.
3. Click the **For Tracing** check box to place a check mark in it.
4. Click **OK** to import the bitmap object.
5. Use the **Zoom** tool to magnify the object so that you can see all of it clearly.
6. If necessary, select the bitmap object with the **Pick** tool. The status line indicates that a bitmap object is selected.

7. Click the **Freehand Pencil** tool. The status line shows that AutoTrace is enabled, and the cursor changes to an elongated cross.

8. Place the cursor to the left of a black area in the object and click the mouse button. CorelDRAW takes a few seconds to trace around the black area.

9. Repeat step 8 until you have traced the entire bitmapped object.

10. Select the **Pick** tool to leave AutoTrace.

11. Select and then delete the original bitmap.

NOTES   It is usually difficult to see which part of a bitmap object has been traced and which is still in its original bitmap form. To overcome this problem, leave the bitmap black and create the tracing in a contrasting color. After you have imported the bitmap, deselect it. Then choose an outline color. Reselect the bitmap and start tracing. Now you will be able to see clearly which parts of your object have been traced and which parts have not.

You can control how accurately AutoTrace traces bitmaps by adjusting values in the Preferences - Curves dialog box:

- **AutoTrace Tracking** controls how closely the Bézier curves produced by AutoTrace follow the edges of the bitmap; low numbers produce more accurate results.

- **Corner Threshold** determines the threshold at which AutoTrace rounds corners; low numbers produce sharper corners.

- **Straight Line Threshold** sets the threshold for deciding between lines and curves; low numbers favor curves.

See *Preferences* for information about changing these settings.

UNDOING, REDOING, AND REPEATING AN OPERATION

You can undo most CorelDRAW operations and then redo an operation that has been undone. You can also repeat operations.

new Undoing Commands

With certain exceptions, you can undo the effect of a sequence of up to 99 commands.

1. Choose **Edit ➤ Undo** to undo the most recent command.

2. Repeat step 1 to undo previous commands in sequence.

NOTES You set the number of undo levels permitted in the Preferences dialog box (see *Preferences*), up to a maximum of 99. The more undo levels you allow, the more memory CorelDRAW requires.

Redoing Commands

After you have undone a command, you can redo it.

1. Choose **Edit ➤ Redo** to redo the most recent undone command.

2. Repeat step 1 to redo previous undone commands.

Repeating Commands

After you have executed a command, you can execute it again:

1. Choose **Edit ➤ Repeat** to repeat the most recently executed command.

2. Repeat step 1 to execute the same command again.

VIEWING AN OBJECT AT DIFFERENT MAGNIFICATIONS

You can use the Zoom tool to view objects at different magnifications.

1. Click the **Zoom** tool to display the five icons shown in Figure 1.30.

2. Click one of the five icons in the Zoom flyout.

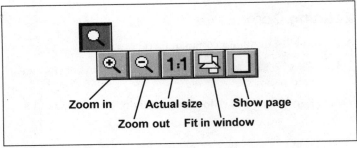

Figure 1.30: The Zoom tool flyout

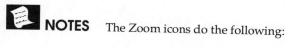 **NOTES**   The Zoom icons do the following:

Icon	Action
Zoom in	Magnifies part of the screen. Click this icon, then marquee-select the area to be magnified. Alternatively, just click a point on the screen to double the magnification around that point.
Zoom out	Halves the magnification of what is on the screen.
Actual size	Displays part of the drawing at the size it will be printed.
Fit in window	Magnifies, or reduces magnification, so that all objects in the drawing are shown on the screen.
Show page	Displays the entire printable page.

WELDING OBJECTS

When objects overlap, you can use the Weld command, a new feature in CorelDRAW 4, to permanently join them at the points where the outlines intersect. Welding also removes sections of the outlines between the intersection points. There is no corresponding Unweld command, but you can use Undo to remove the effect of a weld.

1.   Select the objects to be welded.

2.   Choose **Arrange ➤ Weld** to weld the objects.

Part 2

CorelCHART

With CorelCHART, you can create charts and graphs based on data in a worksheet. In addition to the usual bar, line, and pie charts, you can use CorelCHART to create three-dimensional charts, high-low-close charts, and other specialized types of charts.

You create data for a chart in the Data Manager either by typing values or by importing them from popular spreadsheet or database applications, or as ASCII data. Although not as powerful as a full-featured spreadsheet program, the Data Manager has many of the commonly used spreadsheet capabilities such as calculating cell values based on values in other cells.

After you have created a chart from data in the Data Manager, you can enhance the appearance of the chart by using tools similar to those in CorelDRAW. Also, you can embellish the chart by adding graphics or text created within CorelCHART itself or imported from other applications.

You can also link or embed charts in other OLE-compliant applications by taking advantage of CorelCHART as an Object Linking and Embedding (OLE) server. The Data Manager supports Dynamic Data Exchange (DDE), so you can create links to data in other DDE-compatible applications.

3D TOOL ROLL-UP

Use the 3D Tool roll-up to modify three-dimensional charts.

Activating the 3D Tool Roll-up

1. Display a three-dimensional chart in the Chart window (see *Three-Dimensional Charts*).

2. Choose **Chart ➤ 3D Roll-up** to display the 3D Tool roll-up in one of the four forms shown in Figure 2.1.

3. Click one of the icons at the top of the roll-up to display the form of the roll-up you want to use.

NOTES The 3D Tool roll-up first appears in the form you used most recently.

Moving a Chart

Use the 3D Movement tool to move a chart horizontally or vertically, or to make it larger or smaller to simulate it being closer or further away. To move the chart:

1. With the **Pick** tool, click the **3D Movement** icon at the top left of the 3D Tool roll-up to display the 3D Movement tool in the roll-up.

2. Point onto one of the red arrows in the tool, then press and hold down the mouse button. An outline of the chart moves in the direction of the arrow until you release the mouse button.

3. Repeat step 2 using any of the other arrows in the 3D Movement tool.

4. Click **Redraw** in the roll-up to redraw the chart in the new position, or click **Undo** to redraw the chart in its original position.

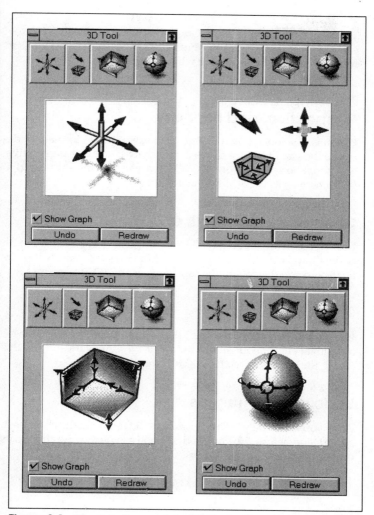

Figure 2.1: The four forms of the 3D Tool roll-up: 3D Movement
(top left), Perspective and Panning tools (top right),
Axis tool (bottom left), Rotation tool (bottom right)

NOTES The Show Graph check box in the 3D View tool is normally checked. Click this button to remove the check mark and replace the chart by its outline while you move it.

Zooming, Changing Perspective, and Panning

Use the three tools shown in Figure 2.1 (top right) to increase or decrease the size of a three-dimensional chart, change its perspective, and pan it horizontally or vertically. Activate and use these tools in the same way as the 3D Movement tool.

Changing Axis Length and Wall Thickness

Use the tool shown in Figure 2.1 (bottom left) to change the length of the three axes and to change the thickness of the chart walls. Activate and use this tool in the same way as the 3D Movement tool.

Rotating

Use the tool shown in Figure 2.1 (bottom right) to rotate a three-dimensional chart about any of the three axes. Activate and use this tool in the same way as the 3D Movement tool.

Undoing 3D Changes

After you have dragged arrows in any 3D tool to make changes to a chart, and before you click Redraw, you can restore the chart to its original state by clicking **Undo**.

ADDING DATA TO A WORKSHEET

CorelCHART creates charts based on data in a worksheet. You can add data to a worksheet in the Data Manager screen by:

- Typing data directly into each cell (see below)

- Importing data created in another application (see *Importing Data*)

- Using Dynamic Data Exchange (DDE) to link data from an application that supports DDE (see *Dynamic Data Exchange*).

See *Screen* for information about the various areas of the Data Manager screen.

A typical worksheet has four parts, as shown in Figure 2.2:

- The array of values used to create charts

- The column headers used as group labels on the chart

- The row headers used as vertical axis labels on the chart

- The text, which becomes the title, subtitle, row and column titles, and footnote on the chart

By default, CorelCHART interprets values in the worksheet's rows as series and values in columns as groups. Figure 2.3 shows a default bar chart of this type.

Alternatively, CorelCHART can interpret values in columns as series and values in rows as groups. Figure 2.4 shows this type of bar chart.

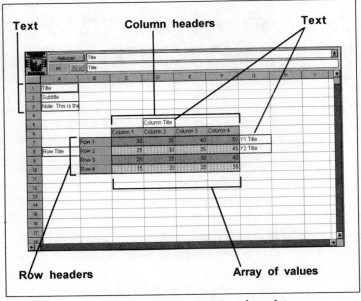

Figure 2.2: A typical worksheet containing chart data

For more information, see the explanation of using columns as series in *Bar Charts*.

Typing Numeric Data and Text into a Worksheet

You can type data into a worksheet the same way you would place data into a spreadsheet. You can also edit data imported from another application.

1. Display a blank Data Manager window, usually as part of the process of creating a new chart (see *File Management*).

2. Optionally, maximize the Data Manager window.

3. Select the rectangular block of cells into which you want to place data (see *Selecting Cells in a Worksheet*).

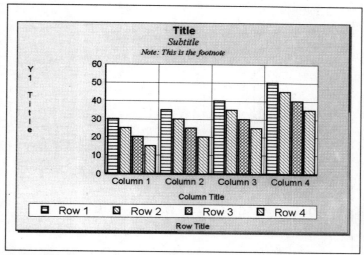

Figure 2.3: A bar chart created from the worksheet in Figure 2.2. Here, values in rows are used as series, and values in columns are used as groups.

4. Type the value or text for the cell at the top left corner of the block of cells. The characters you type appear in the cell and in the Formula bar. If the first typed character is a number or a symbol that can be used with a number, such as +, -, =, ., or (, CorelCHART assumes the value is numeric. If the first typed value is alphabetic or a symbol that cannot be used with a number, Corel-CHART assumes that the value is text.

5. Click the **Enter** button or press ↵ to accept the data. The data disappears from the Formula bar and the next cell is selected (see the note below).

6. Type the value or text for the cell, and click the **Enter** button, press ↵, or press the **Tab** key.

7. Repeat step 6 to add data into the remaining cells.

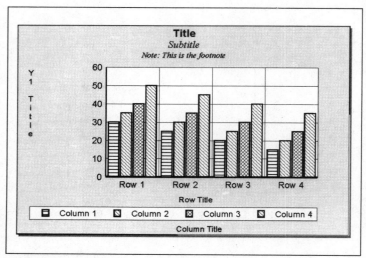

Figure 2.4: A bar chart created from the worksheet in Figure 2.2.
Here, values in columns are used as series, and
values in rows are used as groups.

8. Tag the data so that CorelCHART can create a chart (see
Tagging Cells).

NOTES If you want a cell to have the same value as that
in another cell, type = followed by the cell's address. The equals sign
enables CorelCHART to recognize what you type as an address even
though it starts with a letter.

Each time you click the Enter button or press ↵, the next cell in the
rectangular block is automatically selected. Cells are selected beginning with the top left cell, moving down the column, then moving to the next column, and so on. When you press the Tab key, cells
are selected from left to right.

You can place data into a block of cells without first selecting the
block. Select the first cell, type the data for it, and click the Enter

button or press ↵ to place data into a cell and select the next cell in the column, or you can press one of the arrow keys to place the data into the current cell and select an adjacent cell:

Press	Next Cell Selected
Enter button, ↵, or ↓	One down
↑	One up
←	One to the left
→	One to the right

You can avoid the need for step 8 if you place specific types of data in certain relative positions (see "Using Autoscan" in *Tagging Cells*).

To cancel data you have typed, click the Cancel button.

`new` Typing Calculated Data into a Worksheet

Instead of typing numeric data into a cell, you can use calculated data.

1. Select a cell.

2. Type the calculation preceded by an equals sign, then press ↵. For example, to place the result of multiplying 2.49 by 4.67, type **=2.49*4.67**.

 NOTES You can also place a value into a cell calculated from values in other cells. For example, to place the value calculated by multiplying the value in cell A2 by the value in cell B4, type **=A2*B4**.

Addition (+), subtraction (-), multiplication (*), division (/), and raise to a power (^) operators are supported.

When you place a calculated value into a cell, the cell shows the result of the calculation and the Formula bar shows the calculation.

new Using Functions and Formulas in a Worksheet

You can use formulas to express data. A formula is any text within quotation marks, any combination of numbers, numbers with operators, or functions that result in data which can be placed into a worksheet cell.

Formulas having two or more operators are evaluated in conventional order. For example, multiplication and division occurs before addition and subtraction. You can use parentheses to define the order of evaluation.

Some examples of legitimate formulas are as follows:

Formula	Description
"cat"	Text
1.254	Numeric value
=1.67+7.54	Calculation—numeric values with operator
=1.67*(2.54-1.69)	Calculation—numeric values with operators and with parentheses controlling order of evaluation
=C1	Address of cell containing data
=C1+C4	Calculation—numeric values, represented by the addresses of cells, with operator
=now()	Function with no arguments
=sum(C1,C2,C3,C4)	Function with arguments
=sum(C1..C4)	Function with list of arguments stated as a range

To use a formula to place data into a cell:

1. Select the cell into which you want to write data.

2. Choose **Data ➤ Enter Formula** to display the Enter Formula dialog box shown in Figure 2.5.

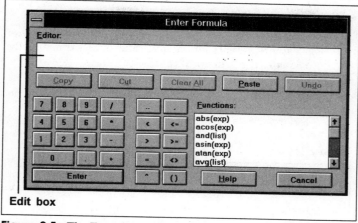

Edit box

Figure 2.5: The Enter Formula dialog box

3. Type the formula into the **Edit** box, using one of the formats listed above.

4. Click **Enter** to write the result of the formula into the selected cell.

To use a function to place data into a cell:

1. Select the cell into which you want to write the result of using the formula.

2. Choose **Data ➤ Enter Formula** to display the Enter Formula dialog box.

3. In the Functions list box, double-click the function you want to display in the edit box. Commas within the parentheses indicate places for arguments.

4. Edit the function to place the appropriate arguments between the commas within the parentheses.

5. Click **Enter** to place the value returned by the function into the selected cell.

The CorelCHART worksheet functions are listed in Table 2.1. In this table:

- *Number* represents a numerical value or an expression that evaluates to a numerical value.

- *List* represents one or more values, or the addresses of cells that contain values.

- *Text* represents a text string.

Table 2.1: CorelCHART functions

Function	Action
abs (number)	Returns the absolute value of *number*.
acos (number)	Returns the arccosine of *number*.
and (list)	Returns TRUE if all arguments in **list** are true, otherwise returns FALSE.
asin (number)	Returns the arcsine of *number*.
atan (number)	Returns the arctangent of *number*.
avg (list)	Returns the average (mean) of numbers in *list*.
char (number)	Returns the character corresponding to *number* interpreted as an ANSI code.
choose (index_num,list)	Returns the value in position *index-num* from a *list* of arguments.
clean (text)	Removes all nonprintable characters from *text*.
cnt (list)	Returns the number of occupied cells in *list*, excluding cells containing error values and text.
cnta (list)	Returns the number of occupied cells in *list*, including cells containing error values and text.
code (text)	Returns the ANSI value of the first character in *text*.

Table 2.1: CorelCHART functions (continued)

Function	Action
columns (list)	Returns the number of columns in the references of *list*.
cos (angle)	Returns the cosine of *angle* expressed in radians.
date (day,month,year)	Returns the Julian value of a date expressed in *day,month,year* format.
day(number)	Returns the day of the month as an integer for a day defined by its serial *number*.
db (cost,salvage,life, period,month)	Returns the depreciation on an asset for a *period*, using the fixed declining balance method.
ddb (cost,sal-vage,life,period)	Returns the depreciation allowance on an asset for a *period* using the double declining method.
dollar (number, decimals)	Returns *number* in currency format with the specified number of *decimal* places.
exp (number)	Returns the exponential of *number*.
false()	Returns the logical value FALSE (0).
find (find_text,within_text ,start)	Returns the position of the beginning of *find_text* in *within_text*, counting from *start*.
fixed (number, decimals)	Returns *number* in text format with a specified number of *decimal* places.
fv (payment,interest, period)	Returns the future value of a periodic *payment* at a fixed *interest* rate over a *period*.
getcell (type,ref)	Returns a specific *type* of information about the cell in the top-left corner of the current range of cells (if *ref* is omitted) or about a range of cells.

Table 2.1: CorelCHART functions (continued)

Function	Action
hlookup (value, array,index_num)	Returns a value in a lookup table where *value* is a column header in the table, *array* is the range of the table, and *index_num* is the row number of the value to be returned.
hour (number)	Returns the hour defined by its serial *number*.
if (expression true,false)	If *expression* evaluates to TRUE, execute *true*, otherwise execute *false*.
int (number)	Returns *number* rounded down to the nearest integer.
left (text,number)	Returns the leftmost character (if *number* is omitted) or leftmost number of characters from *text*.
len (text)	Returns the number of characters, including spaces, in *text*.
ln (number)	Returns the natural logarithm of *number*.
log (number)	Returns the base-10 logarithm of *number*.
lower (text)	Converts all uppercase letters in *text* to lowercase.
max (list)	Returns the maximum value in *list* of numbers.
mid (text,start,num)	Returns a specific *number* of characters from *text*, starting from *start*.
min (list)	Returns the minimum value in *list* of numbers.
minute (number)	Returns the minute defined by its serial *number*.

Table 2.1: CorelCHART functions (continued)

Function	Action
mod (number, divisor)	Returns the modulus (remainder) after *number* is divided by *divisor*.
month (number)	Returns the number of a month defined by its serial *number*.
now ()	Returns the serial number of the current date and time. The digits to the left of the decimal point represent the number of days since January 1, 1990. Numbers to the right of the decimal point represent the time.
nper (payment, interest,principal)	Returns the number of periods needed to repay *principal*.
npv (int,list)	Returns the net present value of an investment based on *list* of payments and a constant interest rate.
or (list)	Returns TRUE if one or more arguments are true, otherwise returns FALSE.
pct (number)	Returns *number* as a percentage.
pi ()	Returns the value of pi accurate to 12 digits.
pmt (principal,int,term)	Returns the periodic payment for *principal* based on constant payments and a constant *inte*rest over a specific *term*.
proper (text)	Returns *text* with the first letter of each word capitalized.
pv (payment, interest,term)	Returns the present value of an investment.
rand ()	Returns a random number greater than or equal to zero, and less than 1.

Table 2.1: CorelCHART functions (continued)

Function	Action
replace (old_text,start, number,new_text)	Replaces *number* characters in *old_text*, starting at *start*, with *new_text*.
right (text,number)	Returns the rightmost character of *text* (if *number* is omitted) or rightmost *number* of characters from a string.
roman (number)	Converts an arabic *number* into a roman number.
round (number, digits)	Rounds *number* to the specified number of decimal digits.
rows (list)	Returns the number of rows in the references of *list*.
search (find_text, within_text,start)	Returns the position of *find_text* in *within_text*, counting from *start*.
second (number)	Returns the second defined by its serial *number*.
sgn (number)	Returns 1 if the *number* is positive, 0 if it is zero, or -1 if it is negative.
sin (angle)	Returns the sine of *angle* expressed in radians.
sln (cost,salvage,life)	Returns the straight-line depreciation of an asset.
sqrt (number)	Returns the square root of *number*.
std (list)	Returns the standard deviation of *list* of numbers.
subst (text,old_text, new_text)	Returns *text* with the substring *old_text* replaced with *new_text*.

Table 2.1: CorelCHART functions (continued)

Function	Action
sum (list)	Returns the sum of *list* of numbers.
tan (angle)	Returns the tangent of *angle* expressed in radians.
time (hour, minute,second)	Returns the serial number for a specific time.
today ()	Returns the serial number for the current day.
trim (text)	Returns *text* with all spaces removed except for single spaces between words.
true ()	Returns the logical value TRUE (1).
type (cell)	Returns a number to indicate a *cell's* type.
upper (text)	Returns *text* in all uppercase letters.
value (text)	Returns *text* as a number.
var (list)	Returns the variance of *list* of numbers.
vdb (cost,salvage, life,start,end)	Returns the depreciation of an asset using the double declining balance method.
vlookup (value, array,index_num)	Returns a value in a lookup table where *value* is a row header in the table, *array* is the range of the table, and *index_num* is the column number of the value to be returned.
weekday (number)	Returns the number of a weekday defined by its serial *number*.
year (number)	Returns the number of a year defined by its serial *number*.

NOTES CorelCHART functions are similar to, but not identical to, corresponding Microsoft Excel functions. In some cases the order of arguments is different.

Some functions operate on a list of values which are arguments of the function. Such arguments can be

- Numeric values

- Individual cell addresses which contain values

- A range of cell addresses which contains values

Importing Data into a Worksheet

CorelCHART can import data from popular spreadsheet and database applications.

1. With an empty worksheet displayed, choose **File ➤ Import** to display the Import Data dialog box.

2. Open the **List Files of Type** list box and click on the type of file to import.

3. In the Directories list box, open the directory which contains the file to be imported.

4. In the File Name list box, click the name of the file to import, and then click **OK**.

5. Tag the cells so that CorelCHART can create a chart from the data (see *Tagging Cells*).

NOTES Data fills the worksheet starting at cell A1 and extending down and to the right, replacing data already in the worksheet.

Moving to a Cell

To move from one cell to another:

- Press an arrow key to move from one cell to another in any direction.

- Use the scroll bars to display a section of the worksheet, then click a cell.

- Choose **Data ➤ Go To** to display the Go To Cell dialog box, type the address of a cell (such as Z5), and click **OK.**

- Press **Home** or **Ctrl+←** to move to the first column of the current row.

- Press **Ctrl+→** to move to the last column of the current row.

- Press **Ctrl+↑** to move to the first row of the current column.

- Press **Ctrl+↓** to move to the last row of the current column.

- Press **End** to move to the last occupied cell in the current row.

- Press **Ctrl+Home** to move to cell A1.

- Press **Ctrl+End** to move to the bottom right corner of the occupied part of the worksheet.

Editing Worksheet Data

Editing worksheet data is similar to placing new data into the worksheet (see above). To change the contents of a cell, select the cell. Its value appears in the Formula bar. You can use the following methods to edit the data:

- Type the first character of the new data. The old data disappears and whatever you type completely replaces the old data.

- Point anywhere into the existing data in the Formula bar and click the mouse button. A flashing insertion marker appears. At this point, press **Backspace** to delete one character at a time to the left of the insertion point, or press **Delete** to delete the character to the right of the insertion point. Any characters you type are inserted at the insertion point. Press the arrow keys to move the insertion point one character at a time to the left or right, press **Home** to move it to the beginning of the data, or press **End** to move it to the end of the data.

- Choose **Edit ➤ Clear** to completely delete data from the selected cell or cells (see *Clearing, Deleting, Inserting, and Moving Worksheet Data*).

ANNOTATING A CHART

Each chart consists of a chart layer and an annotation layer. The chart layer contains everything in the worksheet. The annotation layer contains graphics and text you add to a chart. You can annotate a chart by using CorelCHART's text and graphics tools, or you can import annotations from another application.

Adding Text as an Annotation

Adding annotation text is similar to adding paragraph text in CorelDRAW.

1. With a chart displayed in the Chart window, click the **Text** tool.

2. Move the cross-shaped cursor to the place where the annotation is to start, press and hold down the mouse button, and drag to the right to define the annotation width, then release the mouse button. A gray bar shows the width of annotation, and the text ribbon shows the current text defaults.

3. Select the font, size, style and alignment in the text ribbon.

4. Select a color in the color palette.

5. Type the annotation text. The text wraps when it reaches the right side of the annotation area, the depth increasing automatically to accommodate the text.

6. Click the **Pick** tool. The temporary background behind the annotation disappears.

NOTES To change the font, size, or other attributes of the annotation text, use the Pick tool to select the text, and then use the text ribbon to make changes. To change the text color, select the text and click a color in the color palette. You cannot change the attributes of individual characters in this way.

If you need to control the attributes of individual characters, create the text in an application such as CorelDRAW, save it, and import it into the chart.

Annotating with Imported Text

Import text for use as an annotation in the same way as graphics (see "Annotating with Imported Graphics" below).

Annotating with Rectangles and Ellipses

You can annotate a chart with graphics drawn by the Pencil, Rectangle, and Ellipse tools in the toolbox. Use tools in the same way you use them in CorelDRAW (see *Drawing an Object* in Part 1).

Annotating with Lines, Polygons, Freehand Curves, and Arrows

Use the Pencil tool to draw lines, polygons, freehand curves, and arrows:

1. With a chart displayed, point onto the **Pencil** tool and click the mouse button to display a flyout with four icons

that represent straight lines, polygons, curves, and arrows, as shown in Figure 2.6.

2.   Click the icon representing what you want to draw.

3.   With the cross-shaped cursor, point to where you want to start drawing a line, then press and hold down the cursor button. For a straight line or an arrow, drag to extend the line in any direction (you can press and hold down the **Ctrl** key to create a horizontal or vertical line). For a polygon, click the mouse button at each point of the polygon, and double-click to close the polygon. For a curve, draw the curve with the mouse button held down.

4.   Release the mouse button and the graphic appears with selection handles.

Changing the Size and Attributes of Graphics

See *Resizing* for information about changing the size of a graphic.

Use the **Outline** tool to change line attributes and the Fill tool to change fill attributes (see *Outlining an Object and Filling an Object* in Part 1). Click the color palette with the left mouse button to select a fill color, or with the right mouse button to select an outline color. For more detailed control of colors, click the **Colorwheel** icon in the Outline flyout to display the Outline Color dialog box, or click the

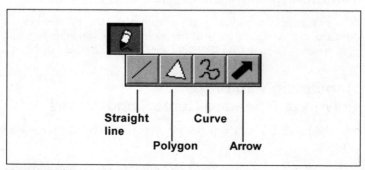

Figure 2.6: The Pencil tool flyout

Colorwheel icon in the Fill flyout to display the Uniform Fill dialog box (see *Color* in Part 1).

To control corners and line caps, click the **Outline** icon in the Outline flyout to display the Outline Pen dialog box (see *Outlining an Object* in Part 1).

To select fill patterns, fountain fills, and textures, click the **Fill** roll-up icon in the Fill flyout to display the Fill roll-up (see *Filling an Object* in Part 1).

Annotating with Imported Graphics

You can import graphics files in many different formats and use them as annotations in charts. See the Appendix for a complete list of supported files.

1. With a chart displayed, choose **File ➤ Import** to display the Import File dialog box.

2. Select the directory that contains the file you want to import.

3. Open the **List Files of Type** list box and click the relevant type of file to display a list of available files in the File Name list box.

4. Click the name of the file and click **OK**. After a few seconds, the graphic appears in your chart with handles around it.

5. Resize and move the graphic as required.

NOTES   If the imported graphic is too large to fit on your chart, CorelCHART displays a message and offers to automatically reduce the size to make it fit.

Duplicating an Annotation

1. Use the **Pick** tool to select the annotation.

2. Choose **Edit ➤ Duplicate** to display a duplicate of the annotation below and to the right of the original. The duplicate is automatically selected.

3. Move the duplicate to the appropriate position.

Deleting an Annotation

To delete an annotation, select it and then choose **Edit ➤ Clear** or press **Delete**.

BAR CHARTS

CorelCHART can create vertical and horizontal bar charts in unstacked and stacked forms. You can create a bar chart based on a template and then make minor or major changes to its appearance.

The explanations of bar chart formats are given here in terms of a side-by-side horizontal bar chart. Other types of bar charts are created in a similar manner.

Creating a Horizontal Bar Chart

A horizontal bar chart shows values for a succession of events or conditions, as in Figure 2.7.

To create a horizontal bar chart:

1. Follow steps 1 through 4 in *Creating a Chart*, choosing **Bar** in step 2 and choosing the first template in the Chart Types box.

2. Place data into the worksheet with the title, subtitle, footnotes, row title, column title, and Y-axis title in the standard positions (see *Tagging Cells*).

3. Place the data values in cells, starting at cell C7, as shown in Figure 2.8.

4. Click the **Chart** icon to display the chart.

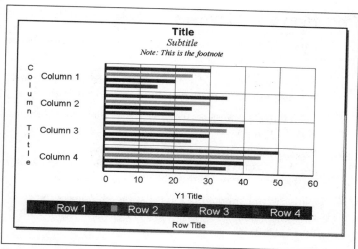

Figure 2.7: Typical horizontal bar chart

	A	B	C	D	E	F	G	H
1	Title							
2	Subtitle							
3	Note: This							
4								
5				Column Tit				
6			Column 1	Column 2	Column 3	Column 4		
7		Row 1	30	35	40	50	Y1 Title	
8	Row Title	Row 2	25	30	35	45	Y2 Title	
9		Row 3	20	25	30	40		
10		Row 4	15	20	25	35		

Figure 2.8: Worksheet for chart in Figure 2.7

Changing Bar Thickness

All the bars in a chart have the same thickness. You can choose from five standard thicknesses.

1. With a chart displayed, use the **Pick** tool to point onto any bar and right-click to display the Bar Riser pop-up.

2. Click **Bar Thickness** to display a flyout that offers a choice of five thicknesses.

3. Press and hold down the left mouse button while you point to various thicknesses. As you do, the thumbnail at the top of the flyout shows the various thicknesses.

4. With the thickness you want displayed, release the mouse button and the bars in your chart change to the new thickness.

Changing Bar Spacing

The spacing between the bars in each series is always the same. You can choose from five standard spacings.

Follow the steps in "Changing Bar Thickness", but in step 3 click **Bar-Bar Spacing** in the pop-up menu and choose one of the spacings.

Reversing Series

You can reverse the series for all types of charts except table charts.

For a bar chart, the sequence of values in a row of a worksheet is known as a series, although you can choose to use the sequence of values in a column as a series (see *Adding Data to a Worksheet*). When you display a bar chart, the series are shown in the order they occur in the worksheet—the first row, then the second, and so on. Reversing a series allows you to reverse the order in the chart so that the last row in the worksheet is the first in the chart, the next-to-last is second, and so on.

1. With a chart displayed, right-click any bar with the **Pick** tool to display the Bar Riser pop-up.

2. Click **Data Reversal** to display a flyout in which you can choose between Reverse Series and Reverse Groups.

3. Click **Reverse Series** to regenerate the chart with the series reversed.

📝 NOTES To revert to the original series order, repeat steps 1 through 3.

Reversing Groups

You can reverse groups for all types of charts except table charts.

In a bar chart, a group is the data in a column of the worksheet. When you display a bar chart, the groups are shown in the order they occur in the worksheet—the first column, then the second, and so on. Reversing groups allows you to reverse the order in the chart so that the last column in the worksheet is the first in the chart, the next-to-last is second, and so on.

To reverse the groups, follow the steps listed under "Reversing Series," but click **Reverse Groups** instead of Reverse Series in step 3.

Using Columns as Series

As explained above in "Reversing Series," a series is normally the sequence of values in one row of a worksheet. To use the sequence of values in columns as a series, do the following:

1. With a chart displayed, click the **Data Manager** icon in the toolbox to display the chart's worksheet.

2. Choose **Data ➤ Data Orientation** to display the Data Orientation dialog box, normally with the **Rows are Series** option button selected.

3. Click the **Columns are Series** option button, click **OK**, then click the **Chart** icon in the toolbox to redisplay the chart.

Changing Bar Shape

By default, CorelCHART shows bars as rectangles. You can replace the rectangles with various shapes, with a different shape for each bar in a series. To do this:

1. With a chart displayed, right-click one bar of a group to display the Bar Riser pop-up.

2. Click **Marker Shape** to display a flyout with a list of 15 shapes.

3. Click one of the shapes to regenerate the chart with all the bars representing the group you selected in step 1 having the new shape.

4. Repeat steps 1 through 4 to create a chart with different shapes for other groups.

Resizing Chart Elements

To resize the chart frame, click on the frame to select it, then drag one of the eight handles. You can also resize the title, subtitle, footnotes, legends, and annotations in the same way (see *Resizing a Chart*).

Changing the Data Axis

CorelCHART automatically chooses a linear scale for bar graphs with the minimum data value as the lowest point on the scale and the maximum data as the highest point on the scale. To change the data axis scale:

1. With a chart displayed, right-click one of the labels in the data axis to display the Data Axis pop-up.

2. Click items in the pop-up to select or deselect them. Each time you click, the chart is regenerated. The options available are

- Display the axis on the top or bottom (or both) of the chart (right or left for vertical bar charts)
- Display the axis as a linear or logarithmic scale

- Change the range of the data axis from automatic to specific minimum and maximum values

- Change the format of numbers in the axis

- Choose to display or not to display grid lines, and to display or not to display tick marks on the axis

- Change the order of values on the axis from ascending to descending

- Change the display of values in the axis so that they are staggered

Changing the Category Axis

1. Right-click one of the labels in the category axis to display the Category Axis pop-up.

2. Click options in the pop-up to select or deselect them. The options available are

   - Display the axis on the right or left (or both) of the chart (bottom of top for vertical bar charts)

   - Choose to display or not to display grid lines, and to display or not to display tick marks on the axis

   - Change the display of values in the axis so that they are staggered

Changing Axis Label Font, Size, Style, Alignment, and Color

Data axis and category axis labels can have different attributes, but all the labels in each axis have the same attributes.

To change axis label attributes:

1. Use the **Pick** tool to select a label in an axis.

2. Click an icon in the Text ribbon to select a font or font size, and choose from the list.

3. Click any combination of **Bold**, **Italic**, and **Underline** icons in the Text ribbon to choose a style.

4. Click the **Left**, **Center**, or **Right** alignment button in the Text ribbon to choose alignment.

5. Click a color in the palette to choose a color.

CASCADING AND TILING WINDOWS

You can display the Data Manager and Chart windows side-by-side or one above the other by choosing **Window ➤ Tile Horizontally**, or **Window ➤ Tile Vertically**.

To return to overlapping windows, choose **Window ➤ Cascade**.

CELL ADDRESSING

Each worksheet cell is identified by an alphabetic column address and a numeric row address. For example, the top left cell in a worksheet is cell A1.

Any cell can refer to the value in another cell by address. You can, for example, place the contents of cell A1 into cell A3 by selecting A3 and then typing =**A1** (the equals sign is necessary so that Corel-CHART recognizes what you type as a cell address, rather than as text).

Cell addresses stated in this way are relative rather than absolute. By typing =**A1** in cell A3, you are telling CorelCHART to use the contents of the cell two cells above the selected cell. This point becomes important when you use the Fill command to copy the contents of one cell to another.

Suppose you copy the contents of cell A3 to cell B3. Now B3 contains the instruction to copy the contents of the cell two cells above B3 into B3. If you look at the Formula bar with B3 selected, you will see =B1.

If you want to copy the contents of A1 into A3, and then copy the contents of A3 into other cells in such a way that these also receive copies of the contents of A1, you must use absolute, rather than relative, addressing. You can use dollar signs to indicate that a cell reference is absolute. There are four ways to refer to the contents of one cell from another cell. In terms of addressing cell A1 from cell B3:

Address in Cell	Meaning
A1	Contents of cell one column to the left and two rows up (column and row are relative)
$A1	Contents of cell in column A and two rows up (column is absolute, row is relative)
A$1	Contents of cell one column to the left and in row 1 (column is relative, row is absolute)
A1	Contents of cell in column A and in row1 (column and row are absolute)

CHANGING THE APPEARANCE OF A WORKSHEET

There are several ways to change the appearance of a worksheet.

Displaying and Hiding Grid Lines

1. Display a worksheet.

2. Choose **Options ➤ Display Grid**.

📖 **NOTES** Alternatively, click the Grid Lines icon in the Text Ribbon.

Changing Column Widths and Row Heights

When CorelCHART creates a worksheet, all the columns are initially 50 points wide and all rows are 16 points high. You can change the widths of columns and heights of rows interactively or with precision. You can also choose to let CorelCHART automatically set appropriate column widths and row heights.

To change the width of a column interactively:

1. Point into the column header and move the cursor onto the dividing line that separates one column button from the next. When the cursor is in the correct position it changes to a double-headed arrow.

2. Press the mouse button and drag to the right or left. As you drag, the line separating the columns moves.

3. When you are satisfied with the column width, release the mouse button.

To change the height of a row interactively, drag the line in the row header that separates the row you want to change from the row below it.

To change the width of columns with precision:

1. Select a column or group of adjacent columns.

2. Choose **Format ➤ Column Width** to display the Column Width dialog box.

3. Choose or type a new column width, then click **OK**. Alternatively, click the **Default Value** check box and then click **OK** to restore the selected columns to the default width.

To change row heights with precision, use a similar method, selecting one or more adjacent rows in step 1 and choosing **Format ➤ Row Height** in step 2.

To have CorelCHART automatically set column widths and row heights:

1. Select columns, rows, or rows and columns.
2. Choose **Format ➤ Best Fit**.

Changing Font, Size, Style, and Color

You can use any TrueType or Adobe Type 1 font installed on your computer.

To change the appearance of characters in any cells:

1. Select the cells in which you want to change characters' appearance.
2. Choose **Format ➤ Font** (or click the **Font** icon in the Text Ribbon) to display the Font dialog box.
3. In the list boxes, choose a font name, style, size, and color, then click **OK**.

Changing Cell Borders and Background

You can choose a separate style and color for the left, right, top, and bottom border of individual cells or groups of adjacent cells.

1. Select the cells for which you want to change the border.
2. Choose **Format ➤ Borders** (or click the **Borders** icon in the Button bar) to display the Borders dialog box.
3. Click any combination of the **Left**, **Right**, **Top**, and **Bottom** check boxes to select the part or parts of cell borders you want to change. Make sure the Outline check box is not checked.

4. Click one of the six line styles.

5. Open the **Color** list box and click a color.

6. Click **OK** to redraw the worksheet, then select a cell other than those you selected in step 1 to see the new cell borders.

To change backgrounds of cells:

1. Select the cells for which you want to change the background.

2. Choose **Format ➤ Borders** (or click the Borders icon in the Button bar) to display the Borders dialog box.

3. Make sure none of the Borders check boxes is checked.

4. Click the **Shaded** check box and then click **Brush**.

5. Click one of the 12 brush styles to select a background pattern.

6. Open the **Foreground** Color list box and select a foreground color.

7. Open the **Background** Color list box and select a background color.

8. Click **OK** to return to the Borders dialog box, click **OK** to redraw the worksheet, then select a cell other than those you selected in step 1 to see the new cell background.

To outline a group of cells:

1. Select the group of adjoining cells which you want to outline.

2. Choose **Format ➤ Borders** (or click the Borders icon in the Button bar) to display the Borders dialog box.

3. Click the **Outline** check box and make sure that none of the Left, Right, Top, and Bottom check boxes is checked.

4. Click one of the six line styles.

5. Open the **Color** list box and click a color.

6. Click **OK** to redraw the worksheet, then select a cell other than those you selected in step 1 to see the outline.

Changing Number Format

When CorelCHART creates a worksheet, it makes certain assumptions about the type of data represented by numbers and formats them accordingly. You can change the format of numbers in individual cells or groups of cells.

See "Creating a Custom Number Format" for information about creating special formats.

To change the number format:

1. Select the cell or cells containing number formats you want to change.

2. Choose **Format ➤ Numeric** (or click the numeric format icon in the Text ribbon) to display the Numeric Format dialog box.

3. Scroll down the Format list box and click the format you want to use. An example of that format appears in the Format text box.

4. Click **OK** to apply that format to the selected cells.

Creating a Custom Number Format

1. Follow steps 1 through 2 in "Changing Number Format."

2. Click a standard format similar to the custom format you want to create.

3. Edit the standard format in the Format text box, using the standard formats listed above as a guide.

4. Click **Add** to add the new format to the list.

5. Click **OK** to apply the new format to the selected cells.

NOTES   After you create a custom number format and save the chart, the new format is available whenever you open the Numeric Format dialog box.

You can delete a custom format by selecting it in the Numeric Format dialog box and then clicking Delete. Be cautious about doing this because you will run into problems if you subsequently open a chart that uses the deleted format.

Changing Data Alignment

When CorelCHART creates a worksheet, all cell data is auto-aligned: numbers are aligned at the right edge of the cell and labels (alphabetic text) are aligned at the left edge. You can select individual cells, or groups of cells, and change their alignment.

1. Select one or more cells.

2. Choose **Format ➤ Alignment** to display the Alignment dialog box.

3. Click **Left**, **Right**, **Center**, or **Auto**.

4. You can also click the **Word Wrap** check box to turn on word wrap.

NOTES Alternatively, you can format selected cells by clicking one of the alignment icons in the Text ribbon.

Sorting Data

You can change the order of columns in a worksheet by sorting according to the values in one row, or the order of rows by sorting according to the values in one column. The row or column on which the sort is based is known as the key. To sort data:

1. Select the cells containing the data to be sorted.

2. Choose **Data ➤ Sort** to display the Sort dialog box.

3. Click the **Rows** option button to sort rows, or click the **Columns** option button to sort columns.

4. If the **Key** text box does not already contain the address of a cell in the key column or row, delete the cell address already there and replace it with the address of a cell in the key column or row.

5. Click the **Ascending** option button to sort in ascending order, or the **Descending** option button to sort in descending order.

6. Click the **Adjust Formulas** check box if the worksheet contains formulas that relate cells, and you want the formulas to maintain the correct cell relationship.

7. Click the **Move Formats** check box if you want cell formatting to move with cells.

8. Click **OK**. The worksheet reappears with the data sorted in the new order.

CHART COMPONENTS

The various types of charts you can create with CorelCHART have many components in common. The components of a typical chart are as follows:

Component	Description
Annotation	Text or graphics in a chart in addition to the data in the worksheet
Category axis	The axis on which the categories of values are represented, often the horizontal axis
Data axis	The axis on which the charted values are represented, often the vertical axis
Footnote	A comment, such as a credit for the data plotted, usually at the bottom of the chart
Grid lines	Horizontal and vertical lines corresponding to values on the axes
Legend	Definitions of colors or hatch patterns that represent data

Component	Description
Subtitle	A secondary name or explanation of the chart, usually placed under the title
Title	The name of the chart, usually placed at the top

CHART FORMATS AND TYPES

CorelCHART can create charts in 12 formats, each with many types. You can choose any of these when you initially create a chart, and you can change an existing chart from one format to another.

The chart formats are as follows:

- Area
- Bar
- High, low, open, close
- Histogram
- Line
- Pictograph
- Pie
- Scatter
- Spectral map
- Table
- Three-dimensional riser
- Three-dimensional scatter

See the CorelDRAW *Manual* for advice on choosing suitable chart formats.

In this book, most of the information is presented as it applies specifically to bar graphs. Significant differences between bar graphs and other types of graphs are noted.

Changing from One Chart Format to Another

1. With a chart displayed in the Chart window, choose **Gallery** to display a menu of chart formats, with the format of the displayed chart checked.

2. Click the name of the format you want to use.

3. Click one of the types of that format to redisplay the chart in the new format.

NOTES   If, in step 2, you click the current format of the chart, the flyout window allows you to choose a different type of that format.

There are too many chart types and their variations to show in this book. You may want to choose those types and variations that interest you and print them for future reference.

CHART TEMPLATES

You can use an existing chart without its data as a template for another chart. The CorelDRAW package contains several templates you can use in this way. When you create a new chart, you can choose the template you want to use from thumbnail-size previews. See *File Management*.

Changing a Chart's Template

To change the appearance of a chart by changing from one template to another:

1.   With a chart displayed in the Chart Window, Choose **File ➤ Apply Template** to display the Open Chart dialog box.

2.   Click the name of the chart you want to use as a template to see it as a thumbnail.

3.   Click **OK** to display the chart based on the selected template.

CLEARING, DELETING, INSERTING, AND MOVING WORKSHEET DATA

When you clear a cell, the cell remains in the worksheet with its original contents replaced by zero. Cutting a cell is similar to clearing it, but it also writes the original contents of the cell into the Clipboard, replacing whatever was previously in the Clipboard.

When you delete a row or column of cells, you remove the cells in that entire row or column (and their contents) from the worksheet.

Clearing Individual Cells, Columns, and Rows

1.   Select the cells to be cleared (see *Selecting Cells in a Worksheet*).

2.   Choose **Edit ➤ Clear**, **Edit ➤ Cut**, or press **Delete** to display the Cut and Clear Options dialog box with all data and format option boxes checked.

3.   Click any data or format option that is not to be cleared so that the check marks are removed, and then click **OK**.

Deleting Columns and Rows

1. Select the columns or rows to be deleted (see *Selecting Cells in a Worksheet*).

2. Choose **Edit ➤ Delete** to delete the selected columns or rows and to move remaining columns to the left or rows up to replace those deleted.

Inserting a Column or Row

1. Select the column or row before which you want to make the insertion.

2. Choose **Edit ➤ Insert**.

Moving a Column or Row

1. Insert an empty column or row in the position to which the column or row will be moved (see the preceding procedure).

2. Select the column or row which is to be moved and cut it to the Clipboard.

3. Select the empty column or row you created in step 1.

4. Choose **Edit ➤ Paste** to paste the Clipboard contents into the empty column or row.

5. Delete the empty column or row from which you cut the data in step 2.

NOTES   You can move more than one column or row using this procedure. In step 1, create enough empty columns or rows to accommodate those to be moved. In step 3, select all the columns or rows into which data is to be pasted.

COLORING CHART OBJECTS

You can apply colors or shades of gray to chart objects either by choosing from a limited range in the color palette at the bottom of the Chart window or by choosing from a more extensive range in the Color dialog box, which you access from the Fill flyout. You can also fill chart objects with patterns, fountain fills, and textures. See *Filling Chart Objects*.

You can separately choose colors for the various objects of a chart such as the background, data series, title, subtitle, and axes.

Using the Color Palette

1. Use the **Pick** tool to select a chart object.
2. Left-click a color or shade of gray in the color palette to change the fill color of the selected object and all like it, or right-click to change the outline color of the selected object and all like it.

NOTES   When you color one bar of a bar chart, one slice in a multiple pie chart, one riser in a three-dimensional chart, or any other marker representing a part of a series, that color is applied to all other markers in the same series.

If you select an outline color and do not see it on the selected object, the probable reason is that the outline has zero width. Use the Outline tool to change the width.

Using Color Dialog Boxes

1. Use the **Pick** tool to select a chart object.
2. Click the **Fill** tool to display the Fill flyout.

3. Click the **Colorwheel** icon to display the Uniform Fill dialog box.

4. Click a color to change the fill color of the selected object and all like it (see *Color* in Part 1 for more information).

5. Click the **Outline** tool to display the Outline flyout.

6. Click the **Colorwheel** icon to display the Outline Color dialog box.

7. Click a color to change the outline color of the selected object and all like it (see *Color* in Part 1 for more information).

COMBINATION CHARTS

You can create combination charts in which two types of chart are shown within the same chart. For example, to display one series in a bar chart as a line:

1. Display a bar chart in the Chart window.

2. Select one of the bars in the series.

3. Choose **Chart ➤ Display As Line** to redraw the chart with the selected series shown as a line.

COPYING CELL CONTENTS

You can copy the fundamental contents of one cell to others.

Copying Cell Contents to Adjoining Cells

The fundamental contents of a cell is the formula that creates the result shown in that worksheet cell. When a cell is selected, its fundamental contents are shown in the Formula bar at the top of the worksheet.

To copy a cell's fundamental contents to adjoining cells:

1. Select the cell containing the formula to be copied, together with one or more cells to the right or below it.

2. Choose **Edit ➤ Fill Right** to copy to cells to the right, or choose **Edit ➤ Fill Down** to copy to cells below.

NOTES If the formula being copied contains cell addresses, make sure that these addresses are expressed as relative, column absolute, row absolute, or column and row absolute according to your intention (see *Cell Addresses*).

Copying Cell Contents to Any Cell

You can cut or copy the contents of a cell to the Clipboard, select another cell, and paste from the Clipboard into that cell. You can also cut or copy from a range of cells into the Clipboard, and paste from the Clipboard into another range of cells.

Using this method, you copy the fundamental contents of cells, rather than the value displayed in the worksheet.

CREATING A CHART

All CorelCHART charts are created in the same general way:

1. Choose **File ➤ New** to display the New dialog box.

2. Click one of the chart formats in the Gallery list box to display thumbnails of types of that format in the Chart Types list box.

3. Click one of the chart types.

4. If the Use Sample Data check box is checked, click it to remove the check mark (see the note below).

5. Click **OK** to display a blank worksheet in the Data Manager window with a thumbnail of the chart format and type in the upper left corner.

6. Place data for the chart into the worksheet (see *Adding Data to a Worksheet*).

7. Tag the data to identify the range of data cells and other cells (see *Tagging Cells*).

8. Click the **Chart View** icon at the top of the toolbox to display the chart.

NOTES If the Use Sample Data check box is checked, when you click OK in step 4 a chart based on sample data is displayed.

DATA MANAGER

The Data Manager contains a worksheet similar in appearance and capabilities to popular spreadsheet applications. The worksheet contains the data from which CorelCHART creates charts. You can type data into the worksheet cells, or you can import or link data from other applications (see *Adding Data to a Worksheet*).

The only way to change chart data is in the Data Manager.

The Data Manager is where you assign tags to indicate how the contents of each cell are used in a chart (see *Tagging Cells*).

DISPLAYING AND HIDING CHART OBJECTS

You can choose which of the objects of a chart to display. To do this:

1. With a chart displayed, choose **Chart ➤ Display Status** to display the Display Status dialog box.

2. Click the appropriate check boxes to check or uncheck the chart objects you want to display or hide. To display all the text, click the **ALL Text** button; to display none of the text, click the **NO Text** button.

3. Click **OK** to regenerate the chart.

NOTES If you check the Data Values box, each data value is displayed on the chart in numbers, as well as by the size of a chart object. You can choose the position and format of these numbers.

If you are working with a three-dimensional chart, the 3D Graph Display Status dialog box appears. This allows you to select which of the three-dimensional background objects you want to include in the chart.

DYNAMIC DATA EXCHANGE

You can set up links between a CorelCHART worksheet and another application in which the data for those charts was prepared, providing that application supports dynamic data exchange

(DDE). You must establish DDE links in the original file. Subsequently, your charts are updated automatically whenever a change is made to the original data. Changes you make to the data in CorelCHART do not affect the original file.

Do the following to create a DDE link between CorelCHART and a spreadsheet file created in a Windows application such as Microsoft Excel:

1. Display the CorelCHART Data Manager screen to which you want to link data, then minimize it.

2. Open the application from which the link is to be established.

3. In that application, open the file containing the data you want to link into CorelCHART and select the range of cells to be linked.

4. Choose **Edit ➤ Copy** to copy the selected cells into the Clipboard.

5. Restore the CorelCHART window, and select the cell where the top left cell of the linked data should be.

6. Choose **Edit ➤ Paste Link** to display the linked data in the worksheet.

7. Optionally, return to the other application, make a change to some of the linked data, save the changed data, and return to the Data Manager window to confirm that the data in the worksheet has changed.

EXPORTING A CHART OR WORKSHEET

You can export a chart or a worksheet as a file, or you can export it by way of the Clipboard.

Exporting to a File

You can export a chart to a file in many different graphics formats and a worksheet as text or as a spreadsheet file (see the Appendix for a list of file formats).

1. Display the chart in the Chart window or the worksheet in the Data Manager window.

2. In the case of a worksheet, select the cells to be exported.

3. Choose **File ➤ Export** to display the Export File or Export Data dialog box.

4. In the Directories list box, select the directory into which you want to write the exported chart.

5. Open the **List Files of Type** list box and click the format in which you want to export the chart or worksheet.

6. Click in the **File Name** text box to create an insertion point and then type the file name. CorelCHART automatically adds the file name extension appropriate for the file format.

7. Click **OK** to write the chart or worksheet to disk.

Exporting a Chart by Way of the Clipboard

To export a chart to a Windows application such as CorelDRAW by way of the Clipboard:

1. Display a chart in the Chart window.

2. Choose **Edit ➤ Copy Chart** to copy the chart into the Clipboard.

3. Open the other Windows application.

4. Choose **Edit ➤ Paste** to copy the entire chart into that application.

Exporting Worksheet Data by Way of the Clipboard

1. Display a worksheet in the Data Manager window.

2. Select the range of cells to be exported.

3. Choose **Edit ➤ Copy** to copy the selected data into the Clipboard.

4. Open a spreadsheet application that runs under Windows.

5. Choose **Edit ➤ Paste** to copy the data into that application.

FILE MANAGEMENT

This section deals with topics concerned with CorelCHART files. It explains opening, saving, and closing files.

Opening a New Chart

See *Creating a Chart*.

Opening an Existing Chart

1. Choose **File ➤ Open**. The Open Chart dialog box appears. Depending on how it was last used, the dialog box may or may not show a chart image in the Preview box.

2. In the Directories list box, select the directory that contains the chart you want to open. The File Name list box shows charts in that directory.

3. In the File Name list box, click a file name to see a thumbnail image of a chart.

4. Click **OK** to open a Chart window showing the chart.

Saving Files

For information about saving a file with its existing name and saving a file with a new name, see *File Management* in Part 1 of this

book. CorelCHART automatically adds the extension .CCH to
chart file names.

You can save a description with your file but, unlike CorelDRAW,
you cannot list keywords.

Closing Files

To close a chart file, you must have the Chart window displayed.

1. If necessary, make the Chart window active.
2. Choose **File ➤ Close**.

NOTES The Chart and Data Manager windows are both
part of the same file. When a file is open, the Chart window is always
on the screen, although it may be partly or entirely hidden by the
Data Manager window. You can display the Chart window with or
without the Data Manager window. However, you cannot remove
the Chart window without closing the file and, at the same time,
removing the Data Manager window.

FILLING CELLS IN A WORKSHEET

See *Copying Cell Contents*.

FILLING CHART OBJECTS

You can fill chart objects with colors, hatch patterns, fountain fills,
bitmap patterns, and textures. You can replace bars in bar charts
with vector graphics. For information about color fills, see *Coloring*

Chart Objects. See *Filling an Object* in Part 1 for information about fountain fills, bitmap patterns, and textures.

Filling with a Hatch Pattern

When you are going to print charts in black and white and the background is white or light gray, outline chart objects in black and fill them with hatch patterns rather than colors.

If necessary, use the procedure "Outlining Bars in Black or Gray" in *Outlining Bars* to create a solid outline around the chart objects.

To fill chart objects with hatch patterns:

1. With the chart displayed and one object of a series selected, click the **Fill** tool to display the Fill flyout.

2. Click one of the hatch patterns to fill all objects of the selected series with that hatch pattern.

3. Repeat steps 1 and 2 for the remaining series, choosing different hatch patterns for each.

Replacing a Bar with a Pictograph

You can replace bars in bar graphs and histograms with vector images known as pictographs.

To replace a bar with a vector image:

1. Create the vector image that will replace a bar using CorelDRAW and save the image as a file.

2. Open the **Fill** flyout and click the **Pictograph** icon to display the Pictograph roll-up.

3. Choose **Chart ➤ Show as Pictograph**. This has no obvious effect because it is a toggle command.

4. Select the bar you want to replace with a pictograph. Instead of the whole bar being selected, only the portion between major grid lines on the data axis is selected.

5. Click **Import** in the Pictograph roll-up to display the Import File dialog box.

6. Select the directory in which you saved the vector image, click its file name, and click **OK** to display the pictograph in the Pictograph roll-up.

7. Click **Apply** in the Pictograph roll-up to replace the selected bar with pictograph images, one image between each major grid line.

NOTES   If Show as Pictograph is not enabled, one pictograph image replaces each bar of the series.

Filling with a Fountain Fill

To fill a bar with a fountain fill:

1. With the chart displayed and a bar selected, click the **Fill** tool to display the Fill flyout.

2. In the flyout, click the **Fountain Fill** icon to display the Fountain Fill dialog box.

3. Choose the fountain fill and click **OK** to apply it to the selected bar (see *Filling an Object* in Part 1).

NOTES   If Show as Pictograph is not enabled, the fountain fill extends over the length of a bar. If Show as Pictograph is enabled, the fountain fill repeats between major grid lines.

Removing a Fill

To remove a fill, replace it with white or any other solid color, as follows:

1. Select the chart object or objects from which you want to remove the fill.

2. Click white, or any other color, in the color palette. The color replaces the fill.

FINDING CELLS IN A WORKSHEET

You can find a cell in a worksheet if you know its address or content.

Accessing a Cell by Address

1. Choose **Data ➤ Go To** to display the Go To Cell dialog box.
2. Type the cell address in the Address text box, and click **OK**.

Searching for a Cell Containing Specific Data

1. Choose **Data ➤ Find** to display the Find dialog box.
2. Type the data you want to find in the Find text box.
3. Click the **Ignore Case** check box to insert or remove a check mark according to whether you want the search to be case-sensitive (check mark present) or case-insensitive (check mark absent).
4. Click the **Whole Cell** check box to insert or remove a check according to whether you want to match the entire contents of cells (check mark present) or match any part of cell contents (check mark absent).
5. Click the **Formulas**, **Values**, or **Text** option button according to the type of data you want to find.
6. Click the **Rows** or **Columns** option button according to the direction in which the search should proceed.
7. Click the **Forward** or **Backward** option button according to whether you want to search from the currently selected cell towards the end or towards the beginning of the worksheet.

8. Click **Find** to find the first occurrence of the data.

9. Choose **Data ➤ Find Next** (or press **F3**) to find the next occurrence of the data, or choose **Data ➤ Find Prev** (or press **Shift+F3**) to find the previous occurrence of the data.

Replacing Data in a Cell

1. Choose **Data ➤ Replace** to display the Find dialog box.

2. Type the data you want to find in the **Find What** text box and the data you want to replace it with in the **Replace With** text box.

3. Follow steps 3 through 6 in "Searching for a Cell Containing Specific Data."

4. Click the **Prompt on Replace** check box to remove or place a check mark in it. With the check mark present, you have the opportunity to decide whether or not you want to replace each occurrence of the found data.

5. Click **Find Next** to find the first occurrence of the text, or click **Replace All** to find all occurrences.

HELP

See *Help* in Part 1 of this book.

HIGH-LOW-OPEN-CLOSE CHARTS

CorelCHART can produce three types of these charts:

- High-low
- High-low-open
- High-low-open-close

Creating a High-Low Chart

A high-low chart shows the range of values above and below a reference value for a succession of events, as in Figure 2.9.

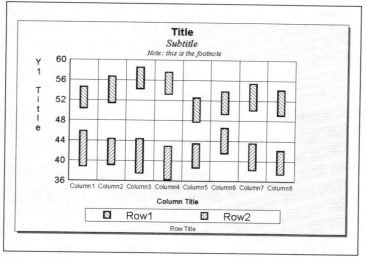

Figure 2.9: A high-low chart

To create a high-low chart:

1. Follow steps 1 through 4 in *Creating a Chart*, choosing **High/Low/Open/Close** in step 2 and choosing the first template in the Chart Types box.

2. Place data into the worksheet with the title, subtitle, footnotes, row title, column title, and Y-axis title in the standard positions assumed by Autoscan (see *Tagging Cells*).

3. For the first column in the chart, place the high and low values for the upper bar in cells D8 and D9, and place the high and low values for the lower bar in cells D10 and D11.

4. Place values for other chart columns in consecutive worksheet columns, as shown in Figure 2.10.

5. Click the **Chart** icon to display the chart.

Creating a High-Low-Open-Close Chart

A high-low-open-close chart is similar to a high-low chart, but with the addition of marks indicating the open and close points on each bar. Use the third template in Chart Types and, in the worksheet, provide open and close data in addition to high and low data. See the sample data supplied with CorelCHART for an example.

	A	B	C	D	E	F	G	H	I	J	K
1	Title										
2	Subtitle										
3	Note: this i										
4											
5											
6						Column Tit					
7				Column1	Column2	Column3	Column4	Column5	Column6	Column7	Column8
8	High		Row1	54.6	56.67	59	57.56	52.5	53.78	55.4	54.1
9	Low	Row Title		50.35	51.43	54.25	53.2	47.7	49.3	50.1	49.1
10	High		Row2	45.8	44.3	44.3	42.83	43.4	46.5	43.5	42.1
11	Low			38.78	39.12	37.5	36.2	38.6	41.5	38.2	37.4

Figure 2.10: Worksheet for high-low chart in Figure 2.9

HISTOGRAMS

A histogram is a chart that shows the number of times each value in a set of data occurs.

Creating a Histogram

A histogram, such as that in Figure 2.11, shows the number of times each value in a set of data occurs. Each bar represents a range of values. The bar between 0 and 10 on the horizontal axis represents all values in the set greater than zero and less than or equal to 10. The height of each bar represents the number of occurrences of those values.

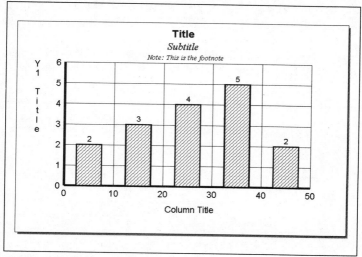

Figure 2.11: A typical histogram

To create a histogram:

1. Follow steps 1 through 4 in *Creating a Chart*, choosing **Histogram** in step 2 and choosing either template in the Chart Types box.

2. Place data into the worksheet with the title, subtitle, footnotes, row title, column title, and Y-axis title in the standard positions assumed by Autoscan (see *Tagging Cells*).

3. Place the data values in an array of cells, starting at cell C7, as shown in Figure 2.12. For a histogram, rows and columns have no significance.

4. Click the **Chart** icon to display the histogram.

IMPORTING DATA

You can import data into the Data Manager from ASCII text files, from dBASE and compatible databases, from Excel and Lotus 1-2-3

	A	B	C	D	E	F	G
1	Title						
2	Subtitle						
3	Note: This						
4							
5				Column Titl			
6			Column 1	Column 2	Column 3	Column 4	
7		Row 1	5	35	40	50	Y1 Title
8	Row Title	Row 2	6	30	35	45	Y2 Title
9		Row 3	20	25	30	40	
10		Row 4	15	20	25	35	

Figure 2.12: Worksheet for histogram shown in Figure 2.11

spreadsheets, and from Harvard Graphics (see the Appendix for details).

1. Display an empty worksheet in the Data Manager window.
2. Choose **File ➤ Import** to display the Import Data dialog box.
3. In the Directories list box, select the directory that contains the file you want to import.
4. In the List Files of Type list box, click the type of file you want to import to display the names of available files of that type in the File Name list box.
5. Click the name of the file to be imported, and then click **OK** to display the imported data in the worksheet.

NOTES All data previously in the worksheet is deleted when new data is imported.

LINKING AND EMBEDDING CHARTS

You can use CorelCHART as an OLE server to embed or link charts into other applications. See *Linking and Embedding Objects* in Part 1 of this book for information about linking and embedding objects.

MENUS

CorelCHART has standard menus as well as context-sensitive menus.

252   CorelCHART

Main Menu Bar

The Main menu bar is different when the Chart window is active and when the Data Manager window is active, as shown in Figure 2.13. Some menus that have the same name in the two menu bars contain different items. See CorelCHART on-line Help for detailed information about menus.

Context-Sensitive Menus

Context-sensitive menus provide fast access to the attributes of chart objects. To display a context-sensitive menu, either point to a

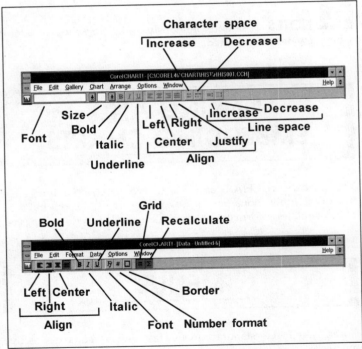

Figure 2.13: Main menu bars when the Chart (top) and Data Manager (bottom) windows are active

chart object and click the right mouse button, or click the **Context-Sensitive Pop-up Menu** tool (the second tool from the top in the toolbox) and then click a chart object. In either case, a pop-up menu appears. Click the item on the menu you want to use, and then choose from a list of alternatives.

MOVING CHART OBJECTS

You can move a chart as well as its title, subtitle, footnote, and legend.

Moving a Chart

To move a two-dimensional chart, leaving the title, subtitle, foot-note, and legend in place:

1. Using the **Pick** tool, point onto a chart, but not onto a specific object within the chart.

2. Press and hold down the mouse button until the cursor changes to a four-pointed arrow.

3. Drag the mouse. A dashed rectangle shows the new position of the chart.

4. Release the mouse button to redraw the chart in the new position.

NOTES   Use the 3D Movement tool to move a three-dimensional chart. See *3D View Tool*.

Moving a Chart Object

To move a chart object, such as the title, point onto that object and then follow steps 2 through 4 above. To move the legend, make sure you point between (not on) components of the legend.

OPENING A NEW OR EXISTING CHART

See *File Management*.

OUTLINING BARS

You can outline bars in a bar chart in black, a shade of gray, or another color to enhance their visibility. All the bars in a chart have the same outline.

Outlining Bars in Black or Gray

Do the following to draw a black outline around all the bars:

1. Use the **Pick** tool to select any bar in the chart.

2. Click the **Outline** tool to display the Outline flyout shown in Figure 2.14.

3. Click one of the ten thickness icons in the top row of the flyout. These icons correspond to thicknesses of ¼, ½, 1, 2, 4, 8, 16, 20, and 24 points.

4. Click the **Outline** tool again.

5. Click the black icon, or one of the gray icons, in the bottom row of the flyout.

6. Click **OK**.

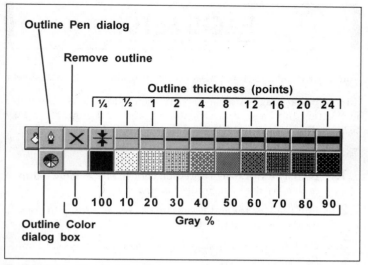

Figure 2.14: The Outline flyout

Outlining Bars in Color

Do the following to draw a colored outline around all the bars:

1. Follow steps 1 through 4 in "Outlining Bars in Black or Gray" above.

2. Click the **Colorwheel** icon, the leftmost icon in the bottom row of the flyout, to display the Outline Color dialog box.

3. Choose a color (see *Coloring Chart Objects*), then click **OK**.

Removing Outlines

1. Follow steps 1 through 3 in "Outlining Bars in Black or Gray" above.

2. Click the X in the top row of the flyout, then click **OK**.

PAGE SETUP

You can separately set up pages for printing charts and worksheets.

To set up chart pages, display a chart, then follow steps 1 through 5 in "Setting the Page Size, Orientation, and Background" in *Page Setup* in Part 1. In step 1, choose **File ➤ Page Setup**.

To set up worksheet pages:

1. Display a worksheet and then choose **File ➤ Page Setup** to display the Page Setup dialog box.

2. Edit the **Header** and **Footer** text boxes according to your needs (see the note below).

3. Click the **Font** button to display the Header/Footer Font Format dialog box.

4. Choose the font, font style, size, effects, and color for the header and footer, then click **OK**.

5. Choose margin sizes.

6. Click check boxes to select or deselect options, then click **OK**.

NOTES   In step 2 you can type codes and text to control what appears in the header and footer of printed pages.

Codes, which consist of characters preceded by an ampersand, control alignment and content of the header and footer.

Frequently used codes are as follows:

Code	Meaning
&C	Text that follows is centered.
&D	Print the date.
&F	Print the file name.
&L	Text that follows is left-aligned.
&P	Print the page number.

Code	Meaning
&R	Text that follows is right-aligned.
&T	Print the time.

Most other text is printed as it appears.

PIE CHARTS

You can create the following types of pie charts:

- Basic pie charts
- Ring pie charts
- Multiple pie charts
- Multiple ring pie charts
- Multiple proportional pie charts
- Multiple proportional ring pie charts

Creating a Pie Chart

Use the procedure in *Creating a Chart*. Figure 2.15 shows a typical pie chart.

To create a pie chart:

1. Follow steps 1 through 4 in *Creating a Chart*, choosing **Pie** in step 2 and choosing the first template in the Chart Types box.

2. Place data into the worksheet with the title, subtitle, footnotes, row title, column title, and Y-axis title in the standard positions assumed by Autoscan (see *Tagging Cells*).

3. Place the pie values in a column of cells, starting at cell C7, as shown in Figure 2.16.

4. Click the **Chart** icon to display the chart.

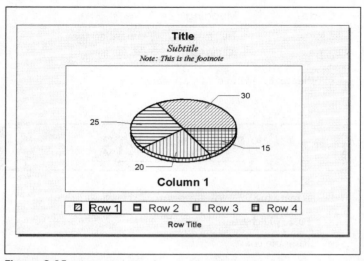

Figure 2.15: A typical pie chart

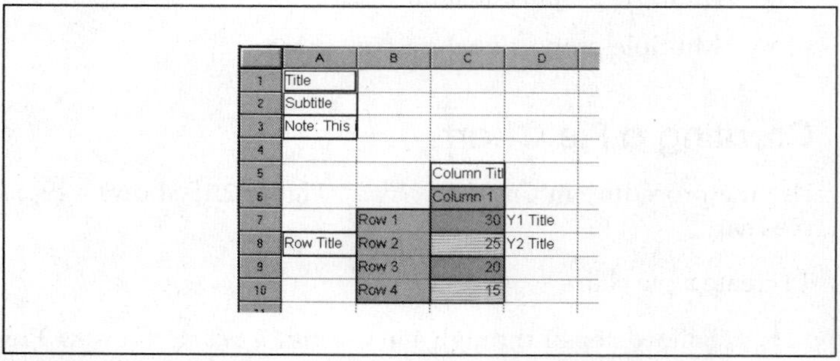

Figure 2.16: Worksheet for chart shown in Figure 2.15

Changing a Pie Chart's Appearance

You can change the overall appearance of a pie chart by modifying the following:

- Tilt
- Pie thickness
- Rotation
- Pies per row (multiple pie charts only)
- Slice feeler size
- Hole size (ring pie charts only)
- Ring total format (ring pie charts only)
- Legend
- Display status

To change a chart's appearance:

1. With a pie chart displayed, point outside the chart (but within the chart frame) and click the right mouse button to display the Pie Chart Frame pop-up.

2. Point onto the pop-up choice you want, and click the left mouse button to display a set of alternatives or a dialog box.

3. Click one of the alternatives, or complete the dialog box and click **OK**, to redraw the pie chart.

Changing the Appearance of an Individual Slice

You can change the appearance of individual slices by:

- Detaching a slice from the pie
- Deleting a slice

- Restoring deleted slices

- Changing the size of an individual feeler

- Showing or hiding an individual feeler

- Showing or hiding an individual slice name

- Showing or hiding an individual slice value

To change the appearance of an individual slice:

1. With a pie chart displayed, point onto a slice and click the right mouse button to display the Pie Slice pop-up.

2. Point onto the pop-up choice you want, and click the left mouse button to activate that choice, display a set of alternatives, or display a dialog box.

3. Click one of the alternatives, or complete the dialog box and click **OK**, to redraw the pie chart.

POP-UPS

In the Chart screen, you can use the right mouse button to display pop-ups, which allow you to select attributes. For example, if you point onto a cell and press the right mouse button, you see a list of menu commands. With the mouse button held down, drag to the command you want to use, then release the button to execute the command or display a dialog box.

The commands and dialog boxes that can be accessed from different parts of the Data Manager screen are as follows:

Screen Component	Commands	Dialog boxes
Cell	Clear, cut, copy, paste, paste special, best fit	Numeric format, font, borders, alignment

Screen Component	Commands	Dialog boxes
Column Header	Insert, delete, clear, cut, copy, paste, best fit	Numeric format, font, borders, alignment, column width
Row Header	Insert, delete, clear, cut, copy, paste, best fit	Numeric format, font, borders, alignment, row height

PREFERENCES

To set preferences, choose **Options ➤ Preferences** to display the Preferences dialog box.

See *Preferences* in Part 1 for an explanation of the preferences.

PRINTING CHARTS AND WORKSHEETS

The facilities for printing charts are similar to those for printing documents in most Windows applications.

Printing a Chart

To print a chart, display the chart and then follow the procedures under *Printing a Drawing* in Part 1 of this book.

Printing a Worksheet

1. Choose **File ➤ Print Setup** and follow the first procedure under *Printing a Drawing* in Part 1 of this book.

2. With the worksheet displayed, choose **File ➤ Print** to display the Print Data dialog box.

3. Type the number of copies to be printed in the **Copies** text box.

4. If you want to print only certain cells, specify the range of cells to be printed in the **Print Cells** group of text boxes.

5. If header or footer text boxes in the Page Setup dialog box contain the code to print page numbers, and you want the first page to be numbered other than 1, type the number of the first page in the **First Page Number** text box. You can click the **Page** button at the bottom of the dialog box to display the Page Setup dialog box.

6. Click the **Two-Sided Printing** check box to place a check mark there if you want to enable two-sided printing.

7. If you want to print only certain pages, type the first and last page numbers into the **From** and **To** text boxes.

8. Click **OK**.

REFRESHING A CHART

Sometimes, after making changes to a chart or an annotation, remnants of the original are left behind. To clear these remnants, choose **Options ➤ Update Chart Now**.

RESIZING A CHART

You can resize a chart, and you can separately resize text in the title, subtitle, footnote, and legend.

Resizing an Entire Chart

1. With a chart displayed, use the **Pick** tool to point within the chart, but not on a specific object, and click the mouse button to select the entire chart. Handles appear at the four corners of the chart and at the mid-points of the top, bottom, and sides.

2. Point onto a corner handle, press and hold down the mouse button, and drag diagonally to change the size of the chart but keep the height and width in proportion. Use a handle at the center of the top or bottom to change the height of the chart but keep the width unchanged. Use a handle at the center of a side to change the width but keep the height unchanged. A dashed outline shows the new size.

3. Release the mouse button to redraw the chart at the new size.

NOTES   You can use the technique described above to change the size of the entire legend.

Resizing Text

To change the size of text in the title or subtitle:

1. Use the **Text** tool to select all the text characters to be changed.

2. Open the **Font Size** list box.

3. Click the new font size.

ROLL-UPS

See *Roll-ups* in Part 1 of this book for general information about roll-ups.

SCATTER CHARTS

Scatter charts show the relationships between two sets of values.

Creating a Scatter Chart

A scatter chart shows values for a succession of events or conditions.

1. Follow steps 1 through 4 in *Creating a Chart*, choosing **Scatter** in step 2 and choosing the first template in the Chart Types box.

2. Place data into the worksheet with the title, subtitle, footnotes, row title, column title, and Y-axis title in the standard positions assumed by Autoscan (see *Tagging Cells*).

3. Place the X-value and Y-value for the first point in cells C7 and D7, the values for the second point in cells C8 and D8, the values for the third point in cells C9 and D9, and so on.

4. Click the **Chart** icon to display the chart.

SCREEN

See *Screen* in Part 1 of this book for information about the parts of CorelCHART screens that are similar to CorelDRAW screens. Screen components unique to CorelCHART are described below.

Chart Screen

Figure 2.17 shows a typical CorelCHART chart screen. The screen components that are different from those in CorelDRAW screens are explained below.

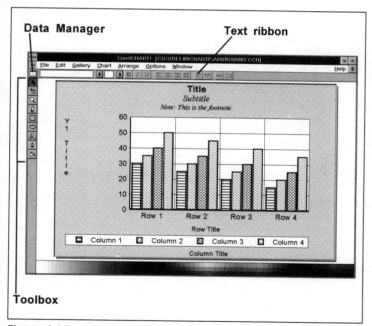

Figure 2.17: A typical CorelCHART chart screen

266   CorelCHART

Component	Purpose
Data Manager icon	With a chart displayed, click the Data Manager icon to access the data on which the chart is based.
Text ribbon	Provides access to the attributes of text on a chart.

Data Manager Screen

Figure 2.18 shows a typical CorelCHART Data Manager screen. The screen components that are significantly different from those in CorelDRAW screens are explained below.

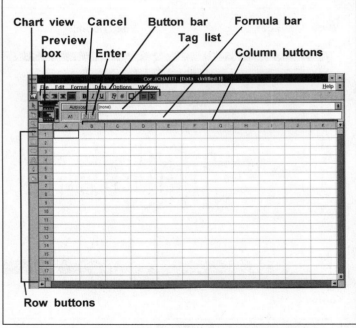

Figure 2.18: A typical CorelCHART Data Manager screen

Component	Purpose
Auto recalc button	Recalculates values displayed in cells.
Bold button	Changes selected text characters to bold.
Border format button	Displays Borders dialog box.
Button bar	Contains buttons used to format cells.
Cancel button	Deletes typed data (used before data is accepted into cell).
Chart view button	Displays the corresponding chart.
Column buttons	Each column is named alpha-betically in the header. The first 26 columns are named A through Z, the next 26 are named AA through AZ, and so on. There can be as many as 240 columns.
Current cell address box	Shows the column and row of the currently selected cell.
Enter button	Accepts typed data.
Font format button	Displays the Font dialog box.
Formula bar	Shows the contents of the active cell.
Grid button	Hides or shows the grid.
Italic button	Changes selected text characters to italic.
Numeric format button	Displays the Numeric Format dialog box.
Preview box	Shows a thumbnail preview of the current chart with currently selected section of chart highlighted.

Component	Purpose
Row buttons	Each row is named numerically in the header. Rows are numbered 1 through 2048.
Tag list box	Displays list of tags.
Toolbox	All toolbox icons are dimmed and not available when the Data Manager window is active.
Underline button	Underlines selected text characters.
Worksheet cells	This area contains the cells in which the Data Manager displays data.

SELECTING AND DESELECTING OBJECTS IN A CHART

You select chart objects in order to make changes to them. You can select individual objects or multiple objects.

Selecting Individual Objects

1. Use the **Pick** tool to point onto an object.

2. Click the mouse button. All previously selected objects are deselected and the object you are pointing onto is selected.

Selecting Multiple Objects

1. Use the **Pick** tool to point onto the first object.
2. Click the mouse button.
3. Point onto another object.
4. Hold down the **Shift** key while you click the mouse button.
5. Repeat steps 3 and 4 to select additional objects.

Deselecting All Selected Objects

1. Use the **Pick** tool to point onto a blank area of the Chart window.
2. Click the mouse button.

Deselecting Individual Objects

1. Point to the object you want to deselect.
2. Hold down the **Shift** key and click the mouse button.

SELECTING CELLS IN A WORKSHEET

You can select individual cells, rectangular blocks of cells, or scattered cells.

Selecting an Individual Cell

1. Point onto the cell.

2. Click the mouse. Dark lines outline the selected box, the
Reference box shows the cell's address, and the Formula
bar shows its contents.

Selecting a Block of Cells

1. Point to the cell at one corner of the rectangular block and
press the mouse button.

2. Drag to the cell at the opposite corner of the rectangular
block and release the mouse button. Dark lines outline the
first selected cell and the other cells in the block become
black with white lettering. The Reference box shows the
first cell's address, and the Formula bar shows its contents.

Selecting a Column or Row of Cells

To select a column or row of cells, click a column button to select a
column of cells, or click a row button to select a row of cells.

NOTES To select two or more adjacent columns or rows,
point onto the first column or row button, press the mouse button,
and drag to include additional columns or rows.

SHORTCUT KEYS

Most procedures in this book are described in terms of selecting from menus, but CorelCHART provides keyboard shortcuts to speed certain actions. Many of these shortcuts appear in dialog boxes. When you find yourself using a command often, look in the dialog box to learn its shortcut. Tables 2.2, 2.3, 2.4, and 2.5 list shortcuts for charts and worksheets.

Table 2.2: Function Key Shortcuts for Charts

Key	Action
F1	Accesses on-line Help
Shift+F1	Displays the help cursor with which you point at the part of the screen on which you want help
Ctrl+F1	Opens the Help Search dialog box
Shift+F4	Executes the Tile Vertically command
Alt+F4	Exits from CorelCHART
F5	Selects the Pencil tool
Shift+F5	Executes the Cascade command
F6	Selects the Rectangle tool
F7	Selects the Ellipse tool
F8	Selects the Text tool
F9	Toggles between Normal and Preview display modes
F11	Opens the Fountain Fill dialog box
Shift+F11	Opens the Uniform Fill dialog box

Table 2.3: Function Key Shortcuts for Worksheets

Key	Action
F1	Accesses Help
F2	Accesses Formula bar
F3	Executes Find Next
Shift+F4	Executes the Tile Vertically command
Alt+F4	Closes worksheet
Shift+F5	Executes the Cascade command
F6	Executes the Tile Horizontally command
F7	Toggles recalculation on and off
Shift+F7	Recalculates spreadsheet
F9	Displays preview of printed worksheet

Table 2.4: Speed Key Shortcuts for Charts

Key	Action
Ctrl+A	Executes the Align command
Ctrl+C	Executes the Copy command
Ctrl+D	Executes the Duplicate command
Ctrl+J	Opens the Preferences dialog box
Ctrl+N	Opens the New dialog box
Ctrl+O	Opens the Open Chart dialog box
Ctrl+P	Opens the Print dialog box
Ctrl+S	Saves the chart under the current file name
Ctrl+V	Executes the Paste command
Ctrl+W	Executes the Refresh Window command
Ctrl+X	Executes the Cut command
Ctrl+Z	Executes the Undo command

Table 2.4: Speed Key Shortcuts for Charts (continued)

Key	Action
Delete	Executes the Clear command
PageDown	Executes the Backward One command
Shift+PageDown	Executes the To Back command
PageUp	Executes the Forward One command
Shift+PageUp	Executes the To Front command

Table 2.5: Speed Key Shortcuts for Worksheets

Key	Action
Ctrl+A	Executes the Align command
Ctrl+B	Changes selected characters to bold
Ctrl+C	Executes the Copy command
Ctrl+F	Displays the Font dialog box
Ctrl+I	Changes selected characters to italic
Ctrl+N	Opens the New dialog box
Ctrl+O	Opens the Open Chart dialog box
Ctrl+P	Opens the Print dialog box
Ctrl+S	Saves the worksheet under the current file name
Ctrl+U	Underlines the selected characters
Ctrl+V	Executes the Paste command
Ctrl+X	Executes the Cut command
Ctrl+Z	Executes the Undo command
Delete	Executes the Clear command

SPECTRALLY MAPPED CHARTS

Spectrally mapped charts are used to display data that has spatial relationships.

Creating a Spectrally Mapped Chart

To create a spectrally mapped chart:

1. Follow steps 1 through 4 in *Creating a Chart*, choosing **Spectral Maps** in step 2 and choosing the only template in the Chart Types box.

2. Place data into the worksheet with the title, subtitle, footnotes, row title, column title, and Y-axis title in the standard positions assumed by Autoscan (see *Tagging Cells*).

3. Place the values to be mapped in an array of cells starting at cell C7.

4. Click the **Chart** icon to display the chart.

STACKING ORDER

You can use the Arrange menu to change the stacking order of objects in the annotation layer of a chart. See *Stacking Order* in Part 1 of this book for information.

STATISTICAL DATA

CorelCHART can calculate statistical data based on values in a series. Use the following steps:

1. Display a bar chart in the Chart window.

2. Use the **Pick** tool to point onto one member of a series.

3. Click the right mouse button. A Bar Riser pop-up menu appears.

4. With the left mouse button, click **Data Analysis**. The Data Analysis dialog box appears, as shown in Figure 2.19.

5. Click one or more buttons in the dialog box to select the statistical data you want.

6. Click **OK**. The chart reappears with a line representing each of the types of statistical data you selected in step 5.

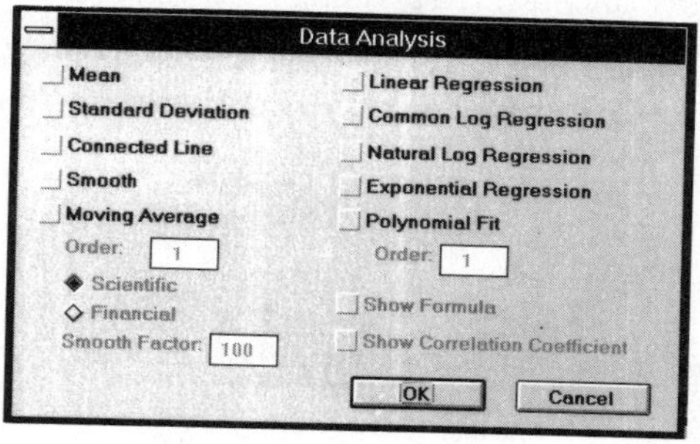

Figure 2.19: The Data Analysis dialog box

NOTES The lines representing the statistical data are in the same color as the series data in the chart. As these lines are not labeled, it is advisable to request only one type of statistical data at a time.

You can also display the Data Analysis dialog box from the Chart menu.

SWITCHING BETWEEN DATA MANAGER AND CHART VIEWS

In a Data Manager window, click the **Chart** icon at the left end of the Button bar to display the corresponding Chart window.

In a Chart window, click the **Data Manager** icon at the top of the toolbox to display the corresponding Data Manager window.

For information about how to display the corresponding Data Manager and Chart windows side-by-side on the screen, see *Tiling Views*.

TABLE CHARTS

CorelCHART presents data in tabular form.

Creating a Table Chart

A table chart presents tabular data.

1. Follow steps 1 through 4 in *Creating a Chart*, choosing **Table Charts** in step 2 and choosing any of the templates in the Chart Types box.

2. Place data into the worksheet with the title, subtitle, footnotes, row title, column title, and Y-axis title in the standard positions assumed by Autoscan (see *Tagging Cells*).

3. Place the data values in cells, starting at cell C7.

4. Click the **Chart** icon to display the chart.

Automatically Coloring Rows and Columns

To control how CorelCHART applies colors to a table chart:

1. With a table chart displayed in the Chart window, choose **Chart ➤ Divisions** to display the Table Chart Divisions dialog box.

2. In the top part of the dialog box, click one of the three buttons to choose **No Color Divisions** (to make all data cells the same color), **Color by Rows**, or **Color by Columns**.

3. If you selected either Color by Rows or Color by Columns, click the **Include Headers** check box in the top part of the dialog box to extend, or not extend, the coloring of data cells into the header.

4. In the bottom part of the dialog box, you can change the numbers in boxes to control how many adjacent rows or columns have the same color, and how many colors are used for these rows or columns.

Manually Coloring Rows and Columns

To choose individual colors for columns or rows:

1. Follow steps 1 and 2 above, selecting either **Color by Rows** or **Color by Columns**.

2. Click close to the edge of a cell. A colored outline appears around the cell. Make sure the entire cell is selected, not just the text or number inside it.

3. Click a color in the color palette at the bottom of the screen. The entire row (if you selected Color By Rows) or the entire column (if you selected Color by Columns) of cells changes to the new color.

NOTES   You can also select a color, or other fill, for cells from the Color dialog box. See *Coloring Chart Objects*.

Coloring Text and Numbers

Follow the three steps under "Manually Coloring Rows and Columns in a Table Chart" except, in step 2, click close to the center of a cell to select the text or number inside it.

Turning Grids and Borders On and Off

You can turn table borders, as well as the grid lines between cells, on or off. To do this:

1. With a table chart displayed in the Chart window, choose **Chart ➤ Grids & Borders**. The Grids and Borders dialog box appears.

2. Click the individual segments of the grids and borders image in the dialog box to change them from black to white. Those segments that are black exist in the table; those that are white are not shown in the table.

3. Click **OK**.

Changing Border and Grid Line Thickness

1. Click the border or a grid line to select it.

2. Click the **Outline** tool. A flyout appears.

3. Click one of the thickness icons to select one of ten preset line thicknesses. The border or grid line changes thickness.

Changing Border and Grid Line Color

1.   Click the border or on a grid line to select it.

2.   Click a color in the color palette. The selected line changes color.

TAGGING CELLS

Worksheet cells must be tagged so that CorelCHART knows which cells contain the chart title, subtitle, column headers, row headers, data, and so on.

You can either use Autoscan to apply tags automatically to cells, or you can tag cells manually.

Using Autoscan to Tag Cells

If you place data into the worksheet in relative positions corresponding to those defined below, and then click the Autoscan button, CorelCHART automatically assigns correct tags to cells.

- Place the title in cell A1.

- Place the subtitle in cell A2.

- Place the footnote text in cell A3.

- Place row headers in a column of cells, with the first in cell B7, the second in cell B8, and so on.

- Place the column headers in a row of cells, with the first in cell C6, the second in cell D6, and so on.

- Place the row title in cell A8.

- Place the column title in cell D5.

- Place the Y1 and Y2 titles in cells in rows 7 and 8, immediately to the right of the worksheet data.

- Place the worksheet data in a matrix of cells, starting at cell C7, and filling cells to the right and down.

Tagging Cells Manually

If the position of cells does not correspond to that assumed by Autoscan, you must tag cells manually. You can tag cells as:

- A title
- A subtitle
- A footnote
- Row headers
- Column headers
- A row title
- A column title
- Y1 title
- Y2 title
- Data range

To tag cells:

1. Select a cell or range of cells.

2. Open the tag list and click a tag for the selected cell or cells.

3. Repeat steps 1 and 2 to tag other cells.

NOTES When you apply a tag, the chart thumbnail at the top left of the worksheet shows the default position of that object in the chart.

To assign the Row Header tag, select any cell in the column that contains row headers. All cells in that column are tagged as row headers.

To assign the Column Header tag, select any cell in the row that contains column headers. All cells in that row are tagged as column headers.

Displaying Existing Tags

To determine what tag is currently applied to a cell, select the cell and the tag name appears in the tag box.

THREE-DIMENSIONAL CHARTS

CorelDRAW has extensive capabilities for creating and modifying three-dimensional charts.

Creating a Three-Dimensional Chart

To create a three-dimensional chart such as that shown in Figure 2.20, use the same procedure for creating a bar chart, except in step 2 click **3D-Riser**. See *Bar Charts*. Alternatively, you can change a chart of another type into a three-dimensional chart.

Changing the General Appearance

Use the techniques described in *Bar Charts* to make changes to a three-dimensional chart. In each case, use the **Pick** tool to point onto an object of the chart, and then press the right mouse button to see a pop-up menu. Choose what you want to change from the items in the pop-up menu.

Changing the Viewing Angle

You can change the viewing angle to enhance the visual appeal of a chart. In some cases, you might have to change the viewing angle

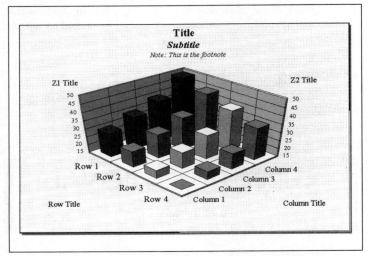

Figure 2.20: A typical 3D-Riser three-dimensional chart

to make certain objects of the chart visible. You can use the steps described here to select one of 16 preset viewing angles, or you can have more detailed control by using the 3D View tool. See *3D View Tool*. Do the following to select a preset viewing angle:

1. Display a three-dimensional chart in the Chart window.

2. Choose **Chart ➤ Preset Viewing Angles**. A flyout menu appears with a list of 16 preset viewing angles (Standard Angle is the default).

3. Click a different viewing angle. The chart is redrawn with the new viewing angle.

TOOLS

CorelCHART tools shown in Figure 2.21 are similar to CorelDRAW tools (see *Toolbox* in Part 1).

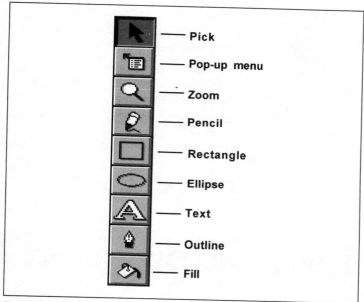

Figure 2.21: The CorelCHART toolbox

There is no Shape tool because you cannot shape objects in Corel-CHART as you can in CorelDRAW. You can create a shaped object in CorelDRAW and import it into a chart.

Use the tools to:

- Ellipse tool: Annotate a chart with ellipses and circles (see "Annotating a Chart with Rectangles and Ellipses" in *Annotating a Chart*)

- Fill tool: Modify a chart objects fill (see *Filling Chart Objects*)

- Outline tool: Modify the thickness and color of outlines of chart objects (see *Outlining Bars*).

- Pencil tool: Annotate a chart with lines, freehand curves, polygons, and arrows (see "Annotating a Chart with Lines, Polygons, Freehand Curves, and Arrows" in *Annotating a Chart*)

- Pick tool: Select, move, or change chart objects

- Pop-up Menu tool: Display and change attributes of chart objects (see "Context-Sensitive Menus" in *Menus*)

- Rectangle tool: Annotate a chart with rectangles and squares (see "Annotating a Chart with Rectangles and Ellipses" in *Annotating a Chart*)

- Text tool: Annotate a chart with text (see "Adding Text as an Annotation" in *Annotating a Chart*) and also to change the attributes of text that originated in the Data Manager (see *Bar Charts*)

- Zoom tool: Change the magnification of a chart (see *Viewing a Chart at Different Magnifications*)

UNDOING OPERATIONS

To cancel your most recent operation and restore your chart to its previous state, select **Edit ➤ Undo**.

VIEWING A CHART AT DIFFERENT MAGNIFICATIONS

Use the Zoom tool to view a chart at different magnifications.

1. Click the **Zoom** tool to display the Zoom flyout shown in Figure 2.22.

2. Click one of the six icons in the flyout.

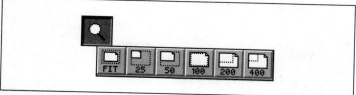

Figure 2.22: The Zoom flyout

Part 3

CorelPHOTO-PAINT

CorelPHOTO-PAINT, as its name suggests, combines painting and photographic retouching capabilities.

You can use CorelPHOTO-PAINT in many ways, such as:

- Creating original artwork using a variety of brush effects

- Modifying existing images that you have as clip art on disk or that you have scanned from other sources

- Capturing screen images and enhancing them

- Combining images from several sources

- Improving images and creating special effects by using retouching tools and filters

Images created or modified within CorelPHOTO-PAINT can be black and white, 8-bit grayscale, 8-bit color, or 24-bit color.

Versatile prepress tools, which CorelPHOTO-PAINT shares with CorelDRAW, allow you to optimize images for printing.

CANVAS

CorelPHOTO-PAINT is supplied with many canvases that you can use as backgrounds for images.

Choosing a Canvas

1. With an image open in its window, open the **Canvas** roll-up shown in Figure 3.1.

2. Click **Load** to open the Load a Canvas from Disk dialog box.

3. If there is no check mark in the Preview check box, click to place a check mark there.

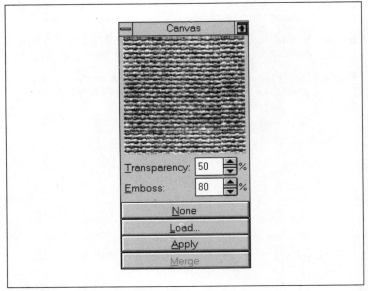

Figure 3.1: The Canvas roll-up

4. Click the name of a canvas in the File Name list box to see a preview.

5. Click **OK** to accept the canvas and show it in the roll-up.

6. Adjust the **Transparency** and **Emboss** percentages to obtain the desired effect (see note below).

7. Click **Apply** in the roll-up to apply the canvas to your images.

NOTES   If you do not click Merge in the roll-up, a canvas appears to overlay images. With a transparency of zero, a canvas is totally opaque, so that underlying images are invisible. With a transparency of 100, a canvas is almost totally transparent and is nearly invisible. Transparency values between 0 and 100 provide intermediate effects.

If you click Merge in the roll-up, images are drawn on top of the canvas.

A canvas can have an emboss factor in the range from 0 to 100 to provide effects ranging from flat to sculptured.

You can superimpose one canvas on top of another.

Changing the Transparency and Emboss Factors

To change the transparency or emboss factors, or both, open the **Canvas** roll-up, type or select new values, and click **Apply**.

CAPTURING A SCREEN

The screen capture facility packaged with CorelDRAW, CCAPTURE, is not a part of CorelPHOTO-PAINT, but it is described in the CorelPHOTO-PAINT section of the Corel *User's Manual* and is also included with CorelPHOTO-PAINT in this book.

CCAPTURE is similar to the Windows screen capture facility. Both can capture an entire Windows screen or just the active window in a Windows screen. In addition, CCAPTURE can capture an active window without its title bar. Windows Capture and CCAPTURE both place the captured image in the Clipboard.

Activating and Deactivating CCAPTURE

To activate CCAPTURE from the Windows Program Manager:

1. With the Windows Program Manager displayed, double-click the **Corel 4** icon to display the Corel 4 program group.

2. Double-click the **CCAPTURE** icon to activate CCAPTURE and display the Corel Screen Capture information box.

3. Click anywhere on the screen to remove the information box, leaving CCAPTURE active.

To deactivate CCAPTURE, repeat steps 1 and 2, but in step 2, click **Yes** in the dialog box to confirm that you want to deactivate CCAPTURE.

Capturing a Screen

With CCAPTURE activated:

1. In any Windows application, display the screen you want to capture.

2. To capture the entire screen, tap **Print Screen**. To capture the active Windows window, hold down the **Alt** key while you tap **Print Screen**. To capture the Client Area of the active window (the active window without its title bar), hold down **Alt** while you tap **Pause**. In each case, the cursor flashes briefly while the captured image is placed in the Clipboard.

Copying a Captured Image into Another Image

See *Importing Images*.

CLEARING A WINDOW

To clear a window to the current background color, choose **Edit ➤ Clear**.

CLONE TOOLS

The toolbox provides access to the three clone tools shown in Figure 3.2.

Use these tools to copy selected parts of an image. You can modify the copied image by using the Impressionist or Pointillist clone tool.

Cloning an Image

To selectively copy an area of an image into the same image or into another image:

1. Click the **Clone** tool in the toolbox and move the clone cursor into the work area.

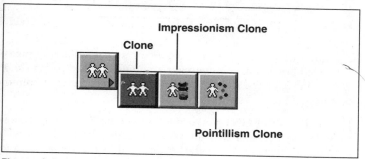

Figure 3.2: The three clone tools

2. Adjust the cloning effect in the Tool Settings roll-up (see *Tool Settings*).

3. Point to the center of the source area you want to clone and click the right mouse button. A flashing cross appears at that point.

4. Point to where you want the clone to appear, then press and hold down the left mouse button.

5. Drag to paint a clone of the first area. As you drag, the cross in the source area moves to show what you are cloning.

NOTES Hold down the Ctrl key while you drag to constrain the lines in vertical and horizontal directions. Press the spacebar to change directions. While you are cloning, you can reposition the source by pointing to the new position and clicking the right mouse button.

Cloning an Image with an Impressionism or Pointillism Effect

Select the **Impressionism** or **Pointillism** clone tool, and then use the steps in the preceding procedure.

COLOR TOLERANCE

Natural colors are not precise. Leaf-green, for example, is a range of colors, all green, but with varying amounts of other colors. Tolerance is a way of specifying how much a color can deviate from the optimum.

In CorelPHOTO-PAINT, you use color tolerance in such operations as replacing one color with another. The color you specify to be replaced, together with all other colors within the color tolerance range, is replaced.

To specify color tolerance:

1. Choose **Special ➤ Color Tolerance** to display the Color Tolerance dialog box.

2. If you want to have the same tolerance values for each of the three color components, leave the **Identical Values** check box checked; otherwise click the box to remove the check mark.

3. For each color component, choose or type negative and positive tolerance values. With Identical Values checked, any change you make to one value is automatically copied to all others.

4. Click **OK** to accept the new color tolerance values.

NOTES   Color tolerance is always specified in terms of the RGB color model.

By default, CorelPHOTO-PAINT has all six color tolerance values set to 15. However, any changes you make to these values apply throughout your current session and are still in effect after you close and reopen CorelPHOTO-PAINT. Always make sure the color tolerance values are correctly set before doing anything that makes use of these values.

COLORS

You can work with CorelPHOTO-PAINT in four color modes. The memory required for a one-inch square image at 300 dots per inch is as follows:

Color	Memory required
24-bit color (16,777,216 colors)	526 kilobytes
8-bit color (256 colors)	174 kilobytes

Color	Memory required
Grayscale (256 shades of gray)	174 kilobytes
Black and white	22 kilobytes

Choose a color mode that matches your requirement and is within the capabilities of your computer.

When you open a color image with less than 256 colors, it is automatically converted to 8-bit color; a 32-bit color image is automatically converted to 24-bit color. You can work with more colors than your hardware supports because CorelPHOTO-PAINT uses dithering to simulate colors not available on your monitor.

Selecting a Color Mode

Choose one of the four color modes when you create a new image (see *File Management*). *You can change an image's color mode (see "Available Colors" below).*

Available Colors

After you open an image or start a new one, you can open the Color Selection roll-up to see the available colors. When you are using black-and-white or grayscale mode, the roll-up shown in Figure 3.3 (left) shows the shades of gray available. When you are using 8-bit or 24-bit color mode, the roll-up shown in Figure 3.3 (right) shows the colors available.

Selecting Shades of Gray from the Palette

The sample box in the roll-up shows the currently selected outline (primary), fill (secondary), and background colors.

Grayscale and black-and-white modes both provide a choice of 256 shades of gray. Whereas grayscale provides true gray, black-and-white simulates gray by dithering. You select a level of gray by choosing from the palette or by specifying the Gray Level in the roll-up's text box.

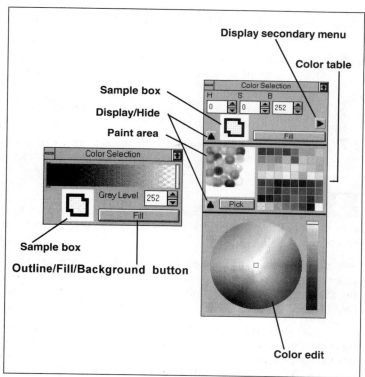

Figure 3.3: The Color Selection roll-up, for black-and-white and grayscale modes (left), for 8-bit or 24-bit color modes (right)

To select colors from the grayscale or black-and-white palette:

1. With an image open in black-and-white or grayscale mode, open the **Color Selection** roll-up.

2. Click the **Outline/Fill/Background** button until it displays Outline.

3. Point into the palette and click the shade of gray to use for the current outline. That shade appears as the outline shade in the sample box.

4. Click the **Outline/Fill/Background** button so that it displays Fill.

5. Point into the palette and click the shade of gray to use for the current fill. That shade appears as the fill shade in the sample box.

6. Click the **Outline/Fill/Background** button so that it displays Background.

7. Point into the palette and click the shade of gray to use for the current background. That shade appears as the background shade in the sample box.

NOTES   In steps 3, 5, and 7, instead of clicking a shade of gray in the palette, you can type or choose a shade in the Gray Level text box.

Selecting a background color does not affect the current background color; it only affects subsequent operations, such as using the Eraser tool or choosing Edit ➤ Clear, that use the background color.

The Color Selection roll-up is also used to select colors for gradient fills (see "Filling with a Gradient" in *Fill Tools*). In this case, the button alternates between From and To, and the sample box shows just two colors, the From color and the To color.

Selecting Colors from the Color Mode Palettes

Eight-bit color mode provides 256 colors. You select a color by choosing from the palette or by specifying the components of the color.

Follow the same general procedure as when selecting from the grayscale palette, with several additional options.

The roll-up is in three sections. You can display only the top (color-selection) section, the top section with the middle (color table) section, or the top, middle, and bottom (color-editing) section. Click the arrow icons at the bottom left corner of the top two sections to display or hide sections of the roll-up.

The top (color-selection) section of the roll-up allows you to select a color by specifying its components. You can work in RGB, CMYK, or HSB color models, and you can choose between the standard palette and the palette of colors used in the current image. To switch from one color model to another:

1. Click the right-pointing arrow at the right edge of the top section of the roll-up to display a secondary menu.

2. Click **RGB**, **CMYK**, or **HSB** according to which color model you want to use.

You know which color mode is currently selected by the designation of the color value boxes in the roll-up. If you choose the RGB or HSB color model, the top section of the roll-up has text boxes corresponding to the three color components. If you choose the CMYK color model, the top section shows text boxes corresponding to the four color components.

To switch between the standard color table and a color table that contains the colors used in the current image:

1. Click the right-pointing arrow at the right edge of the top section of the roll-up to display a secondary menu.

2. Click **Standard Palette** or **Image Palette**.

In addition to the standard color table, you can choose among several tables provided with CorelPHOTO-PAINT and custom tables you have created. To choose among tables:

1. Click the right-pointing arrow at the right edge of the top section of the roll-up to display a secondary menu.

2. Click **Load** to display the Load New Colors From Disk dialog box, which lists available color tables.

3. Click one of the table names, and then click **OK** to display the new table.

There are three ways to select outline, fill, and background colors:

- Click on colors in the color table
- Click on colors in the color-editing section of the roll-up
- Mix colors in the roll-up's paint area (see below)

Mixing Colors

The left side of the color table section of the roll-up is the paint area, which contains the basic colors in the color table. You can mix any of these colors to create new colors. To mix colors:

1. Click the **Pick** button under the paint area to change its name to Edit.

2. Point into the paint area. The cursor changes to the shape of a paint brush.

3. Use the brush to mix colors in the paint area.

4. Click the **Pick** button (now labeled Edit) again to restore the Pick label.

Creating a Custom Color Table

1. With the button under the paint area set to Pick, point onto a color in the paint area.

2. Press the mouse button, drag onto a square in the color table and release the mouse button to replace the original color in that square.

3. Repeat steps 1 and 2 to place additional colors in the color table.

4. Click the right-pointing arrow in the top section of the roll-up to display the secondary menu.

5. Click **Save Colors** to display the Save The Current Colors To Disk dialog box.

6. Type a name for the new color table and click **OK**.

Changing an Image
from One Color Mode to Another

CorelPHOTO-PAINT allows you to change an image from one color mode to another. To change modes:

1. Choose **Image ➤ Convert To**. A flyout menu appears listing the four modes, with the current mode dimmed.

2. Click on the mode you want to convert to. If you choose **24-bit Color, 256 Color,** or **Gray Scale,** another window appears to show your drawing in the new mode—providing your computer has sufficient memory. If there is not sufficient memory for the new mode, the message "Not Enough Memory for Operation" appears. If you choose **Black and White,** another flyout menu appears offering you the choice of **Line Art, Printer Halftone,** or **Screen Halftone**.

3. If you are converting to Black and White, click on the type of black-and-white image you want (see the notes below). A black-and-white version of the image appears in a separate window.

NOTES   When you convert from one color mode to another, two versions of the image appear in separate windows on your screen. You can use the normal Windows techniques to select the one you want to work with. Be careful to select the correct one when you save your image to a file.

To improve CorelPHOTO-PAINT's performance, consider converting to 24-bit color or grayscale modes before applying filters or working with the retouching tools.

When you convert an image to a mode with fewer colors than the original, some colors in the original are lost in the converted version. Changing the converted version back to the original mode does not restore the original colors.

When you convert an image to black and white, choose the Line Art variation for a high-contrast effect, choose the Printer Halftone variation if you plan to print on a laser printer, or choose the Screen Halftone variation for the best on-screen appearance.

Optimizing the Way Colors Are Displayed

CorelPHOTO-PAINT uses dithering to display more colors than your hardware supports. You may be able to improve the appearance of colors on your monitor by enabling Optimize Dithering. However, this does slow your system's response. A check mark to the left of Optimize Dithering in the Display menu shows that optimization is enabled. To turn it on or off, choose **Display ➤ Optimize Dithering**.

COPYING PART OF AN IMAGE

You can copy a part of an image to another place in the same image, to another image, or to another Windows application by way of the Clipboard. You can also copy a part of an image to a file.

Copying a Part of an Image to the Clipboard

1. Select a part of the image as a cutout. See *Selection Tools*.

2. Choose **Edit ➤ Copy** to copy the cutout to the Clipboard.

Pasting from the Clipboard into an Existing Image

1. Choose **Edit ➤ Paste** to display a menu that offers the choice of As New Selection or As New Image.

2. Click **As New Selection** to paste the contents of the Clipboard into the top left corner of the current image. If

necessary, CorelPHOTO-PAINT converts the color mode
of the image in the Clipboard to that of the current image.

NOTES The Clipboard Image is not scaled to fit into the
image window; only the part of it that will fit is shown. If necessary,
you can drag a handle to reduce the size of the image from the Clipboard and then move it so that it fits in the window.

Pasting from the Clipboard into a New Image

1. Choose **Edit ➤ Paste** to display a menu that offers the
   choice of As New Selection or As New Image.

2. Click **As New Image** to create a new image and paste the
   contents of the Clipboard into it.

Copying Part of a Image to a File

1. Select a part of the image as a cutout (see *Selection Tools*).

2. Choose **Edit ➤ Copy To File** to display the Copy a Picture
   to Disk dialog box.

3. Open the **List Files of Type** list box and click your choice
   of file format.

4. If the chosen file format has optional subformats, open the
   File Sub-Format list box and click your choice of subformat.

5. Open the **Directories** list box and select the directory and
   subdirectory into which you want to write the file.

6. Replace the asterisk in the File Name text box with the
   name for the file. Alternatively, to overwrite an existing
   file, click the file name in the File Name list box.

7. Click **OK** to write the cutout to disk.

DELETING PART OF AN IMAGE

1. Select a part of the image as a cutout (see *Selection Tools*).

2. Choose **Edit ➤ Clear** to delete the cutout, replacing it with the current background color.

NOTES If you choose Edit ➤ Clear without selecting a cutout, the window is cleared and replaced with the current background color.

DISPLAY TOOLS

The toolbox provides access to the three display tools shown in Figure 3.4.

Use these tools to change the magnification of an image and to scroll an image in its window.

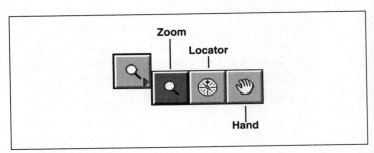

Figure 3.4: The three display tools

Changing Magnification

1. Click the **Zoom** tool icon in the toolbox and move the magnifier cursor to the center of the area of interest in the image.

2. Click the left mouse button to magnify the image, or the right mouse button to reduce it. The new magnification percentage is shown in the title bar.

Alternatively, you can choose **Display ➤ Zoom To Fit** to enlarge the image and its window as much as possible on your screen.

NOTES   To return to the normal size, point onto the Zoom tool icon in the toolbox and double-click. Alternatively, choose Display ➤ 100%.

When you increase magnification, the window remains the same size and only part of the image within the window is displayed. You can use the vertical and horizontal scroll bars to see any part of the image that is hidden.

When you reduce magnification to 50 percent or smaller, the window also becomes smaller. Subsequently, if you restore the image to normal size or larger, the windows remains at the reduced size and only part of the image is visible. To return the window to its original size, drag the window borders.

You can also choose Display ➤ Zoom to choose specific magnifications and reductions, and you can choose Display ➤ Zoom To Fit to resize an image to fit within the current window.

To edit individual pixels, use the Zoom tool to magnify the image to the maximum amount of 1600 percent (see *Pixel Editing*).

Locating a Point on a Duplicate Image

Use the Locator tool to point onto an image and locate the same point on a duplicate image. This is particularly useful when you work on details in a magnified image and want to retain a sense of the overall effect.

1. With duplicate copies (see *Duplicating a Picture*) of an image (one at a larger magnification than the other) on your screen, click the **Locator** tool icon in the toolbox (see *Display Tools*).

2. Point onto the less magnified copy of the image.

3. Click the mouse button. The same area on the more magnified image is displayed.

NOTES   See *Pixel Editing* for more information about using this technique.

Scrolling an Image

When only part of an image is visible within its window, you can scroll to make any part of the image visible.

1. Click the **Hand** tool icon in the toolbox (see *Display Tools*) and move the hand cursor into the work area.

2. Press and hold down the mouse button while you drag in any direction. As you drag, the hand cursor moves and the scroll boxes also move within the scroll bars.

3. Release the mouse button to redraw the image in a new position within its window.

Alternatively, use the standard Windows methods of scrolling with the scroll bars.

DRAWING TOOLS

The toolbox provides access to the three drawing tools shown in Figure 3.5.

Use these tools to draw straight lines, curves, and freehand shapes.

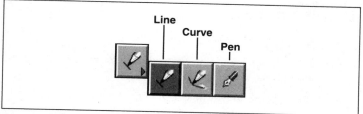

Figure 3.5: The three drawing tools

Drawing a Straight Line

To draw a straight line in the primary color:

1. Click the **Line** tool in the toolbox and move the cross cursor into the work area.

2. If necessary, adjust the size and shape of the tool in the Tool Settings roll-up (see *Tool Settings*).

3. Select a primary (outline) color (see *Colors*).

4. Point within a window to where you want the line to start, then press the mouse button and hold it down.

5. Drag to where you want the line to end, and then release the mouse button.

6. If you want to create another line, joined to the first, right-click the point where that line is to end.

7. Repeat step 6 to create more joined lines.

8. Select another tool to terminate drawing lines.

NOTES Hold down the Shift key while you drag to constrain the line to horizontal, vertical, or diagonal directions.

To draw several lines all radiating from the first point, use the preceding procedure, with the difference that you hold down the Ctrl key while clicking the right mouse button in step 6.

Drawing a Curve

To draw a curved line in the primary color:

1. Click the **Curve** tool in the toolbox and move the cross cursor into the work area.

2. If necessary, adjust the width of the tool in the Tool Settings roll-up (see *Tool Settings*).

3. Select a primary (outline) color (see *Colors*).

4. Point to where you want the curve to start, then press the mouse button and hold it down.

5. Drag to where you want the curve to end, and then release the mouse button. A straight line appears between the two points with square handles at the ends and two circular handles on the line.

6. To shape the line into a curve, point onto one of the circular handles, press the mouse button, and hold it down while you drag in any direction. The curve changes shape as you drag.

7. If necessary, repeat step 6 to drag the other circular handle.

8. Drag the square handles to move the endpoints of the curve.

9. If you want to add another curve, joined to the first, point to where you want that curve to end and press the right mouse button.

10. Repeat step 9 to create additional joined curves.

11. Paste the curve onto your drawing by clicking outside the curve.

12. Select another tool to terminate curve drawing.

NOTES   To draw several curves all radiating from the first point, follow steps 1 through 11, but hold down the Ctrl key while pressing the right mouse button in step 9.

Drawing a Freehand Shape

To draw freehand shapes in the outline or fill color:

1. Click the **Pen** tool in the toolbox and move the pen cursor into the work area.

2. If necessary, adjust the size and shape of the Pen in the Tool Settings roll-up.

3. Select an outline or fill color (see *Colors*).

4. Point on your drawing to where you want to start painting, press the left mouse button, and drag to draw a freehand shape in the outline color, or press the right mouse button to draw to shape in the fill color.

5. Release the mouse button.

6. Select another tool to terminate drawing freehand shapes.

DUPLICATING AN IMAGE

Duplicate screen images are useful when you are working on the detail in a magnified image, but need to see the effect of what you are doing within the context of a larger area. You can create up to 20 duplicates of one image.

To create a duplicate image, choose **Window ➤ Duplicate**.

After you have created a duplicate, you can drag its image so that you can see the duplicate and the original at the same time. You can use the Zoom tool to display duplicates at various magnifications. Any change you make to the original is also displayed in the duplicates.

EYEDROPPER TOOL

The Eyedropper tool allows you to pick up a color and use it some-
where else in an image.

Picking up a Color

To select a color in an image and make it the current outline (primary), fill (secondary), or background color:

1.   Click the **Eyedropper** tool icon in the toolbox.

2.   Point onto the color you want to select in the image.

3.   Click the left mouse button to make the color the current
         primary color, the right mouse button to make the color
         the current secondary color, or hold down the Ctrl key
         while you click the left mouse button to make the color
         the current background color.

NOTES   It is not necessary to have the Color Selection
roll-up open while you pick a color. However, if the roll-up is open,
its sample box provides visual confirmation that you have picked
the intended colors.

FILE MANAGEMENT

CorelPHOTO-PAINT stores images as files on your hard disk. It
can read and write files in many formats (see the Appendix).

Up to eight separate files can be open simultaneously.

Opening a New Image

1. Choose **File ➤ New** to display the Create a New Picture. The dialog box shows the size, resolution, and mode of the most recently open image, as well as the amount of memory available and the memory required for the new image.

2. To change the units in which the size of the new image are specified, open the **Units** list box and select the measurement units.

3. Select or type the **Width**, **Height**, and **Resolution** of the new image.

4. Open the **Mode** list box and select among the Black-and-White, 256-Color, Gray Scale, and 24-Bit Color modes.

5. Compare the Memory required shown in the dialog box with the Memory available. See the notes below for suggestions about what to do if insufficient memory is available.

6. If sufficient memory is available, click **OK** to display a new window with the provisional name New-1.PCX (a different number is used if new images have already been opened).

 NOTES If insufficient memory is available, try the following:

• Make more memory available by closing other images that are open, by closing other Windows applications (including any that are minimized) that are running, and by removing terminate-and-stay-resident (TSR) programs that are occupying memory.

• Reduce the size of the image.

• Change to a mode that uses less memory.

If none of these suggestions is possible or acceptable, you need to increase the amount of virtual memory available to CorelPHOTO-PAINT or install more memory in your computer.

While you have the Create a New Picture dialog box open, select various image sizes and modes to gain an understanding of their memory requirements. This will show you whether your computer has sufficient memory for the types of images you intend to create.

Opening an Existing Image

For information about opening an existing image see "Opening an Existing File" in *File Management* in Part 1 of this book.

Saving an Image

For information about saving a file see "Saving a File with its Existing Name" and "Saving a File with a Specified Name" in *File Management* in Part 1 of this book.

By default, CorelPHOTO-PAINT saves files in the PCX format. If you wish, you can choose an alternative format by choosing File ➤ Save As, opening the List Files of Type list box, and clicking on a different format (see the Appendix for a list of available file formats).

NOTES If you have opened the same file two or more times to simultaneously display it in different modes, be careful to save the correct version.

FILL TOOLS

The toolbox provides access to the four fill tools shown in Figure 3.6.

Use these tools to fill enclosed areas with colors, patterns, gradients, and textures.

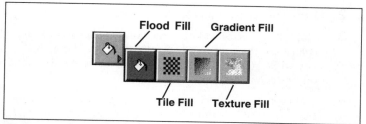

Flood Fill   Gradient Fill

Tile Fill   Texture Fill

Figure 3.6: The four fill tools

Filling with Color

To fill an enclosed area with the primary color:

1. Click the **Flood Fill** tool in the toolbox and move the flood fill cursor into the work area.

2. Select a fill or outline color (see *Colors*).

3. Place the tip of the pouring paint extending down from the bottom right of the flood fill cursor inside the area to be filled, and left-click to fill with the fill color or right-click to fill with the outline color.

NOTES   If the area is not completely enclosed, the fill color will leak into other parts of the image. If this happens, choose Edit► Undo to remove the fill.

To correct the problem, either use the Pen tool to close the gaps through which the leak occurred, or adjust the Color Tolerance values to change the range of colors considered to enclose the area.

Copying a Fill from One Area to Another

You can use a primary or secondary color in one part of an image as a fill for another part. To use an existing color as a fill:

1. Click the **Flood Fill** tool in the toolbox and move the flood fill cursor into the work area.

2. Point onto an existing color in the image.

3. Hold down the **Shift** key while you left-click to pick that color to be the current fill color, or hold down the **Shift** key while you right-click to make that current the current outline color.

4. Follow steps 2 and 3 in the preceding procedure to apply the current fill or outline color to a new area.

Filling with a Tiled Pattern

To fill an enclosed area with a repeating pattern:

1. Click the **Tile Fill** tool in the toolbox and move the tile cursor into the work area.

2. Open the **Fill Settings** roll-up.

3. Click **Load Tile** to display the Load a Tile Pattern from Disk dialog box.

4. Click the name of a file pattern in the File Name list box. If the Preview check box is checked, a preview of the selected tile pattern is displayed.

5. Click **OK** to accept the tile pattern and display it in the roll-up.

6. Place the tip of the arrow extending from the bottom right of the tile cursor inside the area to be filled, and click the mouse button.

Filling with a Gradient

To fill an enclosed area with a gradient (fountain fill) in which the color shades from one color to another:

1. Click the **Gradient Fill** tool in the toolbox and move the gradient cursor into the work area.

2. Open the **Color Selection** roll-up and select a From color and a To color (see *Colors*).

3. Open the **Fill Settings** roll-up and select a type of gradient (see the notes below).

4. Place the tip of the arrow extending down from the bottom right of the gradient cursor inside the area to be filled, and click the mouse button.

5. To change the effect of the gradient fill, choose **Edit ➤ Undo** to remove the fill, make changes in the roll-up, and then repeat step 4.

NOTES With the Gradient tool selected, the Fill Settings roll-up offers a choice between linear, rectangular-radial, or circular-radial gradients. The roll-up shows an example of the selected type of gradient after you click one of the three buttons.

You can change the effect of each type of fill by pointing onto the example in the roll-up and dragging. You can also change the effect by dragging the balance selector to the left or right.

Filling with a Texture

To fill an enclosed area with a texture:

1. Click the **Texture** tool in the toolbox and move the texture cursor into the work area.

2. Open the Fill Settings roll-up and click **Create Texture** to display the Texture Fill dialog box.

3. Click the name of a texture in the Texture List box to see a preview of that texture.

4. Modify the texture as necessary (see "Filling an Object with a Bitmap Texture" in *Filling an Object* in Part 1 of this book).

5. Click **OK** to accept the texture and display it in the roll-up.

6. Place the tip of the line extending down from the bottom right of the texture cursor inside the area to be filled, and click the mouse button.

FILTERING AN IMAGE

Filters allow you to enhance images and create special effects in a complete image or in a cutout. A filter acts on the cutout or, if no cutout is selected, on the entire image.

When using filters, you get the best results with 24-bit color and grayscale modes.

Using Image Filters

All image filters are used in a similar manner. As an example, to control the brightness and contrast of an image:

1. With the image displayed in a window, choose **Image ➤ Color ➤ Brightness and Contrast** to display the Brightness and Contrast dialog box.

2. Select or type a value in one of the text boxes and click **Preview** to see how the change affects the image.

3. Repeat step 2 as often as necessary to optimize the image.

4. Click **OK** to accept the modified image.

NOTES   The various filters allow you to create many specialized effects. In each case, you can use controls to vary the effect. To see what these filters can do, open a 24-bit color image and be prepared to spend many hours in experimentation. Table 3.1 lists filters that are used in a similar manner as the Brightness and Contrast filter.

Table 3.1: The CorelPHOTO-PAINT Filters

Filter	Command to Access	Purpose
Brightness and Contrast	Image ➤ Color ➤ Brightness and Contrast	Controls overall brightness and contrast
Threshold	Image ➤ Color ➤ Threshold	Creates a high-contrast image
Gamma	Image ➤ Color ➤ Gamma	Controls the mid-tone detail as displayed on screen
Hue and Saturation	Image ➤ Color ➤ Hue and Saturation	Controls the hue and saturation of colors without affecting brightness
Sharpen	Image ➤ Sharpen ➤ Sharpen	Sharpens edges
Enhance Detail	Image ➤ Sharpen ➤ Enhance Detail	Enhances detail selectively
Unsharp Mask	Image ➤ Sharpen ➤ Unsharp Mask	Controls edge detail
Adaptive Unsharp Mask	Image ➤ Sharpen ➤ Adaptive Unsharp Mask	Selectively controls edge detail
Smooth	Image ➤ Smooth ➤ Smooth	Smooths differences between adjacent pixels
Soften	Image ➤ Smooth ➤ Soften	Softens image without losing detail
Diffuse	Image ➤ Smooth ➤ Diffuse	Scatters colors as if the image is viewed through ground glass

Table 3.1: The CorelPHOTO-PAINT Filters (continued)

Filter	Command to Access	Purpose
Blend	Image ➤ Smooth ➤ Blend	Smooths and softens colors
Color/Gray Map	Image ➤ Tone ➤ Color/Gray Map	Modifies the effect of lighting an image
Equalize	Image ➤ Tone ➤ Equalize	Stretches the tonal contrast
Pointillism	Effects ➤ Artistic ➤ Pointillism	Creates pointillism effect
Impressionism	Effects ➤ Artistic ➤ Impressionism	Creates an impressionism effect
Edge Emphasis	Effects ➤ Edge ➤ Edge Emphasis	Emphasizes edges
Edge Detect	Effects ➤ Edge ➤ Edge Detect	Adds outline effect
Contour	Effects ➤ Edge ➤ Contour	Creates a high-contrast effect
Outline	Effects ➤ Edge ➤ Outline	Outlines an image
Emboss	Effects ➤ Emboss	Creates an embossed effect
Invert	Effects ➤ Invert	Inverts colors
Jaggie Despecle	Effects ➤ Jaggie Despecle	Randomly scatters colors
Motion Blur	Effects ➤ Motion Blur	Creates motion effect
Add Noise	Effects ➤ Noise ➤ Add Noise	Creates granular effect
Add More Noise	Effects ➤ Noise ➤ Add More Noise	Creates increased granular effect

Table 3.1: The CorelPHOTO-PAINT Filters (continued)

Filter	Command to Access	Purpose
Maximum Noise	Effects ➤ Noise ➤ Maximum	Lightens image by reducing contrast between adjacent pixels
Median Noise	Effects ➤ Noise ➤ Median	Reduces grainy appearance of image
Minimum Noise	Effects ➤ Noise ➤ Minimum	Darkens image by adjusting pixel values
Pixelate	Effects ➤ Pixelate	Creates block-line effect
Posterize	Effects ➤ Posterize	Creates posterized effect
Psychedelic	Effects ➤ Psychedelic	Randomly changes colors
Solarize	Effects ➤ Solarize	Selectively inverts colors

HELP

See *Help* in Part 1 of this book for more information. Shift+F1 and Ctrl+F1 are not available in CorelPHOTO-PAINT Help.

HELP BAR

The help bar at the bottom of the work area, which serves the same purpose as the status bar in CorelDRAW, provides information about the currently selected tool and operation.

The help bar shows

- Current cursor position

- Start position and delta (distance from start position) of the image currently being drawn or effecting being created

- Name of the tool icon currently under the cursor

Positions in CorelPHOTO-PAINT are measured from the top left corner of the drawing area. By default, measurements are in pixels, but you can choose other units (see *Preferences*).

IMAGE INFORMATION

To display information about the current image, choose **Image ➤ Info** to display a dialog box showing the image's:

- File name

- Width and height

- Horizontal and vertical resolution

- Color mode

- Memory occupied

- File format and subformat

For additional information, choose **Special ➤ System Info** to display the Current Operating Statistics dialog box, which shows

- Resolution, size, and color mode of the current image

- Size and color mode of screen

- Printer type and resolution

- Memory installed and remaining

- Disk space installed and remaining

IMPORTING AN IMAGE

CorelPHOTO-PAINT can import images in many formats.

Importing an Image from a File

To import an image from a file into the current image:

1. With an image displayed, choose **Edit ➤ Paste From File** to display the Paste a Picture from Disk dialog box.

2. Select a directory and then click on a file name to select the image in that file.

3. Click **OK** to insert the image into the top left corner of the current image.

NOTES   If an imported 8-bit color image contains colors that are not in the current image's palette, the imported image's colors change. To retain the imported image's colors, change the existing image's palette before importing the new image.

Importing an Image from the Clipboard

You can import an image from the Clipboard into an existing CorelPHOTO-PAINT image, or you can use an image in the Clipboard to create a new CorelPHOTO-PAINT image.

For information about importing an image from the Clipboard into an existing CorelPHOTO-PAINT image, see *Copying Part of an Image.*

MAIN MENU

See *Commands* in on-line Help for a summary of information about Main menu items and roll-ups.

MASKING AN IMAGE

Masks are a new feature of this version of CorelPHOTO-PAINT. You can use masks to protect the background area of an image from changes made to other areas. Use the Selection tools to create a mask (see *Selection Tools*).

You can

- Choose Mask ➤ Select All to select an entire image as a mask
- Choose Mast ➤ Clear Mask to clear the mask
- Choose Mast ➤ Crop To Mask to create a new image consisting only of the masked area

PAINTING TOOLS

The toolbox provides access to the six painting tools shown in Figure 3.7.

Use these tools to create new images and to add effects to existing images.

Painting an Image

To paint in the outline or fill color:

1. Click the **Paint Brush** tool in the toolbox and move the brush cursor into the work area.

2. Select a outline color (see *Colors*).

3. Adjust the brush in the Tool Settings roll-up (see *Tool Settings*).

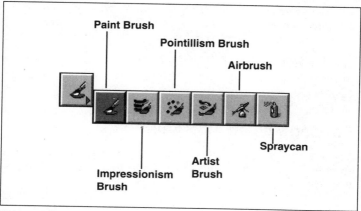

Figure 3.7: The six painting tools

4. Point onto your drawing to where you want to start painting, press the left mouse button, and drag to paint an area with the outline color, or press the right mouse button to pain with the fill color.

NOTES Drag the paint brush fairly slowly so that you do not get ahead of the image as it appears on the screen.

Painting with an Impressionist Brush

Use the same procedure as when painting with the paint brush. The effect varies according to your drawing speed. Slower painting results in heavier lines.

You can create many different effects with this tool by opening the lower part of the Tool Settings roll-up and changing parameters (see *Tool Settings*).

Painting with a Pointillism Brush

Use the same procedure as when painting with the paint brush. The effect varies according to your drawing speed. Slower painting results in more closely placed dots.

You can create many different effects with this tool by opening the lower part of the Tool Settings roll-up and changing parameters (see *Tool Settings*).

Painting with an Artist Brush

Use this brush to give an effect similar to painting with oils. Choose from eight variations of this effect in the Tool Settings dialog box (see *Tool Settings*).

Airbrushing an Image

Use this brush to give an airbrush effect. You can modify the effect by setting parameters in the Tool Settings dialog box (see *Tool Settings*).

As with an actual airbrush, the image has a higher density if you move the tool slowly.

Spraying an Image

Use the Spraycan tool to splatter an image with the current fill or outline color. Press the left mouse button to spray with the outline color or the right mouse button to spray with the fill color.

PIXEL EDITING

You can magnify an image to the extent that you can see individual pixels and change their color. To prepare to edit an area of a drawing:

1. Display an image at 100-percent size in its window.

2. Choose **Window ➤ Duplicate** to create a duplicate of the image.

3. Choose **Display ➤ Zoom To Fit** to enlarge the duplicate image window as much as possible.

4. Choose **Display ➤ Zoom ➤ 1600%** to display a part of the duplicate at 1600-percent magnification with the individual pixels showing.

5. Drag the duplicate window so that it does not cover the original 100-percent image.

6. Select the **Locator** tool, and click on the area in the 100-percent image that you want to edit to show the same area much enlarged in the 1600-percent image.

Now, you can edit the selected area on a pixel-by-pixel basis. For example, to change the color of a pixel to the color of an adjoining pixel:

1. Select the **Eyedropper** tool.

2. Click the adjoining pixel to pick up its color as the outline color.

3. Select the **Pen** tool and set its width to 1 in the Tool Settings roll-up.

4. Click on the pixel you want to change to give it the new outline color.

All changes made to the enlarged image occur also in the 100-percent image. Although you cannot generally see the effect of changes to individual pixels in the 100-percent image, you can see the cumulative effect of changing several pixels.

NOTES   The above is just one example of how you can edit an enlarged image. Some of the other editing techniques you can use are as follows:

- Enlarge the Pen tool and change its size to change the color of more than one pixel at a time.

- Right-click with the Pen tool to change the color of a pixel to the fill color.

- Use the Eraser tool to replace a pixel's color with the current background color.

While you are using any tool, hold down the Ctrl key to constrain its movement to only the horizontal or vertical directions. While using the tool, press the spacebar to change between horizontal and vertical movements.

PREFERENCES

You can make changes in the way CorelPHOTO-PAINT works to suit your preferences.

Choosing What Is Initially Displayed

To choose what is displayed when you open CorelPHOTO-PAINT:

1. Choose **Special ➤ Preferences** to display the Preferences dialog box.

2. Open the **At Startup** list box, click one of the four options, and click **OK**.

 NOTES   The choices are

- Displaying the About information screen for a few seconds
- Displaying the Create a New Picture dialog box
- Displaying the Load a Picture from Disk dialog box
- Displaying the Main menu with nothing selected

Choosing Measurement Units

1. Choose **Special ➤ Preferences** to display the Preferences dialog box.

2. Open the **Units** list box, click one of the six measurement units, and click **OK**.

NOTES   You can choose inches, millimeters, centimeters, points, picas and points, or pixels as measurement units. A point is $\frac{1}{72}$ of an inch; a pica is $\frac{1}{6}$ of an inch. A pixel is one dot on your monitor screen.

PRINTING AN IMAGE

CorelPHOTO-PAINT can print an image using any printer installed under Windows.

Setting Up a Printer

Use a similar method to set up a printer in CorelPHOTO-PAINT as in CorelDRAW (see *Printing a Drawing* in Part 1).

Calibrating a Printer

You can calibrate a printer so that the tonal values in a printed image are satisfactory.

1. Create an image that has a typical range of tones, print it, and compare the printed image with the screen image.

2. Choose **File ➤ Print ➤ Calibrate** to display the Print Calibration dialog box, which shows a calibration curve that relates the density of the printed image for 11 tones ranging from 0 to 100 percent.

3. Adjust the master calibration curve either by dragging the points on the curve or by changing the density values in the text boxes.

4. If necessary, separately select the red, green, and blue calibration curves, and make adjustments to those curves.

5. With any calibration curve displayed, click Print to print sample tones in 10-percent steps.

6. Click **Save** to save the printer calibration with an appropriate name.

NOTES If you use various printers, calibrate each printer separately.

Selecting a Printer Calibration Curve

After you have calibrated your printers, select the appropriate calibration curve before printing.

1. Choose **File ➤ Print ➤ Calibration** to display the Print Calibration dialog box.

2. Click **Load** to display the Load Curve dialog box which lists the available printer calibration curves.

3. Click one of the calibration curve names, and then click **Load** to display that curve in the Print Calibration dialog box.

4. Click **Cancel** to leave the Print Calibration dialog box.

Printing an Image

Options in the Print dialog box allow you to control the position and size of the image on the printed page and to make many other choices about the way the image is printed, including printing color separations. To print an image:

1. Choose **File ➤ Print ➤ Print** to display the Print dialog box.

2. Make any necessary changes in the Location, Units, and scale sections of the dialog box.

3. Click **Options**, and make choices among the options (see "Printing Options" in *Printing a Drawing*, Part 1 of this book). Use the choices here to print color or grayscale separations.

4. Click **OK** to return to the Print dialog box, and then click **Color** to display the SmartColor dialog box, which is similar to the Color dialog box in CorelDRAW.

5. Click **OK** to return to the Print dialog box, then click **OK** to print the image.

NOTES From within CorelPHOTO-PAINT you can access the same prepress tools as in CorelDRAW. Choose File ➤ Prepress to access the Prepress Tools dialog box.

BOX, ELLIPSE, AND POLYGON TOOLS

The toolbox provides access to the eight tools shown in Figure 3.8.

Use these tools to draw hollow or filled boxes, polygons, and ellipses.

Drawing a Hollow Rectangle

To draw an unfilled rectangle or square in the outline color:

1. Click the **Hollow Box** tool in the toolbox and move the cross cursor into the work area.

2. Adjust the width of the outline in the Tool Settings roll-up.

3. Select an outline color (see *Colors*).

4. Point to where you want one corner of the rectangle to be, then press the mouse button and hold it down.

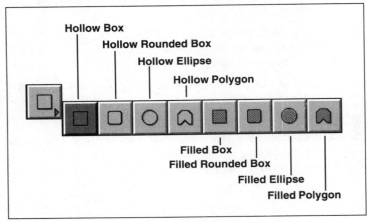

Figure 3.8: The eight box, ellipse, and polygon tools

5. Drag to where you want the opposite corner of the rectangle to be, then release the mouse button.

NOTES Hold down the Ctrl key while you drag to constrain the box to a square.

Drawing a Hollow Rectangle with Rounded Corners

To draw an unfilled rectangle or square with rounded corners:

1. Click the **Hollow Rounded Box** tool in the toolbox and move the cross cursor into the work area.

2. Follow steps 2 through 5 in "Drawing a Hollow Rectangle" above.

NOTES Hold down the Ctrl key while you drag to constrain the box to a square.

Drawing a Hollow Ellipse

To draw an unfilled ellipse or circle in the outline color:

1. Click the **Hollow Ellipse** tool in the toolbox and move the cross cursor into the work area.

2. Adjust the width of the outline in the Tool Settings roll-up.

3. Select an outline color (see *Colors*).

4. Point to where you want the center of the ellipse to be, then press the mouse button and hold it down.

5. Drag away from the center in any direction to create the ellipse, then release the mouse button.

6. To draw another ellipse with the same center point, press and hold down the right mouse button while you drag to create the ellipse.

NOTES   Hold down the Ctrl key while you drag to constrain the ellipse to a circle.

Drawing a Hollow Polygon

To draw a hollow polygon with up to 200 sides in the outline color:

1.   Click the **Hollow Polygon** tool in the toolbox and move the cross cursor into the work area.

2.   Adjust the width of the outline Tool Settings roll-up.

3.   Select an outline color (see *Colors*).

4.   Point to where you want the polygon to start, then click the mouse button.

5.   Point to where you want the first side to end, then click the mouse button.

6.   Point to where you want the next side to end, then click the mouse button.

7.   Repeat step 6 as many times as necessary to draw the remaining sides, but double-click the endpoint of the next-to-last side. Double-clicking completes that side and also closes the polygon by joining that point to the polygon's starting point.

Drawing a Filled Rectangle, Ellipse, or Polygon

Draw filled rectangles, ellipses, and polygons in the same way as hollow shapes, using the equivalent filled tool. The shape is filled with the current fill color.

RESAMPLING AN IMAGE

You can resample an image to create a copy with a different size
and resolution from the original.

Creating a Resampled Image

1. Choose **Image ➤ Resample** to display the Resample Image dialog box. The top left part of the dialog box shows
   the width, height, and size of the original image.

2. Define the size of the copy in either the Resample By Size
   section or the Resample By % section of the dialog box. If
   you leave the Maintain Aspect check box checked, you
   only need to specify the new width. If you click the check
   box to remove the check mark, you can change the aspect
   ratio of the copy.

3. Open the **Process** list box and check the process you want
   to use (see the Notes below).

4. Change the value in the Resolution text box, if required.
   The value here determines the relationship between pixels
   and inches in the printed image; it does not affect the
   screen image.

5. Click **OK** to create the copy.

 NOTES   Choose between the four processes:

Process	Effect
Anti-alias	Removes jaggies from the copy
Average	Creates a smooth picture by averaging duplicated pixels

Process	Effect
Stretch	Creates a rough image by stretching duplicated pixels
Truncate	Creates a rough image by eliminating overlapping pixels

Anti-alias gives the optimum effect in many circumstances. For the most satisfactory results, examine the result of each process in the printed version of your work.

When you resample an 8-bit color image, the resampled copy is a 24-bit image.

RETOUCHING TOOLS

The toolbox provides access to the seven retouching tools shown in Figure 3.9.

Use these tools to make subtle changes to images. You can also use filters to retouch images (see *Filtering Images*).

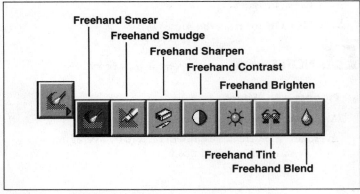

Figure 3.9: The seven retouching tools

The effects of the retouching tools are as follows:

Tool	Effect
Freehand Smear	Smears colors by fading colors into each other
Freehand Smudge	Smudges colors by randomly mixing dots
Freehand Sharpen	Sharpens contrast between colors
Freehand Contrast	Adjusts local contrast
Freehand Brighten	Changes color intensity
Freehand Tint	Tints the image with the current color
Freehand Blend	Smoothes areas

Retouching an Image

1. Select one of the retouching tools in the toolbox and move the cursor into the work area.

2. Adjust the effect of the tool in the Tool Settings roll-up (see *Tool Settings*).

3. Point onto the area of the image that you want to retouch, then press and hold down the mouse button.

4. Drag over the area to be retouched.

NOTES   While you are using a retouching tool, hold down the Ctrl key to constrain its movement to only the horizontal or vertical directions. While using the tool, press the spacebar to change between horizontal and vertical movements.

ROLL-UPS

See *Roll-ups* in Part 1 for general information.

334 CorelPHOTO-PAINT

CorelPHOTO-PAINT has four roll-ups:

- Canvas: See *Canvas*.
- Color Selection: See *Colors*.
- Fill Settings: See *Fill Settings*.
- Tool Settings: See *Tool Settings*.

To display or hide roll-ups:

1. Choose **Display** to display the Display menu, in which currently displayed roll-ups are checked.

2. Click the name of a roll-up to display or hide it.

 NOTES Choose Display ➤ Hide All to hide all roll-ups.

SCANNING

From within CorelPHOTO-PAINT, you can calibrate a scanner and scan images.

Calibrating a Scanner

You can calibrate a color or grayscale scanner to control the relationship between tones in the image being scanned and tones in the scanned image. To calibrate a scanner:

1. Choose **File ➤ Acquire Image ➤ Calibrate** to display the Scanner Calibration dialog box.

2. Click **Color** or **Gray** to specify the type of scanner.

3. Click **Modify** if you want to modify an existing scanner calibration file, or click **New** to create a new scanner calibration file.

4. If you chose Modify in step 3, click the name of the calibration file you want to modify.

5. Click **Master**, **Red**, **Green**, or **Blue** (only Master for a gray-scale scanner) according to which tonal range you want to change.

6. Drag the dots on the tonal range curve to change the calibration.

7. Repeat steps 5 and 6 for other tonal ranges.

8. Click **Save**, and then type a name for the new calibration curve.

9. Click **Save** to save the curve.

Scanning an Image

1. Choose **File ➤ Acquire Image ➤ Acquire** to display the Corel Image Source dialog box, in which you can choose the area to be scanned, the resolution, and other parameters according to the scanner you are using.

2. Respond to the choices in the dialog box.

3. Click **OK** to scan the image.

SCREEN

The normal screen is shown in Figure 3.10. Most of the screen components are similar to those in the CorelDRAW screen (see *Screen* in

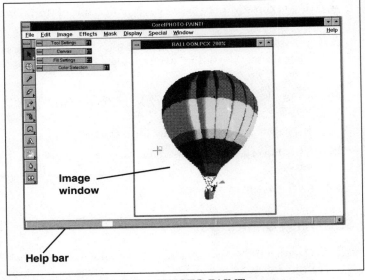

Figure 3.10: A typical CorelPHOTO-PAINT screen

Part 1). Components that are different or in addition to those in the CorelDRAW screen are as follows:

Component	Purpose
Image window	A window in which an image is created or edited. As many as eight windows can be on the screen, but only one window is active at a time.
Help bar	Identifies tools and provides information about the current image. Similar to the CorelDRAW status bar.

Displaying a Full-Screen Image

You can display a full-screen view of an image. To do this, choose **Display ➤ Full Screen Preview** or press **F9**. To return to the normal display, press **Esc**.

Maximizing the Work Area

You can maximize the work area by removing the title bar and menu bar from the screen. To do this, choose **Display ➤ Maximize Work Area**. To return to the normal display, click the button at the right end of the help bar.

SELECTION TOOLS

The toolbox provides access to the four cutout selection tools shown in Figure 3.11.

Use these tools to select an area of an image known as a cutout. You can stretch, shrink, move, copy, cut, delete, tilt, rotate, flip, invert, and outline a cutout; you can paste a cutout into another image; and you can save a cutout as a file. You can also apply filters to a cutout and use it to define the area for a mask.

The cutouts selected by the four tools are

- Box Selection: Rectangular area

- Lasso: Irregularly shaped area

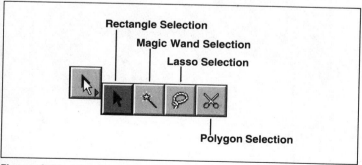

Figure 3.11: The four selection tools

- Polygon: Area bounded by straight edges

- Magic Wand: Area containing similar colors

After selection, a cutout is shown by a dashed outline within a rectangular marquee with handles (known as the gadget box), as shown in Figure 3.12, in which the lasso tool has been used to select the leaf as a cutout.

Creating a Rectangular Cutout

1. Click the **Rectangle Selection** tool icon in the toolbox and move the cross cursor into the work area.

2. Point to the top right corner of the cutout you want to select, then press and hold down the mouse button.

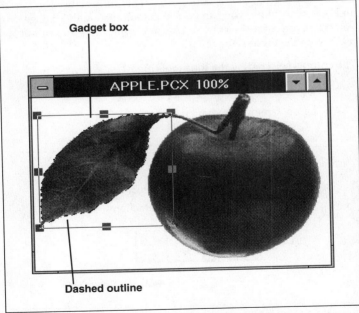

Figure 3.12: An irregularly shaped cutout with its marquee

3. Drag to the bottom left corner of the cutout, then release the mouse button to show the cutout and its marquee (the gadget box).

Creating an Irregularly Shaped Cutout

1. Click the **Lasso** tool icon in the toolbox and move the lasso cursor into the work area.

2. Point to where you want to start drawing the cutout, press and hold the mouse button, and drag to outline the cutout.

3. Release the mouse button to show the cutout and its marquee (the gadget box).

Creating a Polygonal Cutout

To create a polygonal cutout with up to 200 sides:

1. Click the **Scissors** tool icon in the toolbox and move the scissors cursor into the work area.

2. Point to one corner of the cutout and click the mouse button.

3. Point to the next corner of the cutout and click the mouse button to draw a side of the cutout.

4. Repeat step 3 as many times as necessary to draw more sides of the cutout.

5. Double-click the mouse button to close the polygon and show the cutout and its marquee (the gadget box).

Creating a Cutout Based on Color

To create a cutout of an area of an image with similar colors:

1. Click the **Magic Wand** tool icon in the toolbox and move the wand cursor into the work area.

2. Choose **Special ➤ Color Tolerance** to verify the current color tolerance and, if necessary, change it (see *Color Tolerance*).

3. Point to a place on the image that has a color value at the center of the range of colors you want to select, and click the mouse button. A dashed outline shows the cutout area with the selected range of colors. A rectangular marquee outlines the gadget box.

Canceling a Cutout

To cancel a cutout, click on a blank position in the work area.

Using the Gadget Box

After you have created a cutout, you can

- Stretch or shrink the cutout by dragging one of the gadget box handles.

- Move the cutout by pointing inside the gadget box and dragging. You can move the cutout one pixel at a time by pressing the arrow keys.

- Filter or transform the cutout (see *Filtering an Image* and *Transforming an Image*).

- Delete the cutout (see *Deleting Part of an Image*).

- Copy the cutout to the Clipboard (see *Copying Part of an Image*).

After you have completed the operation, click outside the gadget box (but within the window) or choose another tool to make the change permanent.

SHORTCUT KEYS

Most procedures in this book are described in terms of selecting from menus. However, CorelPHOTO-PAINT provides shortcuts to speed certain actions. These shortcuts are shown in Tables 3.2 and 3.3.

Table 3.2: Function Key Shortcuts

Function Key	Action
F1	Accesses on-line Help
Shift+F4	Tiles windows
Alt+F4	Exits CorelPHOTO-PAINT
F5	Displays Canvas roll-up
Shift+F5	Cascades windows
F6	Displays Color roll-up
F7	Displays Fill Settings roll-up
F8	Displays Tool Settings roll-up
F9	Full-screen preview

Table 3.3: Speed Key Shortcuts

Key Combination	Action
Ctrl+1	Displays 100% view
Ctrl+A	Shows or hides all roll-ups
Ctrl+C	Copies to Clipboard
Ctrl+D	Duplicates the current window
Ctrl+J	Displays the Preferences dialog box
Ctrl+N	Displays the Create a New Picture dialog box

Table 3.3: Speed Key Shortcuts (continued)

Key Combination	Action
Ctrl+O	Displays the Load a Picture from Disk dialog box
Ctrl+P	Displays the Print dialog box
Ctrl+S	Saves the picture under the current file name
Ctrl+T	Shows or hides the toolbox
Ctrl+V	Pastes from the Clipboard
Ctrl+X	Cuts to the Clipboard
Ctrl+X	Undoes the most recent action
Esc	Erases some tools' effects before you release the mouse button
←, →, ↑ or ↓	Moves a cutout one pixel at a time

SPLITTING CHANNELS

You can separate an image into its color components, separately edit the components, and then recombine them.

Separating an Image into Color Components

1. Choose **Image ➤ Split Channels To** to display a list of color models.

2. Click one of the color models to display separate images for each of the components of the color model.

Combining Channels

After you have split an image into color channels and modified the individual colors, you can recombine the channels to recreate a color image.

1. Choose **Image ➤ Combine Channels** to display the Combine dialog box.

2. Click the name of the color model, then identify each of the channels in that model.

3. Click **OK** to combine the channels.

TEXT TOOL

Use this tool to add text to an image.

You can edit the text immediately after you have placed it in the image. After you paste the text into the image, it becomes an integral part of the bitmap image and cannot be edited as text.

Adding Text to an Image

1. Select an outline color (see *Colors*).

2. Click the **Text** tool in the toolbox to display the Enter Text dialog box.

3. In the dialog box, select a font, font style, font size, and any effects. As you select, a sample appears in the dialog box.

4. Click an insertion point in the text box at the top of the dialog box, and type the text you want to place in the image.

5. Click **OK** to place the text within a frame in the image.

6. Drag the text frame handles to change the size of the frame.

7. To reposition the frame, point within it so that the cursor changes to the shape of a hand. Drag the hand to move the frame.

8. If you need to reopen the Enter Text dialog box, press the **spacebar**, edit or change the font, and then click **OK**.

9. Click outside the text frame or select another tool to paste the text into the image.

NOTES You can paste text from the Clipboard into the Enter Text dialog box.

Text wraps automatically within the image area. Use Ctrl+↵ to force line breaks.

TOOL SETTINGS

The Tool Settings roll-up allows you to modify the shape and certain other characteristics of many tools. See *Roll-ups* for general information about roll-ups.

To understand the countless effects obtainable by varying tool characteristics, you must be prepared to experiment and evaluate the results in the medium you will use to present your work.

Changing Tool Shape and Size

1. Open the **Tool Settings** roll-up shown in Figure 3.13.

2. Select a tool.

3. In the roll-up, click one of the eight tool shapes.

4. In the roll-up, select or type the tool width.

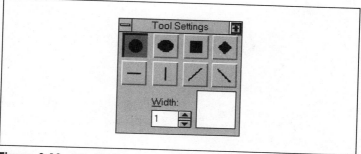

Figure 3.13: The Tool Settings roll-up

NOTES   The sample box in the roll-up shows the current tool shape and size.

The shape and size you select apply to all tools.

Changing Painting Tool and Clone Tool Characteristics

The six painting tools and three clone tools have various characteristics you can choose, an example of which is shown in Figure 3.14. Select or type values for each characteristic.

The best way to see the wide range of effects you can achieve by the painting tools is to experiment with the tool settings.

Changing Rectangle and Ellipse Tool Characteristics

You can change the width, but not the shape, of the tools that draw outlines for rectangles, polygons, and ellipses.

Changing Retouching Tool Characteristics

The seven retouching tools have various characteristics you can control by choosing values in the Tool Settings roll-up. In general,

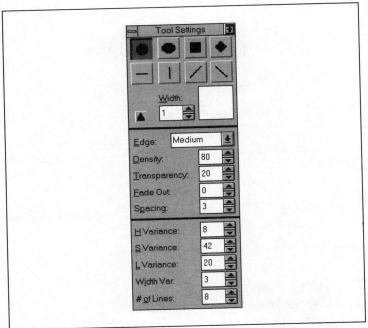

Figure 3.14: The Tool Settings roll-up with the Impressionism Brush selected

these characteristics determine the magnitude of the retouching effect. Experiment to get a feel for these controls.

TOOLBOX

The toolbox, shown in its default configuration in Figure 3.15, contains 11 tool icons. The right-pointing arrows in nine of the tools indicate the availability of flyouts that contain groups of related

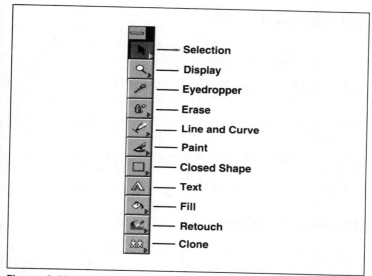

Figure 3.15: The CorelPHOTO-PAINT toolbox default
configuration

tools. By default, the toolbox is vertical and is at the left edge of the
screen.

For information about individual tools, see topics named for each
group of tools.

Selecting a Tool from the Toolbox

To select a tool from the toolbox, move the cursor over its icon and
the name of the tool appears in the help bar at the bottom of the
work area. Click the mouse button to select the tool; its icon becomes darker to show it is selected. When you move the cursor into
the image area, it changes shape to indicate which tool is selected.

Some tools are modified when you double-click on their icons. The
actions of certain tools are constrained if you hold down the Shift
key while you drag the mouse. These modifications and constraints
are described with the information about individual tools.

Selecting a Tool from a Flyout

1. Point onto a tool that has a right-pointing arrow, then press and hold down the mouse button.

2. Drag to the right to select one of the tools in the flyout, then release the mouse button.

When you release the mouse button, the icon from the flyout appears in the toolbox in place of the original icon.

After you have selected an icon from a flyout, that icon continues to appear in the toolbox and does so even when you start a new CorelPHOTO-PAINT session.

Moving the Toolbox

1. With an image open, click the **Control-menu** box at the top left corner of the toolbox to display the Control menu.

2. Click **Upper Left** to remove the check mark.

3. Point onto the black region just to the right of the Control-menu box, then press and hold down the mouse button while you drag the toolbox.

Ungrouping Tools

To display all the tools separately, instead of in groups:

1. With an image open, click the **Control-menu** box at the top-left corner of the toolbox to display the Control menu.

2. Click **Group** to remove the check mark and redraw the toolbox with all tools showing.

Changing the Layout of the Toolbox

Instead of displaying tools in a single column, you can display them in a row or in several rows or columns.

1. With an image open, click the **Control-menu** box at the top left corner of the toolbox to display the Control menu.

2. Click **Layout** to display a flyout in which you can choose from one to six columns or rows.

3. Click one of the layouts to redraw the toolbox in the new layout.

Restoring the Default Toolbox

1. With an image open, click the **Control-menu** box at the top-left corner of the toolbox to display the Control menu.

2. Click **Default Layout** to restore the default format.

TRANSFORMING AN IMAGE

You can transform an entire image, or a part of it, in several ways. If you select a part of an image as a cutout and then apply a transformation, only the cutout is transformed. Otherwise, the entire image is transformed.

Flipping an Image Horizontally and Vertically

To flip an image horizontally about its vertical axis or vertically about its horizontal axis:

1. Select the image to be flipped.

2. Choose **Image ➤ Flip ➤ Horizontally**, or **Image ➤ Flip ➤ Vertically**.

`new` Rotating an Image

You can rotate an image in 90-degree or 180-degree increments, or by any other specific angle.

To rotate an image in 90- or 180-degree increments:

1. Select the image to be rotated.

2. Choose **Image ➤ Rotate ➤ 90 Clockwise, Image ➤ Rotate ➤ 90 Counterclockwise**, or **Image ➤ Rotate ➤180**.

To rotate an image by a specific angle:

1. Select the image to be rotated.

2. Choose **Image ➤ Rotate ➤ Custom** to display the Rotate New Image dialog box.

3. Select or type a rotation angle in the text box, then click **OK**.

To rotate an image manually:

1. Select the image to be rotated.

2. Click the image to display rotation handles and center of rotation, as shown in Figure 3.16.

3. Drag the center of rotation to the required position.

4. Drag any one of the rotation handles to rotate the object.

`new` Distorting an Image

1. Select the image to be distorted.

2. Choose **Image ➤ Distort**.

3. Click on one of the handles at a corner of the selection marquee to display distortion handles shown in Figure 3.17.

4. Drag one of the distortion handles in any direction to distort the image.

Inverting an Image

You can invert an image or a cutout so that all colors are inverted as in a photographic negative.

To invert an image or cutout, choose **Effects ➤ Invert**.

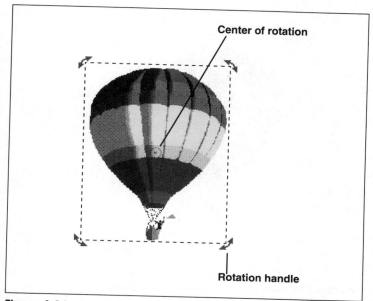

Center of rotation

Rotation handle

Figure 3.16: An image with rotation handles and center of
rotation displayed

Outlining an Image

You can outline shapes within images or cutouts. To outline an image, choose **Effects ➤ Edge ➤ Outline**. Fill colors are replaced with
the current background colors, leaving only lines around areas that
were previously filled.

UNDO TOOLS

The toolbox provides access to the three undo tools shown in Figure 3.18.

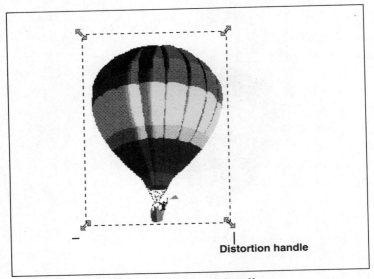

Figure 3.17: An image with distortion handles

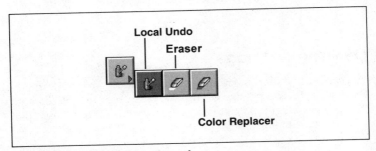

Figure 3.18: The three undo tools

Use these tools to restore an area of an image to a previous state and to remove or replace colored areas.

Depending on the level of detail involved, it is often necessary to enlarge an image before using these tools.

Locally Undoing Changes in an Image

Use the Local Undo tool to restore parts of an image to the state they were in before you last selected a command or tool.

1. Click the **Local Undo** tool in the toolbox, being careful not to double-click (see the notes below). Move the small brush cursor into the image window.

2. If necessary, adjust the size and shape of the tool in the Tool Settings roll-up.

3. Press the mouse button and drag over the parts of the image you wish to restore.

NOTES   Hold down the Shift key while you drag to constrain the movement to horizontal or vertical. Press the spacebar to change direction.

Double-clicking the Local Undo tool icon in the toolbox restores the entire image to the state it was in before you last selected a command or tool.

Erasing Parts of an Image

To replace areas of an image with the current background color:

1. Click the **Eraser** tool icon in the toolbox. Be careful not to double-click (see the notes below).

2. If necessary, adjust the size and shape of the tool in the Tool Settings roll-up.

3. Point to the area you want to erase, press the mouse button, and drag over the area to be erased. As you drag, the area changes to the current background color.

NOTES   By double-clicking the Eraser icon in the toolbox, you can erase the entire image and replace it with the background color. If this occurs by accident, choose Edit ➤ Undo to restore the image.

Replacing Colors

To replace the current primary (outline) color in an area of a picture with the secondary (fill) color:

1.   Click the **Color Replacer** tool icon in the toolbox. Be careful not to double-click. See the notes below.

2.   If necessary, adjust the size and shape of the tool in the Tool Settings roll-up.

3.   Choose the primary color you want to replace and the secondary color you want to replace it with (see *Colors*).

4.   If necessary, choose **Special ➤ Color Tolerance** and, in the Color Comparison Tolerance dialog box, specify the color tolerance for the primary color.

5.   Point to the area you want to erase, press the mouse button, and drag over the area to be changed. As you drag, the area that has the current primary color (or a color within the tolerance specified) changes to the secondary color.

NOTES   Hold down the Shift key while you drag to constrain the movement to horizontal or vertical. Press the spacebar to change direction.

Double-clicking the Color Replacer tool icon in the toolbox changes all occurrences of the primary color in your window to the secondary color.

Undoing Operations

To cancel all changes you made to an image since you last chose a tool or a command, choose **Edit ➤ Undo**.

Part 4

CorelSHOW

With CorelSHOW, you can prepare presentations to show on your computer screen or use to make projection slides, overhead transparencies, or printed images.

All the slides in a presentation have the same background. You create the background as well as the images on each slide in CorelDRAW, CorelPHOTO-PAINT, CorelCHART or any other OLE-server application.

When you are going to show a presentation on a computer screen, you can include animation sequences created in Autodesk, Quicktime, or CorelMOVE formats, and also sound in .WAV format. You can independently control the time each slide stays on the screen and the transition effect from one slide to the next. You can also set timing and transition effects for individual objects on a slide.

With the addition of cues, you can make your on-screen presentation user-interactive.

After you have created a computer slide show with CorelSHOW, you can present the show on any computer on which Windows 3.0 or later is installed, without the need for installing the CorelDRAW package.

ARRANGING OBJECTS

The Arrange menu allows you to alter the stacking order of foreground or background objects (see *Stacking Order* in Part 1).

BACKGROUND

All the slides in a presentation usually share the same background. You can use one of the backgrounds in a library that is provided with CorelSHOW, or you can build backgrounds from objects created in OLE-server applications such as CorelDRAW.

Selecting a Background from a Library

You can choose a background for a new presentation or change the background of an existing presentation from Slide view or Slide Sorter view. To choose a background from a library:

1.   Click the **Background Libraries** button in the toolbox to display thumbnails of libraries in the current default library file.

2.   If you need to look at a different library file, click **Change Library** to display the Open File dialog box. Open the appropriate directory, click the library file name, and then click **OK** to display thumbnails of the backgrounds in that file.

3.   Click the thumbnail you want to use as a background to apply the background to the slides in the presentation.

4.   Click **Done** to remove the thumbnails from your screen.

NOTES   If you installed CorelDRAW normally, the background library provided with CorelSHOW is in a file named SAMPLE.SHB in your C:\COREL40\SHOW\BACKGRDS directory.

Creating a New Background

You create a background in the same way you create a slide. Use the procedures for embedding and linking objects described in *Creating a New Presentation*, the only difference being that you select Background view in the ribbon rather than the Slide view.

You can also create a new background by editing an existing background. Select **Background View**, double-click the background to edit it in the application in which it was created, then choose **File ➤ Exit and Return** (see *Editing Objects*).

Saving a Background

After you have created a background, you can save it and add it to a background library.

1. Choose **File ➤ Save Background** to display the Save Background dialog box.

2. Select the directory C:\COREL40\SHOW\BACKGRDS, in which CorelSHOW saves backgrounds, or another directory if you prefer.

3. To save the new background in the current library, click **Insert In Library**, and then click **OK**. To save the background in a different file, type the file name and then click **OK**.

Controlling the Background for Individual Slides

By default, all slides in a presentation have the same background. However, you can choose to omit the background, or use a different background, for specific slides.

To control a slide's background:

1. In Slide view, select the slide.

2. Right-click the background to display the pop-up menu, then click **Background** to display a submenu.

3. Click **Omit** if you want to omit the background for the selected slide, or click **Independent** if you want to have a different background for the slide.

4. If you chose Independent in Step 3, use the steps in "Selecting a Background from a Library" to choose a background for that slide.

NOTES You can also omit the background for a slide by choosing Edit ➤ Omit Background.

CREATING A NEW PRESENTATION

A presentation consists of a set of images referred to here as slides, although they may be overhead transparencies, pages of a flip chart, or other media. All the slides in a presentation have the same background.

There are six main steps in creating a new presentation:

1. Specify the format.
2. Choose or create a background.
3. Assemble individual slides.
4. Add embellishments such as animation, sounds, and cues.
5. Place the slides in order.
6. Assign time on screen and transition effects to slides and to individual objects on slides.

Each of these steps is explained below.

Specifying the Format

1. Select **File ➤ New** to display a new presentation window.

2. Select **File ➤ Page Setup** to display the Page Setup dialog box.

3. Click either **Portrait** or **Landscape**.

4. Click one of the **Page Size** buttons. For an on-screen presentation, select **Screen**.

5. If you clicked **Custom** in step 4, select or type the horizontal and vertical sizes.

6. Click **OK**.

Choosing a Background

The background, which is usually common to all slides in a presentation, is on a separate layer from the foregrounds of individual slides. You can select a background from an existing library, or create a new background (see *Background*).

You can omit the background or choose a different background for certain slides (see *Background*).

Assembling a Slide

You assemble individual slides from components created in OLE server applications such as CorelDRAW, CorelCHART, and Corel-PHOTO-PAINT. You can embed objects into slides, or link objects to slides.

1. Click the **Slide View** button.

2. Click one of the **Page** icons at the bottom of the screen to select the slide you want to assemble.

3. Embed or link objects into that slide (see "Embedding Objects" and "Linking Objects" below).

4. Size and move the objects as necessary.

NOTES When you start a new presentation, you specify the number of slides. Subsequently, if you want to add more slides, select Insert ➤ New Page. A dialog box appears, in which you can specify the number of new slides you want to add and whether the new slides are to be inserted before or after the currently selected slide. You can insert slides in the Slide or Slide Sorter views.

To delete one or more slides, go to the Slide Sorter view, select the slides you want to delete, and press Delete.

When you resize and move objects on a slide, use the Shift and Ctrl keys to constrain the operation as you do in CorelDRAW. See *Constraining Objects* in Part 1 of this book.

Embedding an Object from a Server Application

1. Select **Slide View**.

2. Choose **Insert ➤ Object** and click the **Create New** option button to display the Insert Object dialog box, which lists available object types.

3. Click the type of object to be embedded, and click **OK**.

4. Use the cross cursor to draw a rectangle of any size within the area of the slide to open the server application.

5. Create the object, or open it if it already exists, in the server application.

6. Choose **File ➤ Exit & Return to CorelSHOW** (or the equivalent) in the server application.

7. If a dialog box asks you if you want to update the embedded object, click **Yes**.

NOTES Instead of choosing the object type from the Insert Object dialog box in steps 2 and 3, you can click one of the source applications in the toolbox.

The size of the object in the slide in many, but not all, cases depends on its size in the server application, not on the size of the rectangle you draw in step 4.

CorelPHOTO-PAINT, used as a server, opens with a minimized CorelSHOW window. Enlarge this window and create the object within it.

Embedding an Object from a File

If the object to be embedded already exists as a file, you can embed it without opening the server application. You can still use the server application to edit it (see *Editing Objects*).

1. Select **Slide View**.

2. Choose **Insert ➤ Object** and click the **Create From File** option button to display the File text box.

3. Type the name of the file to be embedded and click **OK**.

4. Click where you want the object to appear in the slide.

NOTES   As an alternative to step 3, click the Browse button and select the file name in the Browse dialog box.

Embedding an Object by Pasting

You can create an object in a server application, cut or copy it to the Clipboard, and then paste it into a slide. You can still use the server application to edit it (see *Editing Objects*).

1. Create an object in a server application.

2. Cut or copy the object to the Clipboard.

3. Open CorelSHOW.

4. Choose **Edit ➤ Paste** to copy the object into the slide.

Linking an Object

To link from within CorelSHOW:

1. Select **Slide View**.

2. Choose **Insert ➤ Object** and click the **Create From File** option button to display the Link check box.

3. Click the **Link** check box to place a check mark in it.

4. Type the name of the file to be linked and click **OK**.

5. Click where you want the object to appear in the slide. Be patient for a few seconds until the linked object appears in the slide.

NOTES As an alternative to step 4, click the Browse button and select the file name in the Browse dialog box.

new Using Animation

Your presentation can include animations in Autodesk, Quicktime, and CorelMOVE formats. To insert an animation:

1. Select the slide before which you want to place the animation.

2. Select **Insert ➤ Animation** to display the Insert Animation dialog box.

3. Open the **List Files of Type** list box and select the type of animation file you want to use.

4. Select the directory that contains the animation file.

5. Click the file name and click **Preview** to show a part of the first animation frame.

6. Click **Options** to expand the dialog box, as shown in Figure 4.1.

7. Specify the optional parameters.

8. Click **OK** to insert the animation slide.

9. Drag the image to where you want it to appear in the slide.

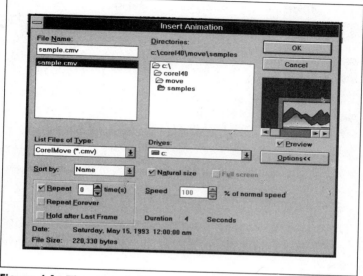

Figure 4.1: The expanded Insert Animation dialog box

new Adding Sound

If your computer has a sound board capable of playing sounds in
.WAV format, you can enhance your presentation with sounds.

1. Select the slide to which you want to add a sound.

2. Choose **Insert ➤ Sound** to display the Insert Sound dialog box.

3. Select a directory containing sound files in .WAV format
and click the name of a sound file.

4. To hear the sound, click **Play**.

5. Click **OK** to attach the sound to the presentation.

NOTES If you installed Windows 3.1 fully, you have four
sound files in your Windows directory. You can use these sounds
effectively in presentations.

Although you initially associate a sound with a specific slide, you can subsequently move the sound so that it occurs at any time during the presentation (see *Timelines*).

new Assigning Transition Effects to a Slide

You can assign an opening transition effect individually to each slide in the Slide or Slide Sorter views. You can also assign opening and closing transition effects to individual objects in a slide.

1.   In Slide or Slide Sorter view, select a slide.

2.   Click the **Frame Transitions** button to display the Transition Effects dialog box.

3.   Scroll if necessary and then click a transition effect.

4.   Click the **Preview** button to see a preview of the selected transition, then click **OK**.

NOTES   As an alternative to step 2, right-click the slide to display a pop-up menu and click Transition Effect to display the Transition Effects dialog box.

new Assigning Transition Effects to an Object in a Slide

1.   In Slide or Slide Sorter view, select a slide.

2.   Use the **Pick** tool to select an object on the slide.

3.   Follow steps 2 through 4 in the preceding procedure, selecting an opening and a closing transition effect in step 3.

Assigning Duration to a Slide

You can assign different durations to each slide.

1.   In Slide view or Slide Sorter view, select a slide.

2.   Open the **Slide Duration** list box and select a slide duration.

NOTES Instead of selecting the slide duration from the list, type the time (in seconds) in the Slide Duration text box.

See *Timelines* for additional information about slide timing.

new Assigning Duration to an Object in a Slide

You can assign different durations to each object in a slide.

1. In Slide view, select a slide and select the object on that slide for which you want to assign a duration.

2. Open the **Frame Duration** list box and select an object duration.

NOTES Instead of selecting the object duration from the list, type the time (in seconds) in the Frame Duration text box.

See *Timelines* for additional information about object timing.

Placing Slides in Order

Use the Slide Sorter view to change the order of slides, either by dragging slides from one position to another or by numbering them. To drag slides:

1. Click the **Slide Sorter View** button in the ribbon to show miniature versions of slides in the presentation.

2. Point onto a slide, then press and hold down the mouse button while you drag the slide to a new position.

3. Release the mouse button.

As an alternative to dragging, you can right-click a slide to select its frame, move the frame to a new position, and then left-click to assign it to that position.

To renumber slides:

1. Click the **Slide Sorter View** button in the ribbon to show miniature versions of the slides in the presentation.

2. Click the **Numbering** tool in the ribbon to redraw the slides with a number panel at the bottom of each.

3. Click the slide which is to be first to change the number in its panel to 1.

4. Click the slide which should be next to change the number in its panel to 2.

5. Continue by clicking the remaining slides in order.

6. After you have clicked the last slide, the slides are automatically rearranged in the correct order and the number panels disappear.

NOTES If you want to stop numbering slides before you have numbered them all, click the Numbering tool. The slides you have numbered are placed in order at the beginning of the presentation with the unnumbered slides following.

CUES

You can use cues to control an on-screen presentation.

new Adding a Cue to a Slide

A cue causes something to happen when a specific condition is satisfied. For example, a simple cue could cause the presentation to pause until you click the mouse button. A more sophisticated cue could cause a several slides to be shown in a specified order when the mouse button is clicked.

1. Select the slide to which you want to add a cue.

2. Choose **Edit ➤ Edit Cue** to display the Cue Information dialog box.

3. Point onto the **Always** button, then press and hold down the mouse button to display a list of conditions.

4. Select from the list of conditions (see below).

5. Point onto **Continue** in the Action box, then press and hold down the mouse button to display a list of actions.

6. Select from the list of actions (see below).

7. Click **Insert** to accept the action.

8. Repeat steps 5 through 7 to place additional actions into the list.

The conditions you can choose are as follows:

Condition Name	Condition to be Satisfied
Always	No condition has to be met, so the action always occurs.
Wait For	The condition is one of four specified events: a specific interval of time, a mouse click, a keypress, or the completion of a sound. After the event, the action occurs.
If Then	The condition is one of the same four specified events as in Wait For. If the condition is not met, another selected action occurs if you have specified one; otherwise nothing occurs.

The actions available are as follows:

Action Name	Description
Continue	The presentation continues.
Goto Time Absolute	Skip to a place in the presentation specified as time from the beginning of the presentation. Click the bar at the right of the action name and type the time.

Goto Time Relative	Skip to a place in the presentation specified as time from the current point in the presentation. Click the bar at the right of the action name and type the time.
Goto Slide	Skip to a slide specified by its number in the presentation. Click the bar at the right of the action name and type the slide number.
End Presentation	The presentation stops. If you are using SHOWRUN, the application terminates.
Play an Object	Show a slide or play a sound. Click the bar at the right of the action name and click Frame Named or Sound Named, then click the next bar to the right and click the frame number or sound name.
Stop Playing an Object	Stop showing a slide or playing a sound. Click the bar at the right of the action name and click Frame Named or Sound Named, then click the next bar to the right and click the frame number or sound name.

NOTES   When you have actions in a list, you can select an action and click Delete to delete it from the list.

new Adding a Cue to an Object in a Slide

You can add a cue to an object in the same way as to a slide. After selecting the slide, select the object and then follow the preceding procedure.

DISPLAY SETTINGS

Background and Slide views allow you to use rulers and guidelines to help align objects, as you can in CorelDRAW.

Setting Up Rulers

You set the measurement units used in the rulers and also set the origin as you do in CorelDRAW (see *Alignment and Placement Aids* in Part 1). To set up the rulers:

1. Choose **Display ➤ Rulers Setup** to display the Rulers dialog box.

2. Select **Horizontal** and **Vertical** measurement units.

3. Set the ruler origin (zero points on the horizontal and vertical rulers) relative to the lower left corner of the page, then click **OK**.

NOTES   Alternatively, you can set the ruler origin by dragging the small square at the intersection of the rulers to the new origin.

Displaying and Hiding Rulers

To display or hide the rulers, choose **Display ➤ Show Rulers**.

Using Guidelines

If you have rulers displayed, you can pull guidelines out of the rulers just as you can in CorelDRAW. You can also specify the position of Guidelines by selecting **Display ➤ Guidelines Setup** (see *Alignment and Placement Aids* in Part 1).

After you have created guidelines you can snap objects to them. To enable snapping to guidelines, choose **Display ➤ Snap To Guidelines**.

Saving Settings

After you have made changes in the Display menu, you can save these settings as defaults by selecting **Display ➤ Save Settings**.

EDITING OBJECTS

Images in slides and backgrounds are objects created in OLE server applications that are embedded into or linked to CorelSHOW. You must use the application in which an object was created to edit it.

Editing an Embedded Object

An embedded object is a copy of the object originally created in the server application. You must open the embedded object from CorelSHOW to edit it. If you open the original object from the server application and make changes, these changes do not affect the embedded object in CorelSHOW. To edit an embedded object:

1. Double-click the object to open the server application with the object displayed.

2. Edit the object in the server application.

3. In the server application, choose **File ➤ Exit & Return** to return to CorelSHOW, or the equivalent command (see the application's documentation).

4. If a dialog box asks you if you want to update the embedded object, click **Yes**.

📝 **NOTES**   If you have a white object on a dark background in a slide and the server application displays objects on a white background, you will not be able to see the object after step 1. The solution to this problem depends on the server application. In CorelDRAW, for example, choose Display ➤ Edit Wireframe so that you can see the object's outline.

Editing a Linked Object

A linked object exists only where it was created by the server. You can access and edit the linked object in the same way as an embedded object. Alternatively, you can open the object directly from the server application to edit it. Any changes you make to a linked object are reflected in all applications to which the object is linked.

FILE MANAGEMENT

Most commands in the File menu are similar to those in CorelDRAW (see *File Management* in Part 1).

📝 **NOTES**   The Save Background command allows you to save a file in the format CorelSHOW uses for backgrounds.

The Page Setup command allows you to choose several formats other than Screen. Use this if you want to make overhead transparencies or printed copies of your slides.

When you print black-and-white transparencies or copies of your slide, you can usually improve them by omitting the background. To do this, select Edit ➤ Omit Background for each slide.

FRAMING OBJECTS

Each object in a slide is contained within a frame that is normally invisible. You can choose to place a visible frame around individual objects.

new Framing an Object in a Slide

1. Left-click an object in a slide to select it.
2. Right-click the selected object to display a pop-up menu.
3. Left-click **Frame Style** to display a submenu.
4. Click one of the available frame styles to apply it to the object.

HELP

CorelSHOW has a Help facility similar to that in other Windows applications (see *Help* in Part 1).

LINKS

See *Linking and Embedding Objects* in Part 1 for information about changing, updating, and canceling links.

MAIN MENU

See *Menus* in on-line Help for information about each of the menus and commands.

OPENING A PRESENTATION

You can open a presentation for editing in the same way you open a CorelDRAW drawing (see *File Management* in Part 1).

PLAYING A PRESENTATION

You can play a slide show from CorelSHOW, or you can use the portable screen show player to present a show on any computer in which Windows 3.0 or later is installed.

Using CorelSHOW to Play a Presentation

1. Open the presentation in CorelSHOW.

2. Select **Display ➤ Presentation Options** to open the Presentation Options dialog box.

3. Click an option button to choose between automatic or manual advance.

4. Click the **Run show continuously** check box if you want the presentation to repeat automatically.

5. Click the **Display pointer onscreen** check box if you want the pointer on screen.

6. Leave the **Generate slide show in advance** check box checked to minimize pauses between slides.

7. Click **OK**.

8. Click the **Screen Show** button to start the show.

NOTES If you choose manual advance in step 3, double-click the left mouse button to advance from one slide to the next. Double-click the right mouse button to go back to the previous slide.

If you choose continuous running in step 4, press Esc to terminate the show.

Using SHOWRUN to Play a Portable Presentation

The CorelSHOW portable screen show player (SHOWRUN.EXE) is an independent Windows application you can use to present a presentation on a computer screen without installing CorelSHOW itself. SHOWRUN is a shareware program that Corel invites you to distribute freely. You can install this program on any personal computer that has Windows 3.0 or higher without violating any software copyrights.

To create a portable screen show:

1. Save your presentation and copy the file to a floppy disk.

2. Copy the file **SHOWRUN.EXE** to a high-density floppy disk. Look in the COREL40\SHOW\SHOWRUN directory, to find SHOWRUN.EXE.

To run the screen show:

1. Create a new directory on the computer and copy your presentation file and SHOWRUN.EXE into it.

2. Start Windows and start SHOWRUN.EXE by one of the standard Windows methods (see Notes below) to display the Open Presentation dialog box.

3. Select the name of the presentation and click **OK**.

4. Choose **File ➤ Presentation Options** to display the Presentation Options dialog box.

5. Select the appropriate presentation options (see the preceding procedure) and click **OK**.

6. Click the **Screen Show** button to start the presentation.

7. To close the presentation file, choose **File ➤ Close**.

8. If you want to show another presentation, choose **File ➤ Open** and then repeat steps 3 through 7.

9. To close SHOWRUN, choose **File ➤ Exit**.

NOTES One way to start SHOWRUN is to display the Program Manager group window, then choose File ➤ Run. In the Command Line text box, type the full path name of the program you want to run, such as C:\SHOW\SHOWRUN.EXE if you have SHOWRUN in a directory called SHOW on the C: drive.

When you are preparing to show a portable presentation, you can change the timing and transition effects for each slide. However, you cannot save these changes; they remain in effect only until you close SHOWRUN.

POP-UP MENUS

Pop-up menus provide fast access to commonly used features.

▊new ▊ Accessing a Pop-up Menu

To display a pop-up menu, right-click a slide background or an object. The pop-up menu for a background provides access to:

- Page setup (see *Creating a New Presentation*)
- Background (see *Background*)
- Cues (see *Cues*)
- Timelines (see *Timelines*)
- Transition effects (see *Transition Effects*)

The pop-up menu for an object provides access to:

- Frame style (see *Framing Objects*)
- Editing cues (see *Cues*)
- Timelines (see *Timelines*)
- Transition effects (see *Transition Effects*)

PRINTING A PRESENTATION

Printing a presentation is similar to printing a CorelDRAW document (see *Printing a Drawing* in Part 1).

SCREEN

Figure 4.2 shows the CorelSHOW Slide view screen. The Background and Slide Sorter views are similar. Many of the screen components are

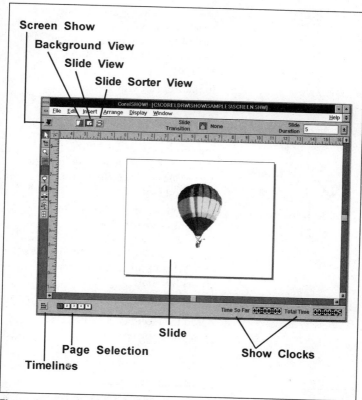

Figure 4.2: The CorelSHOW Slide view screen

similar to those in CorelDRAW. Those that are significantly different are as follows:

Component	Purpose
Page icons	In Slide view and Slide Sorter view, used to select individual slides.
Screen Show button	Used to start a presentation.
Show Clocks	Show the total length of the presentation and the time up to the current slide.

Slide	In Background view and Slide view, area in which background or slide is assembled. In Slide Sorter view, areas in which presentation is assembled.
Slide Numbering tool	In Slide Sorter view, used to put slides in order. Not shown in figure.
Slide Duration box	In Slide view and Slide Sorter view, controls how long individual slides are shown on screen. When an individual object is selected in Slide view, this becomes the Frame Duration box.
Slide Transition box	In Slide view and Slide Sorter view, provides control over how a slide first appears on the screen. When an individual object is selected in Slide view, this becomes the Frame Transition box.
Timelines button	Accesses timelines.
View Selection buttons	Used to select Background, Slide, and Slide Sorter views.

SELECTING A VIEW MODE

There are three view modes:

- Background view, which is used to select, create, or edit a background for all the slides in a presentation

- Slide view, which is used to assemble the components of individual slides

- Slide Sorter view, which is used to change the order of slides in a presentation

To select a view, click the appropriate button.

SHORTCUT KEYS

CorelSHOW provides shortcuts to speed certain actions and, in some cases, to provide extra functions. The shortcut keys are described in Tables 4.1, 4.2, and 4.3.

Table 4.1: Function Key Shortcuts

Key	Purpose
F1	Displays help on the currently selected command or currently open dialog box
Shift+F1	Displays the help cursor with which you point at the part of the screen on which you want help
Ctrl+F1	Opens the Help Search dialog box
F2	Zooms out by a factor of two
F3	Displays the Zoom-out cursor
F4	Changes the magnification so that the slide fits within the window
Alt+F4	Exits from CorelSHOW
Shift+F5	Cascades windows

Table 4.2: Speed Key Shortcuts

Key	Purpose
Ctrl+A	Opens the Insert Animation dialog box
Ctrl+B	Opens the Insert Object dialog box
Ctrl+C	Executes the Copy command
Ctrl+G	Displays the Insert New Page dialog box
Ctrl+N	Opens a new presentation
Ctrl+O	Opens the Open Files dialog box
Ctrl+P	Opens the Print dialog box
Ctrl+R	Runs the presentation
Ctrl+S	Saves the presentation under the current file name
Ctrl+U	Opens the Insert Sound dialog box
Ctrl+V	Executes the Paste command
Ctrl+W	Executes the Refresh Window command
Ctrl+X	Executes the Cut command
Ctrl+Z	Executes the Undo command
Shift+PageDown	Executes the To Back command
Ctrl+PageDown	Executes the Forward One command
Shift+PageUp	Executes the To Front command
Ctrl+PageDown	Executes the Backward One command
Esc	Terminates a running slide show

Table 4.3: Keys for Controlling Presentations

Key	Purpose
IN AUTOMATIC PRESENTATIONS	
F2	Pause presentation. Press again to continue.
F3	Play backwards.
F4	Play forwards.
F9 or Home	Go to first slide.
F10 or End	Go to last slide.
Esc	Terminate presentation.
IN MANUAL PRESENTATIONS	
→ or double-click left mouse button.	Advance to next slide.
← or double-click right mouse button.	Go back to previous slide.

STARTING AND CLOSING CORELSHOW

To start CorelSHOW:

1. Start Windows and display the Program Manager group window.

2. Double-click the **Corel 4** icon to display the Corel 4 group window.

3. Double-click the **CorelSHOW** icon to open CorelSHOW and display the Welcome to CorelSHOW dialog box.

4. Select the **Open an Existing Presentation** or **Start a New Presentation** option button.

5. If you selected Start a New Presentation in step 4, define the options for a new presentation.

6. Click **OK** to display the Open Files dialog box to select an existing presentation (see *Opening a Presentation*), or to display a blank slide ready for you to create a new presentation (see *Creating a New Presentation*).

To close CorelSHOW, choose **File ➤ Exit**.

TIMELINES

You can use the Timelines window to adjust the timing of slides, of individual objects on slides, and of sounds.

new Adjusting a Slide's Duration

You can use the Timelines window to adjust the duration of slides in a presentation:

1. Click the **Timelines** button to display the Timelines window, similar to that shown in Figure 4.3.

2. Click the **Expand Time** button if you want to expand the time axis.

3. Click the **Sounds** button if you want to hide sounds.

4. Click the **Slides** button if you want to hide slides.

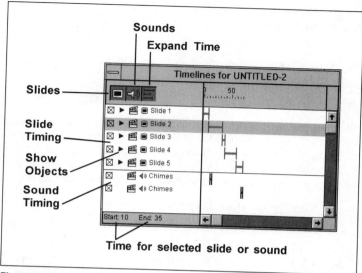

Figure 4.3: The Timelines window showing slide and sound
timing

5. Click on the row that represents the slide or sound you
    want to adjust so that a gray band identifies it and the
    bottom left of the window shows its current starting
    and ending time.

6. Point onto the green timeline that shows the slide dura-
    tion or the blue timeline that shows the sound duration.
    To move the starting time of a sound, point onto the left
    end of the timeline, press the mouse button and drag.
    To move the ending time of a slide or sound, point onto
    the right end of the timeline, press the mouse button
    and drag. The new times are shown at the bottom-left
    of the window.

7. Double-click the **Control-menu** box in the Timeline win-
    dow's title bar to remove the window.

NOTES   When you change the timing for one slide, the symbols for the subsequent slides move automatically.

The Expand Time, Slides, and Sounds buttons are toggles.

Adjusting an Object's Start and Stop Times

You can use the Timeline window to set the start and stop times for individual objects in a slide. With this technique you can create slides in which lines of text or graphics objects are successively added. You have the added flexibility of removing objects at specific times while a slide is being displayed. To set object times:

1.   Click the **Timelines** button to display the Timelines window.

2.   Click on the row that represents the slide that contains objects you want to time.

3.   Click the right-pointing arrow to display a list of objects, each of which is identified by a frame number, as shown in Figure 4.4. The red timelines indicate the start and stop times of the individual objects.

4.   Drag the start and stop point to set the object timing as you did in the preceding procedure.

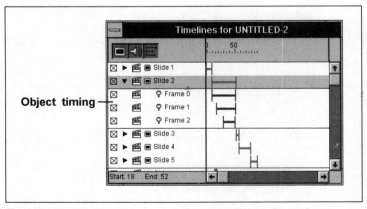

Figure 4.4:   The Timelines window expanded to show object timing

5.   Double-click the **Control-menu** box in the Timeline window's title bar to remove the window.

NOTES   The objects within a slide are numbered in the order you embedded them into, or linked them to, the slide.

You can move an object's timeline by pointing onto its center and dragging.

TOOLBOX

The CorelSHOW toolbox, shown in Figure 4.5, contains nine tools. The toolbox is normally at the left side of the screen. To move

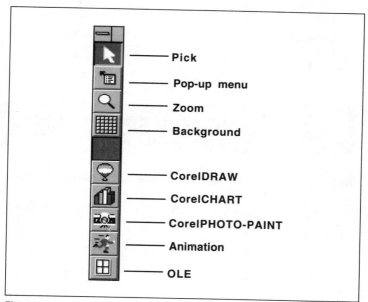

Figure 4.5: The CorelSHOW toolbox

it, choose **Display ➤ Floating Toolbox**, point into the box at the right of the Control-menu bar, and drag. Do the same to restore the toolbox to its normal position.

The purposes of the tools are as follows:

Tool Name	Purpose
Pick	Selects, moves, and resizes objects in background and Slide views. In the Slide Sorter view, it is used to change the order of slides.
Pop-up	Opens pop-up menus.
Zoom	Changes magnification of slide. Similar to CorelDRAW Zoom tool.
Background	Accesses background libraries.
CorelDRAW	Opens CorelDRAW.
CorelCHART	Opens CorelCHART.
CorelPHOTO-PAINT	Opens CorelPHOTO-PAINT.
Animation	Opens Insert Animation dialog box.
OLE	Opens other OLE server applications.

UNDOING OPERATIONS

To undo the most recent operation, select **Edit ➤ Undo**.

Part 5

CorelTRACE

CorelTRACE is a versatile utility you can use to:

- Trace black-and-white, grayscale, and color images, converting them into vector images you can work with in CorelDRAW

- Trace black-and-white bitmapped text and convert it into ASCII format you can edit in a word processor or text editor, and import as text into other applications

- Trace black-and-white images that combine bitmapped text and graphics and convert them into vector images that you can open in CorelDRAW with the text as text objects and the graphics as curve objects

The utility offers a wide selection of trace settings that you can choose from to optimize traced images.

COLOR

You can select a color for traced images when you are using the Woodcut or Silhouette tracing methods.

Selecting a Tracing Color

1. Click the **Tracing Color** button to display the current palette.

2. Click the **More** button in the palette to display the Select Color dialog box.

3. Use the dialog box to select color models and colors within those models (see *Colors* in Part 1).

NOTES As an alternative to selecting a tracing color from a palette, you can use the Eyedropper tool to choose a tracing color from the image that is to be traced.

CONVERTING A BITMAP IMAGE TO A VECTOR IMAGE

There are three stages in converting a bitmap image to a usable vector image:

1. Optimizing the bitmap image.

2. Tracing the bitmap image.

3. Optimizing the vector image.

The more effort you put into optimizing the bitmap image, the less you will have to put into optimizing the vector image. Only experience can teach you how best to split your time between these two activities.

Optimizing the Bitmap Image

Before you can successfully trace most bitmap images, you should optimize them. If you are using a scanner to create bitmap images, you need to experiment with the scanner controls to create an image with good contrast between brightness levels and colors, and with a minimum number of random pixels.

If you are using an existing bitmap image, you can use CorelPHOTO-PAINT to improve the image brightness and color contrast, and to make sure that straight lines and corners are well defined.

To use CorelPHOTO-PAINT from within CorelTRACE:

1. In CorelTRACE, open the image you want to trace.

2. Choose **Edit ➤ Edit Image** to open CorelPHOTO-PAINT.

3. Enlarge the editing window and use CorelPHOTO-PAINT tools to edit the image.

4. Choose **File ➤ Exit**.

5. When the Query dialog box appears, click **Yes** to save the changes and to display the edited image in CorelTRACE.

Tracing the Image

CorelTRACE provides several controls for affecting the way a bitmap image is converted into a vector image. These controls affect the entire image. Set these controls in such a way that CorelTRACE converts your optimized bitmap image into a vector image that needs the least manipulation (see *Settings*).

Optimizing the Traced Image

Depending on the way you optimized the bitmap image, and the controls you chose for the tracing process, the traced image may need more or less attention. In some cases, you may need to convert lines to curves or curves to lines. You might need to combine several objects into one object. The more work you put into providing contrast and continuity in the original bitmap image, the less work you need to put into optimizing the traced image.

CONVERTING AN IMAGE TO WINDOWS BITMAP FORMAT

1. Choose **File ➤ Open** to display the Open Files dialog box.

2. Click the name of the file you want to convert, then click **OK** to load the file into CorelTRACE.

3. Choose **File ➤ Save ➤ Image As** to display the Save Image As dialog box.

4. Type a name for the converted file and click **OK** to save it in Windows bitmap format.

CREATING A BITMAP IMAGE TO BE TRACED

CorelTRACE converts bitmap images into vector images. It accepts bitmap black-and-white, grayscale, and color images in these formats:

- TIFF 5.0 (.TIF)
- PC Paintbrush (.PCX)

- Windows (.BMP)
- CompuServe (.GIF)
- Targa (.TGA)
- Photo CD (.PCD)
- JPEG (.JPG)

You can create bitmap images in these formats by scanning an image, by capturing a screen image, or by working in a paint program such as CorelPHOTO-PAINT. You can also purchase clip art in these formats from many sources. If the image you want to trace is in a different format, you can convert it into one of the formats CorelTRACE accepts with a utility such as Collage Complete or HiJaak.

In order to convert a bitmap image into a vector image, CorelTRACE has to detect definite boundaries in the bitmap image. Bitmap images that have distinct changes in brightness or color produce good results. Those that have gradual changes in brightness or color can be traced less effectively.

HELP

Use Help in the same way as in CorelDRAW (see *Help* in Part 1).

SAVING A TRACED IMAGE

After tracing, CorelTRACE saves vector images as PostScript files in EPS format without an image header. It saves scanned text as ASCII files.

Saving a Traced Image with the Same Name as the Source Image

After you have traced an image using any method except OCR, you can save it in EPS format with the same name as the source image by choosing **File ➤ Save Trace**.

Saving a Traced Image with a New Name

After you have traced an image with any method except OCR, you can save it with a new name in EPS format. After tracing an image using the OCR method, you can save it in ASCII format.

1. Choose **File ➤ Save** to display a secondary menu in which you can choose from Trace As, Text As, or Image As.

2. If you are saving a vector image, click **Trace As** to display the Save Trace As dialog box, type a name for the file, and click **OK** to save it in EPS format.

3. If you are saving text, click **Text As** to display the Save Text As dialog box, type a name for the file, and click **OK** to save it in ASCII format with a .TXT file name extension.

NOTES See *Using Traced Images* for additional information about traced images saved after using the Corel method.

SCANNING ARTWORK

If you are using a scanner to create bitmaps that you are going to trace, there are several points you should be aware of:

• Before you scan, make the artwork as clean as possible. If you are scanning a black-and-white original, use white paint to eliminate any unwanted black or gray before you scan.

- Choose the scanning mode that best suits the original and the way you want to use the scanned image.

- Scan grayscale and color images at 150 dpi or less. You can use a higher resolution with black-and-white images.

- Use the magnification and reduction capabilities of your scanner to scan the original artwork at the size you intend to use it.

- Scan only the part of the original you intend to use.

- If the original artwork has distinct horizontal or vertical lines, make sure the artwork is positioned exactly on the scanner. This usually requires some experimentation.

- When you are scanning black-and-white originals, experiment with the scanner's intensity and contrast controls to get the sharpest possible image.

- When you are scanning grayscale or color images, the settings of the scanner's contrast and intensity controls have a significant effect on the vector image CorelTRACE produces. Be prepared to experiment.

The more effort you put into getting the best possible scanned image, the less time you will have to spend preparing the bitmap for tracing and cleaning up the vector image.

Controlling a Scanner

You can control a scanner from within CorelTRACE just as you can from within CorelPHOTO-PAINT (see *Scanning* in part 3).

SCREEN

Figure 5.1 shows a typical CorelTRACE screen.

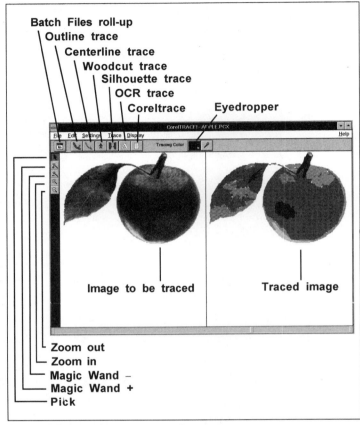

Batch Files roll-up
Outline trace
Centerline trace
Woodcut trace
Silhouette trace
OCR trace
Coreltrace
Eyedropper

Image to be traced

Traced image

Zoom out
Zoom in
Magic Wand –
Magic Wand +
Pick

Figure 5.1: A typical CorelTRACE screen

In many ways, the screen is similar to a CorelDRAW screen. The screen components unique to CorelTRACE are as follows:

Component	Purpose
Batch Files roll-up button	Click to display the Batch Files roll-up

Component	Purpose
Color Selection buttons	Access color palette from which woodcut or silhouette tracing color is chosen
Eyedropper tool	Picks up tracing color from source image
Magic Wand tools	Select and deselect areas of similar color in the source image
Pick tool	Selects area of source image
Tracing buttons	Initiate tracing using a specific tracing method
Zoom tools	Change magnification of source image

SETTINGS

There are many settings you can modify in order to optimize scanned images. Many settings allow you to control how much detail in the original image appears in the traced image. In general, the more detail there is in the traced image, the slower the tracing process and the larger the traced image file.

Changing Settings

1. Choose **Settings ➤ Modify** to display a secondary menu.
2. Click an item on the secondary menu according to which setting you want to change.

The various groups of settings are explained below. Each has a Default button you can click to restore default values.

Image Filtering Settings

When you choose Image Filtering settings, you see a dialog box that has option buttons you can select to:

- Smooth Dithering: When selected, CorelTRACE smoothes dithered pixels in the source image.

- Invert Colors: When selected, CorelTRACE inverts color values in the source image.

- Convert to Monochrome: When selected, CorelTRACE converts the source image to monochrome before tracing, allowing you to set the threshold at which tones are converted to black or white.

- Reduce Colors: When checked, CorelTRACE reduces the number of colors in the source image before tracing to a value you select.

Color Matching

When you choose Color Matching, you can set color tolerance values for use when selecting an area to be traced with the Magic Wand tool (see *Color Tolerance* in Part 1).

Line Attributes

When you select Line Attributes, you can specify outline tracing parameters:

- Curve Precision: Determines how closely the traced image follows curves in the original image

- Line Precision: Controls how straight a line in the original image must be to be traced as a line, rather than as a curve

- Target Curve Length: Controls the length of curves in the traced image, longer curves having less detail

- Sample Rate: Controls how closely the traced image follows small details in the original image

- Minimum Object Size: Allows tracing to ignore small objects in the original

Centerline Method

Select this to modify Centerline tracing parameters:

- Max Line Width: Allows you to specify the width (in pixels) of the widest line that will be traced as a centerline, rather than as an outline.

- Create Lines of Uniform Width: When checked, you can define the width of centerlines created during tracing.

- Horz and Vert Line Recognition: When checked, Corel-TRACE attempts to rotate the page to make lines perfectly horizontal and vertical.

Woodcut Style

Select this to modify the style of tracings made by the Woodcut method:

- Continuous Cut: When selected, cut is made with continuous lines; otherwise the cut fades in bright areas.

- Tapered Ends: When selected, cuts become narrow at the ends.

- Sample Width: Allows you to specify the width of the cut.

- Angle of Cut: Allows you to specify the angle of the cut.

OCR Method

This provides options for OCR tracing:

- Check Spelling: When checked, word-spelling is checked and incorrectly spelled words are not traced.

- Source: Open the list box to choose between Normal, FAX Fine, and Dot Matrix to improve character recognition.

Batch Output

This allows you to specify the directory in which traced images are stored and how file conflicts are handled:

- Select a default output directory: Allows you to specify a directory for traced files.

- Drives: Allows you to specify the disk drive onto which traced files are written.

- Make File Read Only: When checked, traced files are read-only.

- Replace Old Versions: When checked, writes over an existing file with the same name without warning.

- Save OCR as *.TXT: When checked, OCR files are saved with a .TXT extension.

Saving and Using Settings

You can save and reuse any combination of settings. To save settings:

1. Choose **Settings ➤ Save As** to display the Save Settings As dialog box.

2. Type a file name for the settings, choose the directory in which you want to keep it, and click **OK**.

To use previously established settings:

1. Choose **Settings ➤ Load** to display the Load Settings dialog box.

2. Click the name of the settings file you want to use and click **OK**.

 NOTES   Settings have a file name extension .CTR.

SHORTCUTS

Most procedures in this book are described in terms of selecting from menus. However, CorelTRACE provides shortcuts to speed certain actions. These shortcuts are shown in Tables 5.1 and 5.2.

Table 5.1: Function Key Shortcuts

Key	Use
F1	Displays help on the currently selected command or currently open dialog box
Ctrl+F1	Opens the Help Search dialog box
F2	Selects the Zoom-in cursor
F3	Selects the Zoom-out cursor
Alt+F4	Exits from CorelTRACE

Table 5.2: Speed Key Shortcuts

Key	Use
Ctrl+C	Executes the Copy command
Ctrl+O	Displays the Open Files dialog box
Ctrl+S	Executes the Save Trace command
Ctrl+V	Executes the Paste command
Ctrl+W	Executes the Refresh Window command
Ctrl+X	Executes the Cut command
Ctrl+Z	Executes the Undo command

TRACING AN IMAGE

You can accept the default method of tracing an image, or you can modify the way images are traced in many ways.

Tracing an Image with the Default Method

1. Choose **Settings ➤ Default Settings**.

2. Choose **File ➤ Open** to display the Open Files dialog box.

3. Click the name of the image you want to trace, and then click **OK** to display the image in the left side of the Corel-TRACE window.

4. Click the **Outline Trace** button. After a few seconds, the traced outline appears in the right side of the CorelTRACE window.

5. Choose **File ➤ Save Trace** to save the file.

NOTES The file is saved in encapsulated PostScript format with the same file name as the original image and with the file name extension .EPS.

Tracing an Image Using Specific Settings

Use the preceding procedure except, in step 1, choose the settings you want to use (see *Settings*).

Tracing Multiple Images

You can trace several bitmaps consecutively, providing you use the same settings for all of them. To do this:

1. Choose **Settings ➤ Default Settings** or choose alternative settings if appropriate (see *Settings*).

2. Choose **File ➤ Open** to display the Open Files dialog box.

3. Click the name of the first image you want to trace, hold down the **Ctrl** key while you click additional file names, then click **OK** to display the Batch Files roll-up shown in Figure 5.2.

4. Click the icon representing the tracing method you want to use.

5. Click **Trace All** to trace the images one after the other.

NOTES You can use the Batch Files roll-up to delete images from the list to be traced, to add images, to view images, and to display information about images. You can also trace individual images one at a time, choosing a different tracing method for each.

Tracing Part of an Image

1. Select the settings you want to use.

2. Choose **File ➤ Open** to display the Open Files dialog box.

3. Click the name of the image you want to trace, and then click **OK** to display the image in the left side of the Corel-TRACE window.

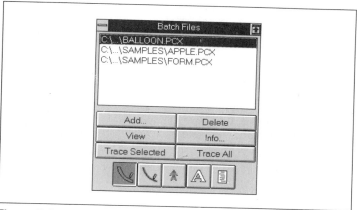

Figure 5.2: The Batch Files roll-up

4. Use the **Pick** tool to outline the part of the image you want to trace.

5. Click one of the tracing buttons. After a few seconds, the traced outline appears in the right side of the CorelTRACE window.

6. Choose **File ➤ Save Trace** to save the file.

NOTES   After you have outlined the part of the image you want to trace in step 4, you can remove the outline by choosing Display ➤ Clear Marquee.

Tracing Areas of Similar Color

You can use this method to create a posterized version of an image. By selecting an area of similar color with the Magic Wand tool, you can trace that area and reproduce it in a color of your choice. Repeating this process with different areas of the original image allows you to build a complete posterized image.

To trace areas of similar color:

1. Choose **Settings ➤ Color Matching** to display the Color Matching dialog box.

2. Click the button at the right side of the dialog box to display the RGB Color Tolerance values (see *Color Tolerance* in Part 1).

3. Choose or type Color Tolerance values according to the range of colors you want to select with the Magic Wand tool, then click **OK**.

4. Click the **Magic Wand +** tool, then click the area in the source image that you want to select to select the area that is within the Color Tolerance range you specified in step 3.

5. Click the **Color** button to display the palette, and click on the color you want to use for the traced image.

6. Click the **Silhouette** tracing tool to trace the selected area and reproduce it in the traced image section of the window.

7. Repeat steps 1 through 6 to trace other parts of the original image.

NOTES   After you have selected an area of the original image with the Magic Wand + tool, you can deselect that are by clicking it with the Magic Wand – tool.

TRACING METHODS

CorelTRACE can use six different tracing methods:

Method	Description
Outline	Traces edges of each element in the source image and fills outlines in a manner similar to that in the source image
Centerline	Treats thin lines in the source image as objects having thickness but no fill
Woodcut	Creates a woodcut effect that has lines across it at a specified angle
Silhouette	Traces an outline of a selected area in the source image and fills it with a single color
OCR	Converts bitmapped text in the source image to characters
Corel	Used to trace images that consist of text, lines, and miscellaneous objects (see *Using Traced Images*)

USING TRACED IMAGES

CorelTRACE saves images traced by all methods except OCR in Encapsulated Postscript (EPS) format without an image header. You can import these files into CorelDRAW and some other vector graphics programs. If you want to use a traced image in a graphics program that does not accept EPS format, import the file into CorelDRAW and then export it in a format the other program can accept. You can also use CorelDRAW to export a traced file as a PostScript file with an image header.

Importing a Traced Image into CorelDRAW

When you import a traced image into CorelDRAW, all the objects are grouped. You must ungroup them before you can edit individual objects.

To import a traced image in EPS into CorelDRAW:

1. In CorelDRAW, choose **File ➤ Import** to display the Import dialog box.

2. Select the name of the traced file you want to import, then click **OK** to import the file with all elements grouped.

3. Choose **Arrange ➤ Ungroup** to ungroup the elements so that you can work with them individually.

NOTES   When you scan an image which combines text, lines, and other bitmap shapes using the Outline, Centerline, Woodcut, or Silhouette methods, the scanned image contains only shapes. When you import the scanned image into CorelDRAW, you can only edit text as vector objects, not as text objects.

When you scan a similar image using the OCR method, the scanned image contains only the text.

It is usually most effective to scan such an image using the Corel method. In this case, the scanned image contains

- Text objects that you can edit as text in CorelDRAW
- Curve objects you can edit using the Shape tool

Part 6

CorelMOVE

You can use CorelMOVE to create and show on-screen animations, complete with sound effects.

Within CorelMOVE, you can create the elements of an animation, actors (the images that move), props (stationary background images), and sounds. You can use actors, props, and sounds created in other applications, or you can use those in the supplied libraries.

You control movement by paths on which points identify each position at which actors are displayed. A graphic display of timing, known as Timelines, allows you to adjust the times at which objects appear and disappear, and when sounds are heard.

Animations created with CorelMOVE can be converted into the AVI format suitable for showing by Video for Windows.

ACTORS, PROPS, AND SOUNDS

An animation consists of visible actors and props, and also sounds. In CorelMOVE, *object* refers to an actor, a prop, or a sound. Actors can move, while props are stationary in the background. There are single-cel actors and multiple-cel actors (*cel* is an abbreviation for *celluloid*, the material on which artists originally drew animations—don't confuse this with *cell*).

There are two ways in which actors can move in an animation. Single-cel and multiple-cel actors can move from point to point along a defined path.

A multiple-cel actor can exhibit a different type of movement; it can change shape, size, and color while remaining at one point in its path, or while moving from point to point. For example, the mouth in a head could move to symbolize talking.

Props are similar to single-cel actors, but cannot move. However, props can enter and leave an animation with various transition effects.

Actors and props exist in layers, one on top of the other. You can control the order in which layers of actors and layers of props are stacked so that one object is in front of, or behind, another. Actors, though, are always on top of props.

An animation can include any number of sounds but, of course, you must have a compatible sound board to take advantage of this. Each sound is an object that can start and stop at any time during the animation.

CONTROL PANEL

The Control Panel shown in Figure 6.1 is at the bottom of the screen.

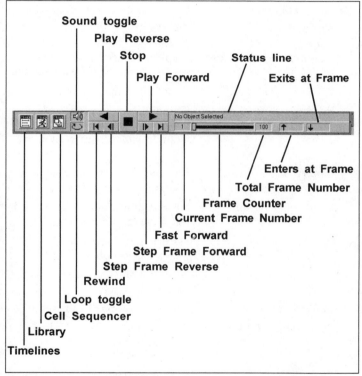

Figure 6.1: The CorelMOVE Control Panel

The purposes of the Control Panel buttons and indicators are as follows:

Button or Indicator	Purpose
Cel Sequencer icon	Displays the Cel Sequencer roll-up (see *Editing an Animation*).
Current Frame Number indicator	Displays the number of the current frame.
Enters at Frame indicator	Displays frame number at which selected actor enters the animation.
Exits at Frame indicator	Display frame number at which selected actor exits the animation.
Fast Forward button	Go to last frame in animation.
Frame Counter	Graphically shows the current position within the animation. Drag the slider to go to another frame.
Library icon	Displays the Library roll-up (see *Creating a New Animation*).
Loop toggle button	Turns continuous play on and off (see *Playing an Animation*).
Play Forward button	Starts playing animation in forward direction.
Play Reverse button	Starts playing animation in reverse direction.
Rewind button	Go to first frame in animation.
Sound toggle button	Turns sound on and off while playing animation (see *Creating and Editing a Sound*).
Status line	Indicates information about the selected object.
Step Frame Forward button	Go to next frame in animation.

Button or Indicator	Purpose
Step Frame Reverse button	Go to previous frame in animation.
Stop button	Stops playing animation.
Timelines icon	Displays the Timelines roll-up (see *Editing an Animation*).
Total Frame Number indicator	Displays the total number of frames in the animation.

CREATING A NEW ANIMATION

You create an animation by drawing individual actors and props either within CorelMOVE or in one or more other applications (or by selecting them from a library), then assembling them into frames, adding action, and adding sounds. These steps are explained in detail in other entries.

NOTES   If you are new to creating animations, start by using actors, props, and sounds in the libraries supplied with CorelDRAW, rather than by creating your own.

Setting the Animation Window Size

Before you begin to create a new animation you must define its on-screen size in the Animation Information dialog box.

Set the size according to the needs of the intended audience. Avoid choosing a larger size than necessary to minimize storage requirements and to optimize on-screen performance.

To set the window size:

1. Choose **Display** ➤ **Animation Info** to display the Animation Information dialog box.

2. Select or type the **Width** and **Height** of the animation in pixels, and click **OK**.

Selecting Animation Options

You can select animation options other than the window size before or during the process of creating an animation.

1. Choose **Display** ➤ **Animation Info** to display the Animation Information dialog box.

2. In the Window section, select or type information in the dialog box, and click **OK**.

The top part of the dialog box shows the number of actors, props, sounds, and cues in the animation. Before you begin assembling the animation, all these are zero.

The center of the dialog box is where you set the size of the animation window.

The bottom part of the dialog box consists of fields where you set the following:

Field	Purpose
Number of Frames	Set this to a number in the range 1 through 9999.
Frame for Thumbnail	Set this to the number of the frame that you want to use as a thumbnail in preview boxes.
Speed (Frames/Second)	Set this to a number in the range 1 through 18. Depending on your computer resources and the complexity of the animation, the actual playback speed may be less than the number you set here.

Field	Purpose
Grid Spacing	Set this to OFF to turn off the grid, or to one of the numbers in the list, which represent grid spacing in pixels. After you select a grid, actors, props, and points on a path are placed on the nearest grid point.

CREATING AN ACTOR OR PROP

You can create single-cel actors, multiple-cel actors, and props using CorelMOVE's Paint Editor, or with other OLE-compatible graphics applications.

Creating a Single-Cel Actor or Prop with the Paint Editor

After step 1 in this procedure, the steps refer explicitly to creating a new actor. Use the same steps to create a new prop.

You create a single-cel actor or prop with the Paint Editor tools, and then apply it to the animation window. To create a new single-cel actor or a prop:

1. Click the **Actor** or **Prop** tool in the toolbox to display the New Actor or New Prop dialog box.

2. Type a unique name for the new actor in the **Object Name** text box.

3. Click the **Create New** option button if it is not already selected.

4. In the Object Type list box, click **CorelMOVE** if it is not already selected, to identify it as the application in which you will create a new actor.

5. Click **OK** to open the Paint Editor window with the name of the new actor in its title bar.

6. Use the Paint Editor tools to create the actor (see the note below).

7. Choose **File ➤ Apply Changes** in the Paint Editor to apply the new actor to the center of the current frame.

8. Choose **File ➤ Exit** in the Paint Editor to close the Paint Editor.

NOTES   The Paint Editor tools are similar to the corresponding CorelPHOTO-PAINT tools (see *Toolbox* in Part 3). You can reach extra functions by double-clicking some of the tools, as follows:

- Any of the closed shape tools to convert them to filled closed shape tools

- The Paintbrush tool to open a palette of brush shapes

- The Airbrush tool to select settings

- The Text tool to display the Font dialog box

- The Eraser tool to erase the entire contents of the Paint Editor window

If you accidentally erase the contents of the Paint Editor window by double-clicking the eraser tool, choose Edit ➤ Undo to restore it.

After step 5, you can choose File ➤ Page Setup in the Paint Editor to change the size of the Paint Editor window. Alternatively, you can drag the borders of the Paint Editor window to change its size.

Creating a Single-Cel Actor or Prop with CorelDRAW or CorelPHOTO-PAINT

To create an actor in CorelDRAW or CorelPHOTO-PAINT:

1. Follow steps 1 through 3 in the preceding procedure.

2. In the Object Type list box, click **CorelDRAW** or **CorelPHOTO-PAINT** to open the application in which you will create a new actor.

3. Use the application to create the object.

4. Choose **File ➤ Exit & Return** to display a dialog box that asks you if you want to update the embedded object.

5. Click **Yes** to return to CorelMOVE with the new object in the Animation window.

NOTES   To edit an object created in CorelDRAW or Corel-PHOTO-PAINT, double-click the object to display the Actor Information dialog box, then click Edit Actor to open the object in the application in which it was created.

Creating a Single-Cel Actor or Prop in Other Applications

To create object in any application that can act as an OLE server:

1. With the CorelMOVE Animation displayed, choose **Edit ➤ Insert New Object** to display a submenu.

2. Click **Actor, Prop,** or **Sound,** according to which type of object you want to create, to display a list of installed applications in which the selected type of object can be created.

3. In the Object Type list box, click the application in which you will create a new actor.

4. Follow steps 3 through 5 in the preceding procedure.

NOTES To edit an object created in another application, double-click the object to display the Actor Information dialog box, then click Edit Actor to open the object in the application in which it was created.

Creating a Multiple-Cel Actor

A multiple-cel actor consists of two or more similar cels usually with only small differences between them. Cycling through the cels gives the illusion of movement.

Start with a single-cel actor. If it is not already in Paint Editor format, double-click to display the Actor Information dialog box, then click Convert to convert it to Paint Editor format.

To create a multiple-cel actor:

1. Use one of the preceding methods to create an actor in the Animation window.

2. Click the actor with the **Pick** tool to select it. A dashed line around the cel indicates it is selected.

3. Choose **Edit ➤ Object** to display the actor in the Paint Editor window.

4. Choose **Edit ➤ Insert Cels** in the Paint Editor window to display the Insert Cels dialog box.

5. In the **Number of Cels to Insert** text box, select or type the number of cels to add.

6. Click **Before Current Cel** or **After Current Cel** as appropriate.

7. Click the **Duplicate Contents** check box to copy the actor into the added cels.

8. Click **OK** to add the cels to create a multiple-cel actor, initially with all cels identical. Notice that the bottom of the

Paint Editor tool box shows the number of cels, and has a scroll bar you can use to move from cel to cel.

9. Select one cel at a time and change it so that the sequence of cels simulates change or movement (see *Editing an Actor or Prop*).

10. Choose **Edit ➤ Apply Changes** to copy the multiple-cel actor to the Animation window.

NOTES As you work, you can add cels to or delete cels from a multiple-cel editor by choosing Edit ➤ Insert Cels or Edit ➤ Delete Cels.

Selecting an Actor or Prop from a Library

See *Libraries* for information about selecting from a library.

Viewing a Multiple-Cel Actor

After you have created a multiple-cel actor, you can see it in action by displaying it in the Animation window and clicking the **Play Forward** button in the Control Panel.

CREATING AND EDITING A PATH

Actors can move from point to point along a path. When an actor is placed in the Animation window it is given a one-point path to which you can add points.

Adding Points to a Path

1. Use the **Pick** tool to select an actor.

2. Select the **Path** tool in the Toolbox to display the Path Edit roll-up shown in Figure 6.2 and to add a black circle showing the first point in the path to the selected actor.

3. If necessary, click **Allow Adding Nodes** in the roll-up so that it is checked.

4. Click points in the Animation window to define points on the path.

NOTES All points except the last on a path are shown by small squares. The first point on the path is slightly larger than the others. The last point on the path is shown as a circle. The selected point on the path is filled; the others are hollow.

Selecting Points on a Path

To make changes to a path you select points. Click any point to select it. After you have selected one point, press **Shift** while you click another point to select that point and all between that point and the first point. Selected points are indicated by becoming filled.

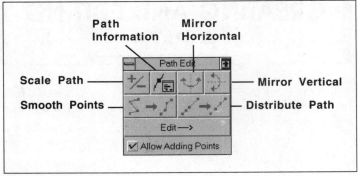

Figure 6.2: The Path Edit roll-up

Editing a Path

To edit a path, select one point to edit the entire path, or select two or more points if you want to edit a specific range of points, and then:

Operation	Procedure
Add points	Click the position for the new point anywhere in the Animation window.
Cut or copy, then paste points	Click Edit in the Path Edit roll-up, then click Cut Point(s) or Copy Point(s). Select a new point, click Edit in the Path Edit roll-up, then click Paste Point(s).
Delete points	Press Delete.
Designate loop point	Double-click a point, then click Loop To Here in the Point Information dialog box (see Notes).
Distribute points	Click Distribute Path in the Path Edit roll-up.
Mirror points	Click Mirror Vertical or Mirror Horizontal in the Path Edit roll-up.
Move points	Drag one of the selected points. Alternatively, click Point Information in the Path Edit roll-up, then select or type new horizontal and vertical positions in the Point Information dialog box.
Remove path	Click Edit in the Path Edit roll-up, then click Clear Whole path.
Scale points	Click Scale Path in the Path Edit roll-up, then select or type the new number of points in the Scale Path dialog box.
Select all points	Click Edit in the Path Edit roll-up, then click Select All Points.

Operation	Procedure
Smooth points	Click Smooth Path in the Path Edit roll-up.
Undo most recent path edit	Click Edit in the Path Edit roll-up, then click Undo Path Operation.

NOTES   Each point on the path corresponds to a frame in the animation. The loop point is the point on a path to which an actor loops back when it reaches the end of the path. You can designate any point as the loop point.

Setting an Actor's Registration Point

The registration point associated with an actor is the point that moves along the path. By default, the registration point is the top left corner of the rectangle that encloses the actor. You can move the registration to anywhere within the actor or outside it.

By positioning registration points for several actors, you can have them move along the same path without overlapping.

1. Select the actor in the Animation window.

2. Choose **Edit ➤ Object** to display the actor in the Paint Editor window.

3. Choose **Edit ➤ Registration** to display the object's current registration point flashing at the top left of the Paint Editor window.

4. Click where you want the new registration point to be.

5. Choose **File ➤ Apply Changes** to apply the new registration point to the actor.

6. Choose **File ➤ Exit** to return to the Animation window.

NOTES   After step 2, the actor occupies the top left corner of the Paint Editor window. If you want to position the registration point above, or to the left of, the actor, select the actor and drag it down and to the right before step 3.

CREATING AND EDITING A SOUND

If you have a sound board, you can add sounds to your Corel-MOVE animations.

Creating a Sound

1. From the Animation window, choose **Edit ➤ Insert New Object ➤ Sound** to display the New Wave dialog box.

2. Type a unique name for the sound.

3. Click the name of the application to be used to create the new sound in the Object Type list box, then click **OK** to open the application.

4. In the application, start recording, record the sound, and then stop recording.

NOTES   If you select CorelMOVE in step 3, you can use the Wave Editor dialog box to record a sound.

Editing a Sound

1. Click the **Timelines** icon in the Control Panel to open the Timelines roll-up.

2. Double-click the sound name in the roll-up to display the Sound Information dialog box shown in Figure 6.3.

3. Adjust the parameters in the dialog box.

4. Click **OK** to accept the edits or, if you want to see or adjust the sound waveform, click **Edit Sound** to display the Wave Editor dialog box. After editing the waveform, choose **File ➤ Exit**.

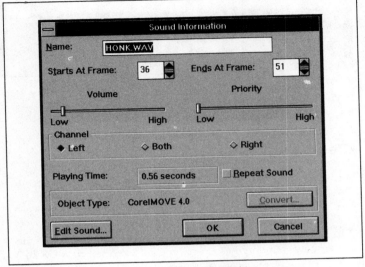

Figure 6.3: The Sound Information dialog box

NOTES The Priority setting allows some sounds to override others. If your sound board has a single channel, during any frame only the sound with the highest priority is heard. If your sound board has two channels, the two highest priority channels are heard.

If the Repeat Sound check box is unchecked the sound continues until it is finished or until the end frame. If the check box is checked, the sound repeats until end frame.

EDITING AN ACTOR OR PROP

Edit an actor or a prop using the application in which it was created.

Editing an Actor or Prop with the Paint Editor

1. Display the actor or prop in the Animation window.
2. Use the **Pick** tool to select the object you want to edit.
3. Choose **Edit ➤ Object** to display the object in the Paint Editor window.
4. Use the Paint Editor tools to edit the object.
5. Choose **File ➤ Apply Changes** to apply the changes to the object in the Animation window.

NOTES   The Paint Editor tools are similar to the corresponding CorelPHOTO-PAINT tools (see *Toolbox* in Part 3). See *Creating an Actor or Prop* for details.

You can convert an object that was created in another application into CorelMOVE format so that you can edit it with the Paint Editor. To do so, double-click the object to open the Actor Information or Prop Information dialog box, click Convert, and then click OK.

Editing an Actor or Prop Created in Another Application

1. Double-click the object to display the Actor Information dialog box.
2. Click **Edit Actor** to open the object in the application in which it was created.

3. Use the applications tools to edit the object.

4. Choose **File ➤ Exit & Return** to return to CorelMOVE.

EDITING AN ANIMATION

After you have created actors, props, and sounds, you can use CorelMOVE's editing capabilities to assemble your presentation.

Moving Objects in the Animation Window

To move an object in the Animation window, select it with the **Pick** tool, and drag. Alternatively, double-click on an object in the Animation window or double-click on an object's name in the Timelines roll-up to edit the data in the Actor Information or Prop Information dialog box.

Arranging Layers

By default, actors and props are placed one on top of another. To change the stacking order select an actor or prop and use the Arrange menu (see *Stacking Order* in Part 1).

Deleting Objects

To delete an object, select it and press **Delete**.

Cutting, Copying, and Pasting Objects

Use standard Windows techniques to cut or copy objects to the Clipboard, and to paste objects from the Clipboard.

Duplicating an Object

To duplicate an object, select it, and choose **Edit ➤ Duplicate** to display the Duplicate Actor or Duplicate Prop dialog box. Type a name for the duplicate, and click **OK** to display it.

Cloning an Object

Clones in CorelMOVE are similar to clones in CorelDRAW (see *Clones* in Part 1). To clone an object, select it, and choose **Edit ➤ Clone** to display the Clone Actor or Clone Prop dialog box. Type a name for the clone, and click **OK** to display it.

Adding Prop Transitions

Props can enter and leave an animation in several ways. To select prop transitions:

1. With the **Pick** tool selected, double-click on a prop to display the Prop Information dialog box.

2. Click **Edit** in the Transition section of the dialog box to display the Transitions for Prop dialog box.

3. Click an Entry Transition and an Exit Transition, then click **OK** to return to the Prop Information dialog box.

4. Click **OK** to return to the Animation window.

NOTES   If you select a Scroll, Zoom, or Zoom Rectangles transition, you can modify the transition by clicking Edit.

Sequencing Cels

Cel sequencing is the process of assigning cels to frames of an animation. By default:

- A single-cel actor that has a single-point path stays in the same position from frame to frame.

- A single-cel actor that has a multiple-point path moves to successive points on the path from frame to frame.

- A multiple-cel actor that has a single-point path stays in the same position showing successive cels from frame to frame.

- A multiple-cel actor that has a multiple-point path moves to successive points on the path, showing successive cels from frame to frame.

By taking control of cel sequencing, you can modify these defaults. For example, you can control the order in which cels of a multiple-cel actor appear from point to point on a track. You can also use cel sequencing to change the size of a cel as it moves from frame to frame.

Controlling Cel Sequence

The following procedure assumes you have a four-cel actor and a seven-point path, and you want the actor to show the specified cells at the specified points:

Point No.	Cell No.
1	1
2	2
3	1
4	3
5	1
6	4
7	1

To set up this cel sequence:

1. Click the **Cel Sequencer** icon in the Control Panel to display the Cel Sequencer roll-up shown in Figure 6.4.

2. Display the first cell of the actor and use the **Pick** tool to select it.

3. Open the **Apply To** list box in the Cel Sequencer roll-up and click **Frame Number**. The roll-up changes to show a frame number and a cell number.

4. Set the frame number to 1, and the cell number to the cell you want to show in that frame, 1 in this case, then click **Apply**.

5. Set the frame number to 2, and the cell number to the cell you want to show in that frame, 2 in this case, then click **Apply**.

6. Set cel numbers for the remaining frames in the same way.

NOTES You can check cell sequences by successively clicking the Step Frame Forward button in the Control Panel to display one frame after another.

There are many other ways in which you can set the sequence of cels. See *Cel Sequence* in CorelMOVE Help for detailed information.

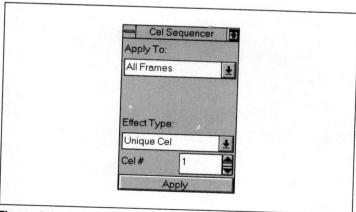

Figure 6.4: The Cel Sequencer roll-up

Adding Cues to an Animation

Cues can be used in an animation in much the same way as in a CorelSHOW on-screen slide presentation. To add a cue:

1. Click the **Cue** tool in the Toolbox to display the Cue Information dialog box.

2. Add Cue information to the dialog box (see *Cues* in Part 4), then click **OK**.

Timing an Animation

You can modify the timing of an animation using Timelines in much the same way as you can in CorelSHOW (see *Timelines* in Part 4).

1. Click the **Timelines** icon in the Control Panel to display the Timelines roll-up, then click the right-pointing arrow to expand the roll-up to display timing, as shown in Figure 6.5.

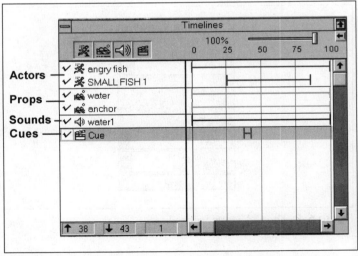

Figure 6.5: The Timelines roll-up expanded to display timing

2. Drag the start and stop times of objects to change their timing.

EXPORTING AN ANIMATION

You can export an animation to the Video for Windows AVI format and then use CorelPLAYER or Video for Windows to play it.

Exporting to AVI Format

To export an animation to an AVI file:

1. Choose **File ➤ Export To Movie** to display the Export To Movie dialog box.

2. Select the drive and directory, type a file name, and click **OK**.

FILE MANAGEMENT

Opening and saving files is similar to the same operations in CorelDRAW (see *File Management* in Part 1).

IMPORTING OBJECTS

You can build animations by importing actors, props, and sounds from other applications.

Importing Objects from Other Applications

1. Choose **File ➤ Import** to display a submenu.

2. Click **Actor**, **Prop**, or **Sound** according to what you want to import, to display the Import Actor, Import Prop, or Import Sound dialog box.

3. Select the drive, directory, file type, and file name, and click **OK** to display the Import Imaging Options dialog box.

4. If you are importing an actor or prop and want to take advantage of dithering to reproduce colors, click the **Perform High Quality Dithering** check box.

5. If you are importing an actor or prop, click one of the **Transparent Color Options** (see the note below).

6. Click **OK** to import the object.

NOTES In step 5, all the white in the imported object becomes transparent if you click White, all the black in the imported object becomes transparent if you click Black, no colors in the imported object become transparent if you click None.

LIBRARIES

CorelMOVE is supplied with libraries of actors, props, and sounds. You can add objects to these libraries and you can create additional libraries of objects.

Retrieving an Object from a Library

When you install CorelDRAW from floppy disks, a selection of clip-art libraries of actors, props, and sounds is copied onto your hard disk. When you install CorelDRAW from a CD-ROM, most libraries are not copied onto your hard disk, but are directly accessible from the CD-ROM.

To select an object from a library:

1. If you are selecting an object from a library on CD-ROM, make sure the CorelDRAW CD-ROM Disk 2 is installed in your CD-ROM drive.

2. Click the **Library** icon in the Control Panel to display the Library roll-up, then click the right-pointing arrow to display the Library menu, as shown in Figure 6.6.

3. Click **Open Library** to display the Open Library dialog box.

4. Select the drive and directory that contains a CorelMOVE library to display a list of available libraries.

5. Click the name of the library you want to use, then click **OK** to display the first object in the selected library in the roll-up.

6. Use the scroll bar to find the object you want to use.

7. Click any combination of the **Actor**, **Prop**, and **Sound** buttons at the top of the roll-up according to what you want to see.

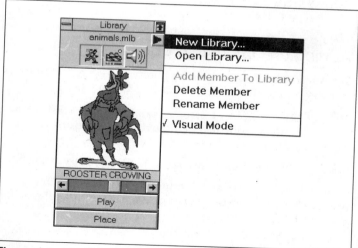

Figure 6.6: The Library roll-up with its menu

8. If you wish, click **Play** to see the object with animation or to hear the sound, then click **Stop Playing**.

9. Click **Place** to place the object in the animation.

NOTES When the Library roll-up first appears in step 2, it may show the most recently selected object, as shown in the figure, or it may show a list of object names. Click Visual Mode in the Library menu to switch between displaying objects and names.

Most of the libraries supplied with CorelMOVE contain multiple-cel actors and sounds. Those named PROPS1, PROPS2, and PROPS3 contain props.

Creating a Library

1. Click the **Library** icon in the Control Panel to display the Library roll-up, then click the right-pointing arrow to display the Library menu.

2. Click **New Library** to display the New Library dialog box.

3. Select a directory and subdirectory for the new library, type a name for it, and click **OK**.

Adding an Object to a Library

You can add objects to an existing library, though not, of course, to a library on a read-only medium such as a CD-ROM.

1. Click the **Library** icon in the Control Panel to display the Library roll-up, then click the right-pointing arrow to display the Library menu.

2. Click **Open Library** to display the Open Library dialog box.

3. Select the drive and directory that contains the library, click on the library name, and then click **OK** to display the first object in that library in the roll-up.

4. Use the **Pick** tool to select the object you want to add to the library.

5. Click the right-pointing arrow in the Library roll-up to display the library menu, and then click **Add Member To Library**.

NOTES After you have added an object to a library, it appears in alphabetical order in that library.

Deleting and Renaming Library Objects

You can delete or rename library objects providing the library is not stored in a read-only medium.

1. Follow steps 1 through 3 in the preceding procedure.

2. Scroll through the library to select the object to be deleted or renamed.

3. Click the right-pointing arrow in the Library roll-up to display the library menu, and then click **Delete Member** or **Rename Member**. In either case a dialog box appears.

4. Either click **Yes** to confirm the deletion, or type the new name and click **OK**.

PLAYING AN ANIMATION

To play an animation, set the playback options, then click the **Play Forward** button in the Control Panel.

Setting Playback Options

1. Choose **Display ➤ Playback Options** to display the Playback Options dialog box.

2. Click the check boxes to check or uncheck them as you wish.

434 CorelMOVE

The playback options are as follows:

Playback Option	Purpose
Mouse Button Click	When checked, playback stops when you click the mouse button.
Ctrl Break	When checked, playback stops when you press Ctrl+Break.
Hide Tools	When checked, toolbox is hidden during playback.
Hide Menu Bar	When checked, menu bar is hidden during playback.
Hide Cursor	When checked, cursor is hidden during playback.
Enable Sounds	When checked, sound is enabled during playback.
Auto Replay	When checked, animation plays repeatedly.

SCREEN

Figure 6.7 shows a typical CorelMOVE screen which is similar to the CorelDRAW screen. Screen components unique to CorelMOVE are as follows:

Component	Purpose
Animation window	Used to build animation
Control Panel	Provides access to roll-ups and controls animation playback (see *Control Panel*).

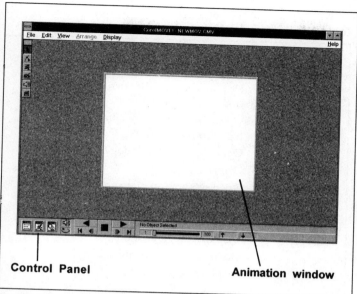

Figure 6.7: The CorelMOVE screen

SHORTCUTS

Most procedures in this book are described in terms of selecting
from menus. However, CorelTRACE provides shortcuts to speed
certain actions. These shortcuts are shown in Tables 6.1 and 6.2.

Table 6.1: Function Key Shortcuts

Key	Use
F1	Displays help on the currently selected command or currently open dialog box
Ctrl+F1	Opens the Help Search dialog box
Alt+F4	Exits from CorelMOVE
F5	Opens New Actor dialog box
Shift+F5	Displays first frame
F6	Opens New Prop dialog box
Shift+F6	Displays last frame
F7	Opens New Wave dialog box
Shift+F7	Displays previous frame
F8	Opens Cue Information dialog box
Shift+F8	Displays next frame
F9	Play forward
Shift+F9	Play reverse
F10	Opens Path Edit roll-up

Table 6.2: Speed Key Shortcuts

Key	Use
Ctrl+C	Executes the Copy command
Ctrl+D	Executes the Duplicate command
Ctrl+K	Opens Playback Options dialog box
Ctrl+N	Opens Select Name For New File dialog box
Ctrl+O	Display the Open File dialog box
Ctrl+S	Executes the Save command
Ctrl+W	Executes the Refresh Window command
Ctrl+X	Executes the Cut command
Ctrl+Z	Executes the Undo command

STARTING AND CLOSING CORELMOVE

To start CorelMOVE:

1. Start Windows and display the Program Manager group window.

2. Double-click the **Corel 4** icon to display the Corel 4 group window.

3. Double-click the **CorelMOVE** icon to display the Corel-MOVE screen.

To close CorelMOVE:

1. Choose **File ➤ Exit**. If you have already saved your animation, CorelMOVE immediately closes. Otherwise, a dialog box gives you the opportunity to save your animation before CorelMOVE closes.

2. Click **Yes** to save your animation, click **No** to close Corel-MOVE without saving your animation, or click **Cancel** if you do not want to close CorelMOVE.

TOOLBOX

The CorelMOVE toolbox, shown in Figure 6.8, is normally at the left side of the screen. To move it, point onto the empty box at the top of toolbox and drag.

The purposes of the tools are as follows:

Tool Name	Purpose
Pick	Used to select objects
Path	Used to select points in an actor's path
Actor	Used to create a new actor
Prop	Used to create a new prop
Sound	Used to add a sound
Cue	Used to add a cue

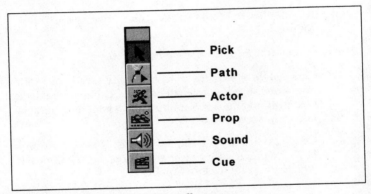

Figure 6.8: The CorelMOVE toolbox

Appendix

File Formats Supported by Corel Graphics

As this appendix shows, the applications in the CorelDRAW package are compatible with a large number of text and graphics file formats. However, a word of warning about compatibility is appropriate.

File formats are of two types: those that are proprietory, such as CorelDRAW's native CDR format and WordPerfect's WPG graphics format, and those that are widely used, such as TIFF (Tag Image File Format). You can expect total compatibility between the way the individual CorelDRAW applications handle CDR files because Corel owns and controls that format.

In the case of a file format, such as WPG, that is owned by another company, total compatibility is dependent on the extent to which the company that controls the format is willing to share the specification with other companies. Also, the controlling company may modify the specification to suit its own needs, so the degree of compatibility may change.

Widely used formats, such as TIFF, are a different matter. The TIFF specification is a broad outline of how a graphics file may be structured. As a result, there are significant differences between TIFF files generated by the many applications that use them. While you will probably find that CorelDRAW is compatible with most TIFF files, you may encounter some that are not totally compatible.

See CorelDRAW Help for recommendations about which file formats to use when importing from, and exporting to, other applications.

Table A.1: File Formats Supported by CorelDRAW

Format	Source	Read	Write
*	MacWrite Text	✓	
*	Microsoft Word for Mac	✓	
*	WordPerfect Text	✓	
*	WordPerfect for Windows Text	✓	
ABK	CorelDRAW Auto Backup	✓	✓
AI	Adobe Illustrator	✓	
BAK	CorelDRAW Backup	✓	✓
BMP	Windows or OS/2 Bitmap	✓	✓
CDR	CorelDRAW Drawing	✓	✓
CGM	Computer Graphics Metafile	✓	✓
DOC	Microsoft Word	✓	
DOC	Microsoft Word for Windows	✓	
DRW	Micrografx Draw	✓	
DXF	AutoCAD	✓	✓
EPS	Encapsulated PostScript	✓	✓
GEM	Graphic Environment Manager	✓	✓
GIF	CompuServe	✓	✓
IPL	CorelDRAW Color Palette	✓	✓
JPG	JPEG Bitmap	✓	✓
PAL	CorelDRAW Color Palette	✓	✓
PAT	CorelDRAW Pattern	✓	✓
PCC	CorelPHOTO-PAINT, etc.	✓	✓
PCD	Kodak Photo CD	✓	
PCT	Macintosh Picture	✓	✓
PCX	CorelPHOTO-PAINT, etc.	✓	✓
PFB	Adobe Type 1 Font	✓	✓

Table A.1: File Formats Supported by CorelDRAW (continued)

Format	Source	Read	Write
PIC	Lotus 1-2-3 Graphic	✓	
PIF	IBM Graphics	✓	✓
PLT	Hewlett-Packard Plotter	✓	✓
PRN	Print File		✓
PS	EPS Thumbnail	✓	
RTF	Rich Text Format	✓	
SAM	Ami Professional	✓	
SCD	Matrix/Imapro SCODL		✓
TGA	Targa	✓	✓
TIF	Tag Image File Format	✓	✓
TTF	TrueType Font	✓	✓
TXT	Text	✓	
WFN	CorelDRAW Symbols	✓	✓
WK?	Lotus 1-2-3 Worksheet	✓	
WMF	Windows Metafile	✓	✓
WPG	WordPerfect Graphic	✓	✓
XLS	Excel for Windows	✓	

Table A.2: File Formats Supported by CorelCHART

Format	Source	Read Data	Read Graphics	Write
AI	Adobe Illustrator		✓	
BMP	Windows Bitmap		✓	✓
CCH	CorelCHART	✓	✓	✓
CDR	CorelDRAW		✓	
CGM	Computer Graphics Metafile		✓	✓

Table A.2: File Formats Supported by CorelCHART (continued)

Format	Source	Read Data	Read Graphics	Write
CHT	Harvard Graphics	✓		
CSV	ASCII (comma separated)	✓		
DBF	Borland dBASE	✓		
DXF	AutoCAD		✓	✓
EPS	Encapsulated PostScript		✓	
GEM	Graphical Environment Manager		✓	✓
GIF	CompuServe		✓	✓
PCC	PC Paintbrush		✓	✓
PCT	Macintosh		✓	✓
PCX	CorelPHOTO-PAINT, etc.		✓	
PIC	Lotus 1-2-3 Graphics		✓	
PIF	IBM Graphics		✓	✓
PLT	Hewlett-Packard Plotter		✓	✓
PRN	Print File			✓
RTF	Rich Text Format			✓
SCD	Matrix/Imapro SCODL			✓
TGA	Targa		✓	✓
TIF	Tag Image File Format		✓	✓
TXT	Text (comma or tab separated)	✓		✓

Table A.2: File Formats Supported by CorelCHART (continued)

Format	Source	Read Data	Read Graphics	Write
WK1	Lotus 1-2-3 Spreadsheet	✓		
WK3	Lotus 1-2-3 Spreadsheet	✓		
WKS	Lotus 1-2-3 Spreadsheet	✓		✓
WKS	Microsoft Works Spreadsheet	✓		
WMF	Windows Metafile		✓	✓
WPG	WordPerfect Graphics			✓
XLS	Excel for Windows	✓		✓

Table A.3: File Formats Supported by CorelPHOTO-PAINT

Format	Source	Read	Write
BMP	Windows Bitmap	✓	✓
CCH	CorelCHART	✓	
EPS	Encapsulated PostScript	✓	✓
GIF	CompuServe	✓	✓
MSP	Microsoft Paint	✓	
PCX	CorelPHOTO-PAINT, etc.	✓	
PRN	Print File		✓
TGA	Targa	✓	✓
THB	CorelPHOTO-PAINT Thumbnail	✓	✓
TIF	Tag Image File Format	✓	✓

Table A.4: File Formats Supported by CorelSHOW

Format	Source	Read	Write
CDR	CorelDRAW	✓	
CMV	CorelMOVE	✓	
FLI	Autodesk Animation	✓	
MOV	Quicktime Animation	✓	
SHB	CorelSHOW Background	✓	✓
SHW	CorelSHOW Presentation	✓	✓
WAV	Sound	✓	

Table A.5: File Formats Supported by CorelTRACE

Format	Source	Read	Write
BMP	Windows Bitmap	✓	
EPS	Encapsulated PostScript		✓
GIF	CompuServe	✓	
ICB	Targa Bitmap	✓	
JFF	JPEG Bitmap	✓	
JPG	JPEG Bitmap	✓	
JTF	JPEG Bitmap	✓	
PCC	PC Paintbrush	✓	
PCD	Kodak CD-ROM	✓	
PCX	CorelPHOTO-PAINT, etc.	✓	
PRN	Print File		✓
SEP	Tag Image File Format	✓	✓
TGA	Targa	✓	
TIF	Tag Image File Format	✓	
TXT	Text		✓
VDA	Targa Bitmap	✓	
VST	Targa Bitmap	✓	

Table A.6: File Formats Supported by CorelMOSAIC

Format	Source	Read	Write
AI	Adobe Illustrator	✓	
BMP	Windows Bitmap	✓	✓
CCH	CorelCHART	✓	
CDR	CorelDRAW	✓	
CLB	Corel Library	✓	✓
CLC	Corel Catalog	✓	✓
CMV	CorelMOVE	✓	
DIB	Windows Bitmap	✓	
EPS	Encapsulated PostScript	✓	✓
FLI	Autodesk Animation	✓	
GIF	CompuServe	✓	
JPG	JPEG Bitmap	✓	
MID	Microsoft MIDI	✓	
PCC	CorelPHOTO-PAINT, etc.	✓	
PCD	Kodak Photo CD	✓	
PCX	CorelPHOTO-PAINT, etc.	✓	✓
SHB	CorelSHOW Background	✓	
SHW	CorelSHOW Presentation	✓	
TGA	Targa	✓	
TIF	Tag Image File Format	✓	
WAV	Microsoft Audio	✓	

Table A.7: File Formats Supported by CorelMOVE

Format	Source	Read	Write
AVI	Video for Windows	✓	✓
BMP	Windows Bitmap	✓	
DIB	Windows Bitmap	✓	
FLI	Autodesk Animation	✓	
CMV	CorelMOVE	✓	✓
GIF	CompuServe	✓	
ICB	Targa Bitmap	✓	
JFF	JPEG Bitmap	✓	
JPG	JPEG Bitmap	✓	
JTF	JPEG Bitmap	✓	
MWF	Motion Works Animation	✓	
PCD	Kodak Photo CD	✓	
PCX	CorelPHOTO-PAINT, etc.	✓	
RLE	Windows Bitmap	✓	
SEP	Tag Image File Format	✓	
TGA	Targa Bitmap	✓	
TIF	Tag Image File Format	✓	
VDA	Targa Bitmap	✓	
VST	Targa Bitmap	✓	
WAV	Microsoft Audio	✓	

Index

452 Index

CorelDRAW Speed Key Shortcuts

KEY	USE
Ctrl+<0–9>	Applies style to paragraph text
Ctrl+A	Opens the Align dialog box
Ctrl+B	Opens the Blend roll-up
Ctrl+C	Executes the Copy command
Ctrl+D	Executes the Duplicate command
Ctrl+E	Opens the Extrude roll-up
Ctrl+F	Opens the Fit Text To Path dialog box
Ctrl+G	Executes the Group command
Ctrl+J	Opens the Preferences dialog box
Ctrl+K	Executes the Break Apart command
Ctrl+L	Executes the Combine command
Ctrl+N	Opens a new drawing
Ctrl+O	Opens the Open Drawing dialog box
Ctrl+P	Opens the Print dialog box
Ctrl+Q	Executes the Convert To Curves command
Ctrl+R	Executes the most Recent command